Fine WoodWorking
TECHNIQUES 1

Selected by the Editors
of Fine Woodworking Magazine

The Taunton Press
Newtown, Connecticut

Typeface: Compugraphic Garamond
Paper: Mead Offset Enamel 70 lb.
Printer: Connecticut Printers, Bloomfield, Conn.
Binder: Haddon Craftsmen, Scranton, Pa.

First Printing: September 1978
Second Printing: April 1980
Third Printing: January 1981
Fourth Printing: July 1981

The Taunton Press, Inc.
52 Church Hill Rd.
Box 355
Newtown, Connecticut 06470

Fine Woodworking® is a trademark of The Taunton Press, Inc.,
registered in the U.S. Patent and Trademark Office.
International Standard Book Number 0-918804-02-7
Library of Congress Catalog Card Number 78-58221
Printed in the United States of America

CONTENTS

INTRODUCTION

FINE WOODWORKING TECHNIQUES is the best from *Fine Wood-working* magazine: 50 articles about wood, woodworking tools, joinery, finishing, turning, marquetry, shaping and carving. Each of the 34 craftsmen in this book writes about his work and passes his expertise on to you.

In this collection, *Bob Stocksdale* relates his experiences with exotic woods; wood science professor *Bruce Hoadley* tells you about wood, drying your own lumber, and using different types of glues; luthier *William Cumpiano* explains guitar joinery; *Robert Whitley* tells which woods were traditionally used for chairs and why; English woodturner and teacher *Peter Child* demonstrates the basic methods of bowl turning; *Tage Frid* shows how to make a workbench, cut the basic carcase joints, and use a scraper; *Mark Lindquist* describes how he harvests and uses spalted wood; *Paul Bois* gives his plans for building a solar wood-drying kiln; restoration specialist *Tommy Bargeron* tells how to make shaper knives to cut any desired molding pattern; *Edward Hasbrouck* shows how to carve Gothic tracery; *Jere Osgood* tells how to bend laminated wood; and *R.E. Bushnell* discusses carving traditional fans.

This book also includes selections from the Methods of Work column of the magazine. These reader-submitted tips often complement a longer article, providing hints on some detail of a technique or showing how to make a special tool that renders the task easier.

Each article has been reprinted in full as it originally appeared in *Fine Woodworking*. However, the articles have been regrouped into five categories, allowing the reader to compare articles that would have been separated in a strictly chronological presentation. Also, footnotes have been added where a reference is made to an article that is also reprinted in this book. These notes appear in small type at the bottom of the column where the reference is made.

We hope that this book will provide one durable and easily referred to storehouse for the timeless information presented in *Fine Woodworking*. We intend to assemble similar reference collections of other articles from *Fine Woodworking* as the opportunity arises.

—The Editors
Fine Woodworking

WOOD

Wood

A look at this fundamental material

by R. Bruce Hoadley

Wood comes from trees. Not forgetting this obvious statement will help us work with wood as it really is, not as we wish it were. For wood has evolved as a functional tissue of plants, not as a material to satisfy the needs of woodworkers.

For example, we all know that most of the wood we use comes from the trunk, bole, or stem, as it is sometimes called, not from the unseen root system below or the crown of limbs, branches and twigs that support the foliage. Some of the most prized wood does come from crotches and irregularities, such as burls or knees, but for the most part we prefer the regular grain found in straight trunks.

But sometimes we come across a board that is different from other boards. It warps severely, or pinches our saw blade as we rip it, or doesn't take a finish quite like the other boards. What we're working with is a piece of reaction wood — wood taken from a trunk that is leaning or from a branch that doesn't grow straight up (by definition most branches are made of reaction wood).

This is an extreme case, but it does illustrate why it's important to remember where wood comes from and also to know something about its anatomical structure. As woodworkers, we usually know far more about our tools than we do about our materials. But as the architect Frank Lloyd Wright once said, "We may use wood with intelligence only if we understand it."

Understanding the difference between sapwood and heartwood, between earlywood and latewood, between "hardwoods" and "softwoods," between ray cells and longitudinal cells, between ring-porous woods and diffuse-porous woods, between vessels and fibers, and so on, may give us a better understanding of why wood behaves as it does, especially when we're trying to shape it, finish it, or preserve it.

Perhaps the best place to start is at the molecular level. Wood is a cellulose material, as is cotton. And because it's cellulosic, it is hygroscopic — it absorbs water readily and swells and shrinks accordingly (therein much of the problem of the "movement of wood").

The cellulose material that wood is composed of is pretty much the same for all species. It's not until we start looking at wood at the cellular level that different woods start to look "different." (And even here this is not necessarily the case. The sapwood of many species can look very much alike. Then it's not until the sapwood turns into dead heartwood that differences among some species really become apparent).

In any event, the cellulosic material is arranged into tubular cells that run longitudinally along the length of the trunk or branch. There are three varieties of such cells — vessels, tracheids, and fibers. Vessels have a large diameter, thin walls, and are very short (but they stack together like drainage tiles). At the other extreme are fibers — narrow diameter, thick walls, and long. In between are tracheids — moderate diameter, moderate thickness, and also very long.

Because they're so large in diameter, vessels are good for conducting sap up the tree, but their thin walls don't contribute much to mechanical support. On the other hand, the thick walls of fibers make them good for support, but their narrow diameter doesn't do much for sap conduction.

In between are the all-purpose tracheids, which can provide both sap conduction and physical support moderately well. In fact, one distinction between the so-called hardwoods and softwoods is this difference in cell structure. Softwoods, or conifers, are composed mainly of all-purpose tracheids. They are believed to have evolved earlier than hardwoods. Hence their more primitive structure, with no cell specialization. On the other hand hardwoods, or deciduous trees, do have cell specialization — vessels for sap conduction, fibers for support, and tracheids for both.

The tracheids of conifers are about 100 times as long as they are wide. Thus their excellent paper-making qualities. Among

| *Cherry (diffuse porous)* | *Black walnut (semi-ring porous)* | *Red oak (ring porous)* |

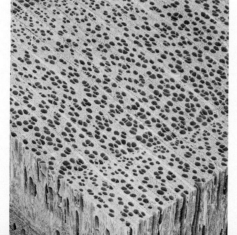 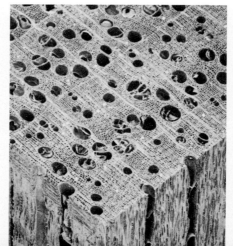 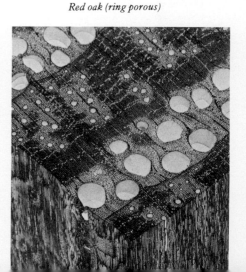

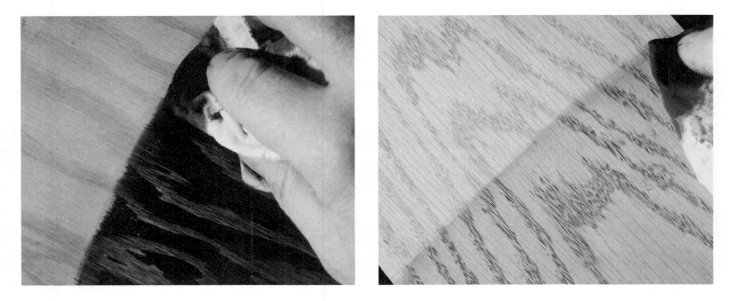

Variations in porosity between earlywood and latewood can create problems in staining. Conifers such as Douglas fir (left) have earlywood that is lighter but more porous than the latewood. Therefore, stain reverses the grain effect, as in a photographic negative. With hardwoods like red oak (right), the earlywood pores are already darker. Lines in the light latewood are rays.

conifer species, however, there can be a three-fold range of diameters, from fine red cedar to coarse redwood. This texture range due to tracheid diameter also affects the smoothness of surface or evenness of staining that can be achieved in woodworking.

If wood were composed strictly of these longitudinal cells, whether vessels, tracheids, or fibers, it would be much less complex than it really is, and really much different, for consider how and where a tree grows.

Growth occurs in the thin layer of reproductive tissues, called the cambium, that separates the wood from the bark. This tubular reproductive sheath, several cells thick, migrates ever outward, leaving behind layers of newly formed wood (which remain fixed in place forever), and also forms new bark in front of it (which will eventually be crowded out by the newer bark cells, and by the ever-expanding girth).

The cambial cells vary in content with the growing seasons. During growth the content is quite fluid; during dormancy there is a thickening. As a result, wood cut in summer usually loses its bark upon drying, while winter-cut wood does not, an important fact for those wishing to incorporate bark into their woodworking projects.

In addition to vertical movement through the sapwood, there must be provision for horizontal sap movement. That's where the ray cells come in. They are oriented radially outward from the center or pith and are stacked vertically in

groups called rays to form flattened bands of tissue. The rays not only carry the nutrients horizontally through the sapwood, but also store carbohydrates during the winter.

The rays are not great in number — typically they represent less than 10 percent of the wood volume — but they are significant for more than food conduction and storage. Their size — ranging from microscopically small in all softwoods to visibly big in many hardwoods — helps in wood identification. (For example, in red oak rays are less than one inch high; in white oak, they're one to four inches.) And structurally they influence the shrinkage of wood and the formation of checks.

Wood cells shrink and expand mainly across their girth, not their length, as they give off or take on moisture. That's why wood moves across the grain, not with the grain. But because ray cells are aligned across the grain (radially) they inhibit the longitudinal cells from expanding as much in a radial direction (towards or away from the center) as in a tangential direction (around the circumference). In effect, the radial cells act as restraining rods imbedded in the wood. That's why wood contracts or expands only half as much radially as tangentially.

The rays also form planes of weakness in hardwoods. End and surface checks, as well as internal honeycombing, will regularly develop through the rays in woods like oak.

So far we've discussed mainly the shape of wood cells, not

Eastern white pine (even grain)

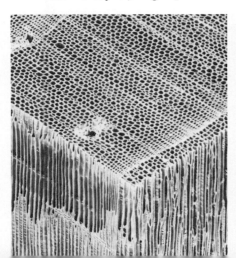

Southern yellow pine (uneven grain)

Earlywood/latewood variations are clearly visible in scanning electron microscope photographs. All the samples are oriented the same way, with the growth rings parallel to the right-hand face. Large "holes" in the pines are resin canals that help in sealing over injuries in the living trees. Pictures are from Structure and Identification of Wood, *by Core, Cote, and Day, a book to be published by the Syracuse University Press.*

Red oak half-cross-section (before shrinkage) shows pith dot at center, dark heartwood, light sapwood, and cambium sheath where bark and sapwood meet. Rays are clearly visible in the heartwood radiating outward. At right is the section from a leaning hemlock tree. Reaction wood appears as abnormally wide latewood on lower side of rings.

whether they're alive or dead. Live cells, called parenchyma, contain living protoplasm and are capable of assimilating and storing carbohydrates. In softwoods or conifers, the parenchyma are generally limited to the ray cells, but in hardwoods, longitudinal vessels and tracheids, as well as ray cells, can be parenchyma. It differs from species to species.

But in general, most longitudinal cells lose their protoplasm soon after development by the cambium and become non-living prosenchyma useful for sap conduction or mechanical support, but not for food storage. (When such a

change takes place, the cell wall structure remains unchanged. Only the protoplasm in the center cavity of the cell disappears.)

Thus the wood nearest the cambium, where sap conduction and food storage can take place, is called sapwood. As the tree grows and the oldest sapwood is no longer needed for water conduction, a gradual transition to heartwood occurs. This transition is accompanied by the death of parenchyma and loss of both food storage and conductive functions, with the heartwood serving the tree only as a supporting column.

Heartwood formation is accompanied by the deposition in the cell walls of chemical additives called extractives which can change the color of the wood. Whereas most sapwood is a cream to light yellow or light tan color, extractives are responsible for any rich browns, reddish or other contrasting dark colors the heartwood may have, as is characteristic of species like walnut, cherry, or red cedar. In some woods, such as spruce or basswood, the extractives may be insignificant or colorless so that there is little color difference between heartwood and sapwood.

Heartwood extractives can make changes other than color. Some extractives may be toxic to decay fungi and thus impart decay resistance to heartwood, as in redwood. Sapwood not only lacks decay resistance, but is attractive to stain fungi and certain powder post beetles because of the stored carbohydrates in the parenchyma cells.

In some species the original sapwood moisture content is remarkably higher, but the permeability of sapwood is usually greater, so that it loses moisture faster, but also absorbs preservatives or stains better. On the other hand, because of the bulking effect of extractives — they occupy molecular space within the cell wall — the shrinkage of heartwood may be less than that of sapwood.

For the woodworker, the heartwood-sapwood distinction is important. But what about the more general "hardwood-softwood" distinction? The names themselves are misleading because balsa wood is really a "hardwood" and hard southern pine is really a "softwood." While softwoods are generally evergreens, and hardwoods are generally deciduous, this is not always the case. The precise distinction is that the seeds of softwoods (gymnosperms — all conifers plus the familiar ginkgo tree) are naked (as in a pine seed), while for

Specific Gravity

Gymnosperms	Angiosperms
	Lignum vitae
	Ebony
Water: 1.0	Rosewood
	Purpleheart
	Domestic "Hardwoods"
	Hickory
Domestic "Softwoods"	Hard maple, Birch, Beech, Oak
	White ash
Southern yellow pine	Black walnut
Douglas fir	Black cherry
Eastern red cedar	
Hemlock, Redwood	Chestnut, Yellow poplar
White pine	Butternut, Aspen
White cedar	Basswood
0.1	Balsa

Differences in the specific gravity (the density relative to water) shows that the range of densities of domestic "hardwoods" and "softwoods" overlaps.

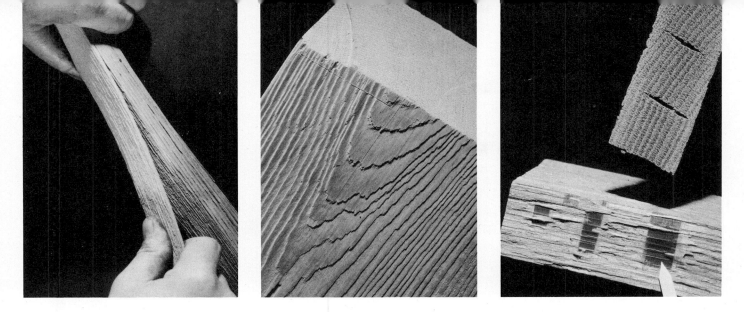

Basketmakers take advantage of weak earlywood (after pounding) of quarter-sawed ash to separate it into strips (left). Severely raised grain on pith side of flat-sawed hemlock (center) results from harder latewood being compressed into softer earlywood during planing, then springing back later. Honeycomb checks in red oak (right) can cause failure along large ray.

hardwoods (angiosperms), they are encapsulated (as in a walnut or acorn).

The hardness and softness of wood does come into play when we consider earlywood and latewood. Earlywood is that grown early in the season, when the moisture needed for rapid growth is present. In conifers, this means those longitudinal tracheid cells have thinner walls and larger cavities to favor conduction of sap. As latewood develops later in the growing season, the tracheids develop thicker walls (and in effect, denser wood). In other words, there is less airspace in latewood.

To a woodworker, what is also important is how this transition between latewood and earlywood occurs. Soft pines (e.g. eastern white, western white, and sugar) are characterized by fairly even grain, with gradual transition from earlywood to latewood. The result is fairly low average density with pleasing uniformity of wearing and working properties. By contrast, species such as the hard pines (e.g. southern yellow pine, pitch pine, red pine) Douglas fir, larch and hemlock are notably uneven-grained. In southern yellow pine there is a three-to-one ratio in the densities of the latewood versus earlywood. Thus the difficulty of machining it and the woodcarver's preference for the soft pines.

The latewood-earlywood differentiation can also present problems in staining — especially in conifers. In natural wood the latewood appears dark, the earlywood light. But earlywood is more porous, so that it absorbs stain more readily and thus stains darker than the latewood. The effect is to reverse the grain pattern, giving us the grain that would appear in a photographic negative. We've probably all seen this happen in the conifers such as pine or Douglas fir. However, in certain hardwoods, the large vessel size found in early wood makes it appear darker. Therefore, stain merely accentuates this darkness, rather than reversing it.

Hardwoods have a wider variety of longitudinal cells so there is less consistency in the differentiation between early wood and latewood. Rather than a change in the size of the tracheids, there is a change in the distribution of the larger vessels and smaller fibers. In some woods, the large vessels appear only during early growth, the fibers mainly during late growth (along with smaller vessels). This results in sharply defined rings of growth and the classification "ring-porous

hardwoods" (such as oak, elm, ash, chestnut, catalpa). As in southern yellow pine, there is a sharp difference in the densities of the earlywood and latewood.

By contrast, there are also the "diffuse-porous hardwoods" (where the pores or vessels are evenly distributed throughout the growth ring). The relative pore size, or "texture," may vary from the finest (or invisible) pores in gum, maple or aspen, to medium (or barely visible) in birch, and to coarse (or conspicuous) in mahogany. Although the vessels remain open in many species (e.g. red oak), in other species (e.g. white oak, locust) the vessels of the heartwood become blocked by bubble-like obstructions called tyloses that occur as sapwood changes to heartwood. These tyloses have a profound effect on the liquid permeability of the wood. That's why white oak is good for casks, but red oak is not.

The last distinction of interest to woodworkers is that of "reaction wood" found in leaning trees and in branches. The usual symptoms are eccentricity of ring shape and abnormally high longitudinal shrinkage, causing severe warpage in drying, as well as unexpected hidden stresses. In softwoods, the reaction wood is found on the underside and is called compression wood. It's also brittle. In hardwoods, it's found on the upper side, and is called tension wood, which machines with a microscopic wooliness resulting in a blotchiness when stained.

Perhaps all this shows that wood is no simple subject to talk about. Take the word "grain" for example. Normally, we mean the alignment of the longitudinal cells, because wood splits "along the grain." In the same context we have such terms as spiral grain, cross grain, wavy grain and interlocked grain. But grain can also refer to the uniformity of the growth ring structure. Douglas fir is an "uneven-grained" wood while basswood is "even-grained." Sometimes grain refers to the ray cell structure, as in the "silver grain" of white oak cut radially — slicing along the rays, in effect. And sometimes we refer to the "open grain" of oak and the "closed grain" of cherry when we're really talking about the texture caused by the presence or absence of large vessels. Finally, there is the "grain" of rosewood — not really grain, but figure, caused by the extractives in the heartwood.

So the word "grain" is not so clearcut and simple as it seems. Neither is the study of wood.

Water and Wood

The problems of a difficult pair

by R. Bruce Hoadley

What is the relative humidity in your workshop? Or in your garage where you are "seasoning" those carving blocks? Or in the spare room where you store your precious cabinet woods? Or for that matter, in any other room in your house or shop?

If you're not sure, you may be having problems such as warp, checking, unsuccessful glue joints, or even stain and mold. For just as these problems are closely related to moisture content, so is moisture content a direct response to relative humidity. Water is always present in wood so an understanding of the interrelationships between water and wood is fundamental to fine woodworking. In this article we'll take a look at water or moisture content in wood and its relationship to relative humidity, and also its most important consequence to the woodworker—shrinkage and swelling.

Remember that wood is a cellulosic material consisting of countless cells, each having an outer cell wall surrounding an interior cell cavity (see *Fine Woodworking*, Summer 1976). A good analogy for now is the familiar synthetic sponge commonly used in the kitchen or for washing the car. A sopping wet sponge, just pulled from a pail of water, is analogous to wood in a living tree to the extent that the cell walls are fully saturated and swollen and cell cavities are partially to completely filled with water. If we squeeze the sopping wet sponge, liquid water pours forth. Similarly, the water in wood cell cavities, called free water, can likewise be

squeezed out if we place a block of freshly cut pine sapwood in a vise and squeeze it; or we may see water spurt out of green lumber when hit with a hammer. In a tree, the sap is mostly water and for the purposes of wood physics, can be considered simply as water, the dissolved nutrients and minerals being ignored.

Now imagine thoroughly wringing out a wet sponge until no further liquid water is evident. The sponge remains full size, fully flexible and damp to the touch. In wood, the comparable condition is called the fiber saturation point (fsp), wherein, although the cell cavities are emptied of water, the cell walls are fully saturated and therefore fully swollen and in their weakest condition. The water remaining in the cell walls is called bound water. Just as a sponge would have to be left to dry—and shrink and harden—so will the bound water slowly leave a piece of wood if placed in a relatively dry atmosphere. How much bound water is lost (in either the sponge or the board), and therefore how much shrinkage takes place, will depend on the relative humidity of the atmosphere.

A dry sponge can be partially swollen by placing it in a damp location, or quickly saturated and fully swollen by plunging it into a bucket of water. Likewise a piece of dry wood will regain moisture and swell in response to high relative humidity and can indeed be resaturated to its fully

This block of catalpa had a moisture content of 114% and weighed almost 60 pounds when cut. It has been dried to 8% moisture content for carving and now weighs only 30 pounds. The gallon jugs

show the actual amount of free water (F) and bound water (B) which were lost in drying. Some bound water, equivalent to B', still remains in the wood.

Average Moisture Content (Percent) of Green Wood		
	HEARTWOOD	SAPWOOD
Ash, white	46	44
Beech	55	72
Birch, yellow	74	72
Maple, sugar	65	72
Oak, northern red	80	69
Oak, white	64	78
Walnut, black	90	73
Douglas fir	37	115
Pine, white	62	148
Pine, sugar	98	219
Pine, red	32	134
Redwood	86	210
Spruce, eastern	41	172

SEE PAGE 8

swollen condition. Some people erroneously believe that kiln drying is permanent, but lumber so dried will readsorb moisture. There is a certain amount of despair in the sight of rain falling on a pile of lumber stamped "certified kiln dried"!

It is standard practice to refer to water in wood as a certain percent moisture content. The weight of the water is expressed as a percent of the oven dry wood (determined by placing wood in an oven at 212-221°F until all water is driven off and a constant weight is reached). Thus if a plank weighed 115 pounds originally, but reached a dry weight of 100 pounds in an oven this would indicate 15 pounds of water had been present and the original moisture content would have been 15 ÷ 100 or 15%.

The fiber saturation point averages around 30% moisture content (higher in some species, lower in others). Living trees always have moisture content in excess of this level, although the moisture content (MC) may vary widely. Hardwoods commonly have original moisture contents ranging from 50 to 100%. In softwoods there is usually a noticeable difference between sapwood and heartwood; heartwood moisture content being just over the fiber saturation point whereas the sapwood commonly exceeds 100% moisture content—that is, the sapwood may be more than half water by weight.

When wood dries, all the free water is eventually lost as well as some of the bound water, depending on the relative humidity. When the bound water moisture content is in balance with the atmospheric relative humidity, the wood is said to be at its equilibrium moisture content (emc).

When lumber is left out-of-doors in well-stickered piles, protected from soaking rain and direct sun, it eventually becomes "air-dry". In central New England, the relative humidity (RH) averages around 77%, so air dry lumber will have a moisture content of 13 to 14%.

In heated buildings, in coldest winter weather, the relative humidity may drop quite low. The actual moisture content of thin pieces of wood or unprotected wood surfaces may be as low as 2 to 3%, only to return to 10 to 12% in muggy August weather. Therefore, for indoor uses, average moisture content should be attained to begin with. A moisture content of 6 to 8% is usually recommended for furniture manufacture in most northern and central regions of the United States. In the more humid southern and coastal regions the appropriate average equilibrium moisture content might be somewhat higher; in the arid southwest, somewhat lower. The only way commercially to get lumber this dry (that is, below air dry) is to dry it in a kiln; hence "kiln dried" lumber suggests this sufficient degree of drying. The drying can also be accomplished by simply leaving wood exposed indoors until it assumes the proper emc—remembering, of course, that it fluctuates as indoor relative humidity does.

Certain common terms which have been associated with drying are unfortunately misleading. "Curing" lumber suggests the involvement of some chemical reaction as in the

Approximate Shrinkage (as percent of green dimension) from green to oven-dry moisture content			
	TANGENTIAL	RADIAL	T/R
HARDWOODS			
Ash, white	7.8	4.9	1.6
Basswood	9.3	6.6	1.4
Beech, American	11.9	5.5	2.2
Birch, yellow	9.5	7.3	1.3
Butternut	6.4	3.4	1.9
Catalpa	4.9	2.5	2.0
Cherry, black	7.1	3.7	1.9
Hickory	11.5	7.2	1.6
Maple, sugar	9.9	4.8	2.0
Oak, northern red	8.6	4.0	2.2
Oak, white	10.5	5.6	1.9
Sycamore	8.4	5.0	1.7
Walnut, black	7.8	5.5	1.4
Mahogany	5.1	3.7	1.4
Teak	4.0	2.2	1.8
SOFTWOODS			
Cedar, northern white	4.9	2.2	2.2
Douglas fir	7.6	4.8	1.6
Hemlock, eastern	6.8	3.0	2.3
Pine, eastern white	6.0	2.3	2.6
Pine, sugar	5.6	2.9	1.9
Pine, red	7.2	3.8	1.9
Redwood	4.4	2.6	1.7
Spruce, red	7.8	3.8	2.1

Cross sectional discs of red pine (left) and catalpa (right) after drying to 6% moisture content. Radial slits were sawn into green discs; width of cracks indicates the relative instability of the two species. At right, the seasoning checks in a butternut half-log illustrates that shrinkage is sometimes greater in sapwood than in heartwood.

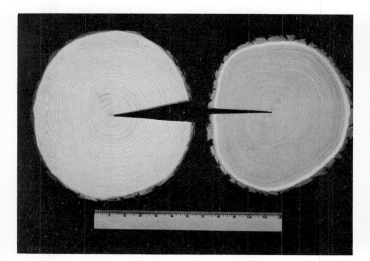

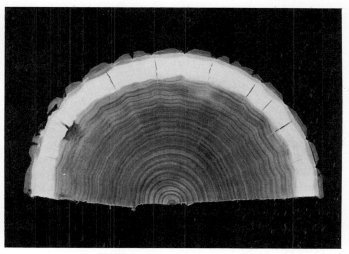

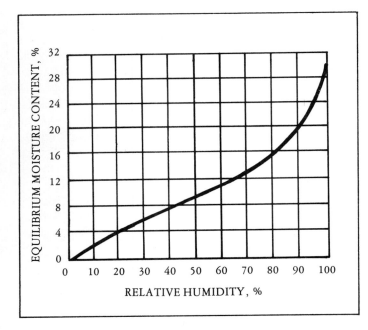

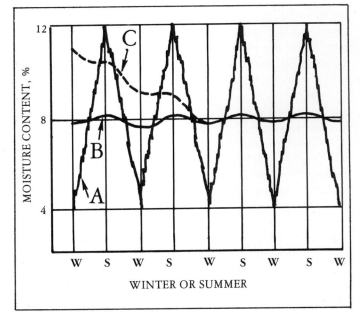

Curve at left shows the approximate relationship between relative humidity and equilibrium moisture content for most woods. At right, the curves show the seasonal indoor variation of moisture content in wood. A is unfinished thin veneers or wood surfaces, B is furniture of kiln-dried lumber and well coated with finish, and C is furniture of air-dried lumber and well coated with finish.

CALCULATING WOOD SHRINKAGE OR SWELLING

The approximate dimensional change expected in a piece of wood can be estimated by application of the following formula:

$$\Delta D = D_o \times S \times \Delta MC \div fsp$$

where ΔD = Change in dimension
D_o = Original dimension
S = Shrinkage percentage (from tables)
ΔMC = Change in moisture content
fsp = Average value for fiber saturation point, approximately 30%

Example: How much will a 14-inch wide, unfinished colonial door panel attempt to "move" (shrink and swell) if made from flat-sawed Eastern white pine?

Solution: Original dimension (width), D_o is 14 inches.
S (from tables) is 6.0% = 6/100 = 0.06
Assuming the humidity may fluctuate such that moisture content will vary from 4% in winter to 12% in summer, then ΔMC = 8%.

$$\Delta D = (14 \text{ inches})(0.06)(8\% \div 30\%) = 0.224 \text{ inches}$$

The door panel will thus attempt to change width by nearly a quarter-inch during seasonal humidity changes. Loose framing to allow the panel to move, or finishing with a moisture-impervious finish are therefore recommended.

The formula clearly suggests ways of reducing the consequences of shrinkage and swelling. For example, reducing the dimensions (D_o) of the members: Narrow flooring will surely develop smaller cracks between boards than wide flooring. Choosing a species with a small shrinkage percent (S) can obviously help; e.g. catalpa is obviously more stable than hickory. Reducing the moisture variation is best accomplished by starting with wood of the correct moisture content and giving the completed item a coat of moisture-impervious finish.

setting of resin, or the curing of hides or meat. To some persons, the term "seasoning" suggests the addition of an appropriate chemical or some special aging process to others; it probably originated in connection with certain seasons of the year when natural drying was optimum for efficiency and quality of drying. But in reality, the drying of lumber is basically a water removal operation that must be regulated to control the shrinkage stresses that occur.

The claim that lumber is kiln dried can probably assure only that the lumber has been in and out of a kiln; it does not assure that the lumber has been dried properly (to avoid stresses), that is has been dried to the desired moisture content, or that subsequent moisture regain has not taken place. On the other hand, lumber which has been kiln dried *properly* is unsurpassed for woodworking.

The woodworker's success in dealing with moisture problems depends on being able to measure or monitor either the moisture in the wood directly, or the relative humidity of the atmosphere, or both. Direct measurement of moisture content is traditionally done by placing a sample of known initial weight into an oven (212-221°F) until constant weight is reached (usually about 24 hours for 1-inch cross-sectional wafer). Reweighing to obtain oven-dry weight enables determination of moisture loss and calculation of moisture content (moisture loss ÷ oven-dry weight). By so determining the moisture content of wafers taken from the ends of a sample board, the board moisture content can be closely approximated. Simply monitoring the sample board weight in the future will then indicate changes in moisture content.

An interesting application of this idea is to suspend a wood sample of known (or approximated) moisture content from one end of a rod, horizontally suspended on a string at its balance point. As the wood looses or gains moisture, the inclination of the rod will give a constant picture of changing moisture content. Such an improvisation can be calibrated (by adding known weights) to make a "moisture meter". Of course, there are also commercially made moisture meters, which are surprisingly accurate and simple to operate and will take the guesswork out of measuring moisture content.

Measuring and controlling relative humidity in the shop can be equally important. Simple and inexpensive wet and dry bulb hygrometers give accurate readings. Common sense will indicate where humidifiers or dehumidifiers (or some improvised means) are necessary to control humidity. One summer I suspected the humidity in my cellar workshop was high. I distributed 1/8-inch thick spruce wafers around and after several days determined their moisture content by the oven-dry technique. To my horror it was up to 21%! I immediately installed a dehumidifier and within a few weeks the emc was lowered to about 9%.

For the woodworker, then it is important either to obtain lumber of proper dryness or to be able to dry it properly (a subject we must leave to the next issue). Further, once having dried wood to the proper moisture content and built something out of it, some consideration must be given to future moisture exchange with the atmosphere. To some extent, design should allow for lumber movement, but usually the principal measure should be that of sealing the finished piece to *prevent* exchange of moisture and avoid the highs and lows of seasonal humidity fluctuation by holding close to the original average. Somehow the notion has prevailed that "wood has to breathe". Unfortunately, the term "breathe" suggests something positive or even necessary for the well being of the wood, but in reality, depriving wood of its tendency to adsorb and desorb moisture in response to humidity fluctuation is the best course of action.

Finishing materials vary widely in their ability to seal off wood surfaces and prevent moisture exchange with the atmosphere. Among the least effective is linseed oil. So-called penetrating oil finishes vary from low to moderate in moisture excluding capability depending on resin content and, as with linseed oil, give improved results when many coats are applied. Shellac is also relatively permeable to moisture. Lacquers are even better, but modern varnishes, such as the urea alkyd or urethane types, offer the best clear-finish protection against moisture adsorption. For end sealing lumber during drying or storage, aluminum paint or paraffin provide the ultimate in moisture barriers, as do commercial end sealing compounds.

Moisture extremes—either too high or too low—sometimes give rise to problems in chemical bonding of adhesives and finishes or high moisture (above 20%) may invite mold, stain or decay. But clearly the most common trouble-maker is the dimensional change—shrinkage and swelling—which accompanies moisture variation over the range below fiber saturation point.

As we begin to unravel the subject of shrinkage, three considerations should be taken into stride: *when* (over what moisture content range), *where* (in what direction relative to cell structure) and *how much* (quantitively in terms of actual dimensions). In the first consideration, as with a sponge, wood shrinks (or swells) as bound water escapes (or is picked up) in seeking its balance with the atmosphere. So only moisture change below fiber saturation point (about 30% MC) results in dimensional change, which is directly proportional to the amount of moisture lost. In considering *where* and *how much*, we must leave our sponge analogy, because a sponge has similar structure and properties in all directions; wood on the other hand, has oriented structure related to the "grain

Various shapes of red pine are shown, after drying, superimposed over their original positions on an adjacent log section. The greater tangential than radial shrinkage causes squares to become diamond shaped, cylinders to become oval. Quarter sawn boards seldom warp but flat-sawn boards cup away from the pith. Camera perspective does not show full extent of shrinkage that occurred.

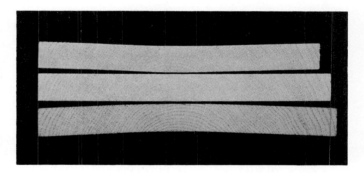

These three strips of wood were cut in sequence from the end of an air-dry red oak board. As shown by the middle strip, it measured 9-1/2-inch wide at a moisture content of 14 percent. The top strip has been dried to below 4 percent moisture content, the lower strip has been allowed to readsorb to over 20 percent moisture content and thus warps in an opposite direction.

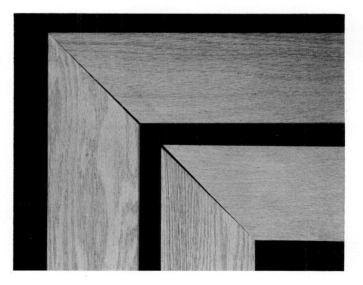

These two red oak frame corners were tightly mitered when originally assembled. The upper one was dried, the lower one dampened. Since wood is stable along the grain, but shrinks and swells across the grain, joints open as shown.

direction'' (predominant longitudinal cells) and to the growth rings. Longitudinal shrinkage (i.e., along the grain) is drastically different from shrinkage across the grain; shrinkage across the grain in turn is variable from the radial direction (perpendicular to growth rings) to tangential (parallel to growth rings).

Shrinkage in wood is commonly expressed as a percentage loss in dimension due to loss of bound water, that is, in drying from the fiber saturation point to the oven dry condition. Parallel to the grain, shrinkage is only about 1/10 of one percent, and in most cases can be neglected. However, in juvenile wood (near the pith) or in reaction wood (in limbs and leaning stems) longitudinal shrinkage may be up to ten times the normal amount, and variable—resulting in extreme warp.

The greatest concern is transverse (across-the grain) shrinkage, which averages about 4% radially and 8% tangentially. However, there is considerable variation among species, ranging from 2% to about 12% (see chart).

These values indicate the degree to which some species are apparently ''more stable'' than others. However, the greatest cause of trouble arises from the difference between radial and tangential shrinkage. As a result, cylinders of wood may become oval, squares may become diamond shaped, and flat sawn boards cup. This shrinkage difference also accounts for wood containing the pith cracking open, as anyone who has tried to dry cross-sectional discs of wood well knows. For it is impossible for wood to shrink more *around* the growth rings than *across* them without the development of stress. We also realize why edge-grain (quarter sawn) boards remain flat and shrink less across the width and are therefore preferable for many uses such as flooring.

Shrinkage in wood tissue results when water molecules leave the microstructure of the cell walls and the cellulosic structure is drawn more closely together. As sapwood transforms into heartwood, molecules of extractives (which usually give heartwood its darker color) may occupy this space and thus reduce total shrinkage. For this reason, woods with high extractive content may tend to be more stable (e.g. redwood, mahogany). At the same time, in a particular piece of wood there may be a troublesome difference between shrinkage of heartwood and sapwood, resulting in noticeable difference in shrinkage or even checking of sapwood.

The woodworker has several options and approaches, which can be applied singly or in combination, for dealing with the instability of wood. First, the wood can be preshrunk, i.e., properly dried to optimum moisture content. And secondly, the subsequent dimensional response to the atmosphere can be reduced or virtually eliminated by proper finishing. Third, sensible design can allow for dimensional change to occur without consequence; the classic example being the traditional feather-edge paneling allowed to move freely within each frame. Fourth, shrinkage and swelling can be overpowered or restrained, as the veneers making up a plywood sheet mutually do, or as the battens on a cabinet door will do. Fifth, chemical treatments may stabilize wood, although this approach is probably least convenient.

Controlling moisture content—and therefore dimensional change—involves an awareness of relative humidity and also the dimensional properties of wood. Understanding and mastering wood/moisture relationships should be looked upon as an integral part of woodworking expertise.

Drying Wood

The fundamental considerations

by R. Bruce Hoadley

It is ironic that our environment has us surrounded by trees—yet wood seems so inaccessible and expensive for the woodworker. Actually, abundant tree material is available to those who seek it out from such sources as storm damage cleanup, construction site clearance, firewood cuttings and even direct purchase from local loggers. With chain saws, wedges, band saws and a measure of ingenuity, chunks and flitches for carving or even lumber can be worked out. Also, it is usually possible to buy green lumber, either hardwood or softwood, at an attractive price from small local sawmills.

But what to do next? Many an eager woodworker has produced a supply of wood to the green board stage, but has been unable to dry it to usable moisture levels without serious ''degrade'' or even total loss. Certainly, the most consistent and efficient procedure would be to have the material kiln dried. Unfortunately, however, kilns may simply not be available. The cost of custom drying may be prohibitive, or the quantity of material too meager to justify kiln operation. But by understanding some of the basic principles of drying requirements and techniques, the woodworker can dry small quantities of wood quite successfully.

The so-called ''seasoning'' of wood is basically a water-removal process. Wood in the living tree has its cell walls water saturated and fully swollen with ''bound'' water and has additional ''free'' water in the cell cavities. The target in drying is to get the wood moisture content down to the equilibrium level of dryness consistent with the atmosphere in which the finished product will be used (*Fine Woodworking*, Fall 1976). In the Northeast, for example, a moisture content of about seven percent is appropriate for interior cabinetwork and furniture; in the more humid Southern states, it would be higher; in the arid Southwest, lower. Since removal of bound water is accompanied by shrinkage of the wood, the object is to have the wood do its shrinking *before*, rather than *after*, the woodworking.

Wood dries first at the outside surface, creating a moisture imbalance. This moisture gradient of wetter interior and drier surface zone is necessary to cause moisture in the interior to migrate to the surface for eventual evaporation. On the other hand, if a piece of wood is dried too quickly, causing a ''steep'' moisture gradient (i.e., extreme range between interior and surface moisture content), excessive surface shrinkage will precede internal shrinkage; the resulting stress may cause surface checking or internal defects (collapse or

R. Bruce Hoadley is a wood technologist at the University of Massachusetts and a carver who is never without a pile or two of drying wood.

SEE PAGE 12

16

later honeycomb). Gradual drying with a moderate moisture gradient allows moisture from the interior to migrate outward, replacing moisture as it evaporates from the surface, thus maintaining gradual and more uniform shrinkage. Shrinkage in wood per se is a natural and normal part of drying which should be expected and accommodated; *uneven* shrinkage due to uncontrolled drying, however, is the culprit which we must deal with. On the other hand, drying cannot be too slow or unnecessarily delayed, lest fungi causing decay, stain, or mold have a chance to develop. In other words, the key to drying is manipulating conditions of humidity, temperature and air circulation to attain a compromise drying rate fast enough to prevent fungal development, but slow enough to prevent severe uneven shrinkage.

The practice of drying includes (1) proper cutting and preparation of the pieces, (2) appropriate stacking and location to allow regulated drying (and in lumber, restraint of warp), and (3) systematic monitoring of the drying progress. Let's review the application of these basic concepts to typical situations of drying small quantities of wood. We will consider the drying of short log segments or short thick stock, commonly used for wood carvings or stout turnings, as well as regular lumber or boards. We will also assume that fairly small quantities such as several log chunks or up to a few hundred board feet are involved—as occurs when one suddenly falls heir to a storm-damaged tree or purchases enough lumber for a single piece of furniture.

First let's look at proper preparation of the material. Selection of pieces should favor those with normal structure and straight grain. If possible, avoid pieces with large obvious defects. Lumber from trees with special grain will invariably twist upon drying. Irregularities such as crotch grain or burls are esthetically interesting but chancy to dry, since their cell structure usually has unpredictable shrinkage. Knots are troublesome if they are large enough to involve grain distortion. Logs with sweep or from leaning trees having an eccentric cross-sectional shape probably contain reaction wood and will almost surely develop warp and stress due to abnormal shrinkage.

Whether preparing lumber or carving blocks, remember that normal shrinkage is about double tangentially as radially. My initial rule in splitting carving chunks from logs is to avoid pieces containing the pith. A half log or less which does not contain the pith can dry with a normal distortion of its cross-sectional shape (like slightly closing an oriental fan).

Another advantage of not boxing in the pith is being able to see if any overgrown knots are present which may not have been apparent from the bark side. Every knot-causing branch developed from the pith, so it is important to examine pieces from the pith side to discover hidden branch stubs, especially if they have decay. Additionally, the pith area is often abnormal juvenile wood that might best be eliminated.

In sawing lumber, cup will be minimized by favoring quartersawed boards, which have no tendency to cup, or flatsawed boards taken furthest from the pith. Boards sawed through the center of the log, containing the pith or passing very close to it, will usually cup severely (or split open if restrained) along the center and might as well be ripped into two narrower boards before drying.

End drying is about 12 times as fast as drying through side-grain surfaces. Consequently, the regions near the ends of pieces drop below the fiber saturation point first. As the ends begin to shrink while the rest of the piece is still fully swollen, end checking usually results. In boards that are relatively long compared to their thickness, most moisture will leave slowly via the side surfaces; the influence of the end-checking problem is confined to a zone near each end of the board (about 6 inches from the ends of 1-in. boards). With relatively thick material, e.g., an 8 x 8-in. chunk 20 in. long, the end checking under uncontrolled drying can extend inward so far from each end that it riddles the entire piece.

To prevent the rapid end drying which will ruin carving chunks and the ends of lumber, the end-grain surface should be coated. Any relatively impervious material (such as paraffin, aluminum paint or urethane varnish) in ample thickness will do nicely. End coating can be applied to relatively wet surfaces by giving a primer coat of latex material first. It is important to end coat as soon as possible after sawing, before even the tiniest checks can begin to develop. Once a check develops, the cell structure failure will always be there even if it later appears to have closed. Also, when normal drying stress develops, a small check can provide the stress concentration point for further failures which otherwise might not have even begun in check-free wood. The purpose

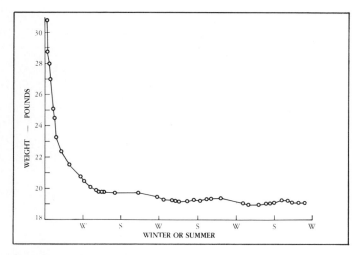

Periodic weights of drying wood plotted on a graph show equilibrium moisture content has been reached.

As shown in this cherry log, the greater tangential than radial shrinkage is relieved by radial cracking.

of end coating is to force all moisture loss to take place from lateral surfaces.

In some species, radial drying may be significantly faster than tangential drying. Therefore, if the bark on larger carving blocks is tight (as with winter-cut wood), it may best be left on to slow the radial drying. If the bark has been removed from a heavy slab, it should be watched carefully during the early drying stages for signs of surface checking. Another reason for prompt end coating is to prevent ever present airborne fungal spores from inoculating the surface. If the bark is loose, it should be removed; otherwise the layer of separation will become a fungal culture chamber with undesirable results.

Don't forget to mark a number and date on each piece. It is amazing how easily your memory can fail once you have several batches of wood in process.

Next, consideration must be given to the correct piling and location of the material so proper drying will result. Piling must ensure maximum air circulation around virtually every surface of the material. Some means of elevating the bottom of the stacks should be provided and some sort of sticker strips are usually recommended to separate adjacent pieces. With irregular carving blocks, merely piling them loosely may suffice, as long as flat surfaces do not lie against one another. No attempt should be made to restrain distortion of large chunks. With lumber, however, carefully designed systematic piling is best.

The usual piling method is to arrange boards in regular layers or courses separated by narrow strips or stickers. This permits the free movement of air around the lumber, uniformity of exposure of the surfaces, and restraint to minimize warp. The stickers should be dry and free of fungi and at least as long as the intended width of the pile. In planning the pile, stickers should be placed at the very ends of each course and at least every 18 inches along the length of the boards, since loose ends hanging out of the pile lack restraint and dry too rapidly (resulting in excessive warp). It is best to have lumber uniform in length, but if random lengths are unavoidable, they should be arranged in a pile as long as the longest boards; within each course, stagger the position of alternate boards so their alternate ends are lined up with the end of the pile. This "boxed pile" system prevents excessive drying of overhanging ends. To prevent excessive drying degrade to the top and bottom courses or layers, extra outer

courses of low-grade lumber or even plywood might be added to the pile. Stickers should be lined up in straight vertical rows. To ensure uniform restraint in a course, lumber and stickers should be as uniform in thickness as possible.

In large piles, the majority of the boards are restrained by the weight of others above. In small piles, extra weight (old lumber, bricks, cinder blocks, etc.) should be placed atop the pile. An alternate method of applying restraint is to assemble rectangular frames to surround the pile. The pile can be wedged against the frames and the wedges tapped further in to maintain restraint as the pile shrinks. Obviously the weighting or wedging should not be so extreme as to prevent shrinkage of the boards across their width.

In a commercial dry kiln, the operator can manipulate air circulation, temperature and humidity to dry the lumber gradually. He begins with a moderately low temperature and high relative humidity until the lumber (based on monitored samples) drops to a certain moisture content, say, near the fiber saturation point. He then establishes a slightly higher temperature and drier condition which he holds until the next lower prescribed moisture content is reached. Then he again establishes another warmer, drier level and so on until the lumber is dried. The so-called "kiln schedule" is a sequence of successively drier conditions which are regulated according to the moisture content of the lumber.

In home drying of wood, we must therefore try to choose locations or regulate conditions to allow only moderate drying at first, followed by more drastic conditions once the lumber has reached a lower moisture level. One logical starting place is out-of-doors. Except for especially arid regions, the relative humidity is usually moderately high. For example, in the New England area the humidity averages around 75 to 80 percent, which would give an equilibrium moisture content of 12 to 14 percent. Piles of blocks or stacks of lumber should be kept well up off the ground to avoid dampness, and should be protected from direct rainfall and sun rays as well. Any unheated building which has good ventilation, such as a shed lacking doors and windows, is ideal. Most garages serve well and even unheated basements are suitable if plenty of air space around the pile is provided. In air drying out-of-doors, some rather obvious seasonal variations will be encountered. In many Eastern areas, slightly lower humidity and more prevalent winds favor drying in spring months. In winter, if temperatures drop to near or below freezing, drying may be

End grain surface of a basswood half log which was not end coated in time shows a large number of end checks.

Cross-cutting has revealed that the surface checks have penetrated deep into this white oak board.

brought to a standstill. You must therefore interpret conditions for each particular area. If wood is intended for finished items that will be used indoors, outdoor air drying will not attain a low enough equilibrium moisture content. The material must be moved indoors to a heated location before it is worked.

Surface checking should be closely watched. Minor shallow surface checking that will later dress out can be ignored. However, deeper checks should be considered unacceptable. The worst type are those which open up but later reclose. Often they go unnoticed during subsequent machining operations only to reveal themselves when staining and finishing of a completed piece is attempted. If any serious end checks develop, don't pretend they don't exist, or will ever get better or go away. For example, if a large carving block develops a serious check, this indicates fairly intensive stress; it is probably best to split the piece in half along the check, thus helping to relieve the stresses, and be satisfied with smaller pieces.

If wood must be located indoors from the very start, drying may be too rapid. Any signs of surface checks in the material suggest that some retardation may be necessary. This can be accomplished by covering the entire pile with a polyethylene film. Moisture from the lumber will soon elevate the humidity and retard the drying. However, this arrangement must be closely watched, since air circulation will likewise be stopped. Moisture condensation on the inside of the plastic covering or any mold on the wood surfaces may mean the pile has been turned into a fungi culture chamber and signals the need for speeding up the drying again. Common sense and intuition will suggest how often to check the wood and how to modify the storage location to speed up or slow down the drying. The seasonal humidity fluctuation commonly encountered in heated buildings must also be allowed for in determining the equilibrium moisture level.

Drying progress can be monitored by weight. Weights should be taken often enough to be able to plot a fairly coherent graphical record of weight against time. Weighing should be accurate to within one or two percent of the total weight of the piece. A large chunk in the 100-pound range can be weighed on a bathroom scale. Pieces in the 10 to 25-pound category can be weighed with a food or infant scale. Small stacks of boards can be monitored by simply weighing the entire pile if this is convenient. In larger piles, sample boards can be pulled and weighed periodically. Electrical moisture meters are perhaps the simplest means of keeping track of the drying progress in boards.

The last stage of drying should be done in an environment similar to the one in which the finished item will be used. The weight of the pieces will eventually level out and reach a near constant equilibrium with only faint gains and losses of weight in response to seasonal humidity fluctuations.

When material comes into equilibrium weight with the desired environment, it's ready. Don't pay attention to overly generalized rules like "one year of drying for every inch of thickness." Such rules have no way of accounting for the tremendous variation in species' characteristics or in atmospheric conditions. Basswood or pine decoy blanks four inches thick dry easily in less than a year, whereas a four-inch thick slab of rosewood may take much longer to dry without defects. In general, the lower density woods are easier to dry than higher density woods. Since the average cell wall thickness is less, moisture movement is greater and this results in faster drying. In addition, the weaker cell structure is better able to deform in response to drying stresses, rather than resisting and checking. After some experience is gained for a particular species and thickness dried in a certain location, a fairly reliable estimate can be made as to the necessary drying time. Here, the initial date you marked on the piece will serve you well.

Whether drying log sections or boards, remember that the drying must be somewhat regulated; usually at the beginning, indoor drying proceeds too quickly and needs slowing down.

In drying your own lumber or carving wood, one common problem is hesitation. You can't wait! If you do, fungi or checks will get ahead of you. Try to think out all the details *before* you get your wood supply; don't wait until you get it home to decide how you are going to end coat or where you are going to stack it.

But perhaps the greatest pitfall is greed. Most woodworkers never feel they have enough material put aside and tend to overstock if the opportunity presents itself. With green wood, this can be disastrous. Don't try to handle too much. Don't even start if you can't follow through. More material is ruined by neglect than by lack of know-how.

Finally, in drying wood, nobody has ever proved that it doesn't pay to cross your fingers.

Chair Woods

Lessons from the past on choosing the right woods

by Robert C. Whitley

I stared at one hundred and fifty chairs, every one of them so loose as to be dangerous to sit in. "I have tried everything to no avail," the owner said. "Do you know the glue they advertise on TV where one drop between two blocks of wood holds a car suspended in the air?" he asked me in exasperation. "Well I must have used half a pint on each chair, and they still came apart." I nodded. "I'll admit you cabinetmakers have some secrets. Will you fix the chairs for me?" I said no, explaining that the chairs were made out of the wrong kind of wood and that they would never hold together for any length of time. He stalked off, obviously convinced I was out of my mind.

The preceding is a true account of a conversation between myself and the owner of a large, beautiful restaurant located on the banks of the Delaware River. The chairs in question are normally referred to as "captain's chairs." The original chair from which these were copied has proved to be a sturdy and

practical design, made since the early 1800's. Why then were the chairs I was asked to repair not only falling apart, but incapable of restoration? Because the complete chair—legs, seat, spindles and back—was all of soft white pine!

It seems impossible that a large manufacturer would devote great sums of money and many man hours of work producing chairs with such an obvious fault. And yet, hardly a week goes by that I don't come in contact with chairs made with the wrong choice of wood.

A chair, especially the plank-seated chair, takes greater stresses, strains and shocks than any other piece of furniture used in the home because of its everyday use in kitchens, dining rooms and general living areas.

Imagine the stress placed on the legs and back of a chair that a 200-pound person sits in three times a day while eating. First, the chair is dragged across the floor, then the body lowers into the seat, shoving forward a few inches with

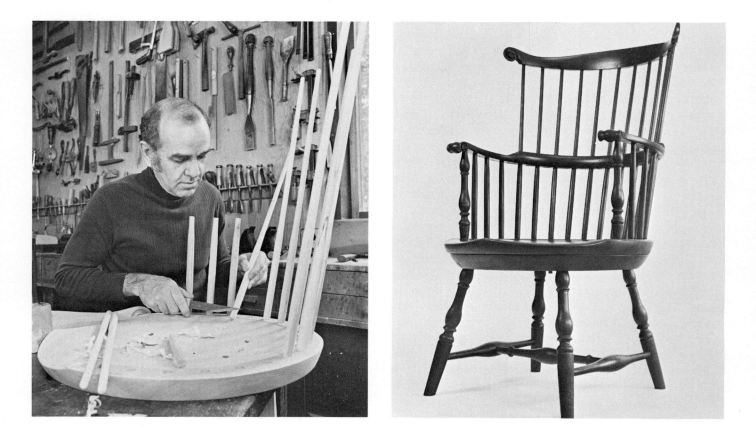

The author making a reproduction (right) of the chair Thomas Jefferson sat in when writing the Declaration of Independence. All woods are the same as the original: maple legs and arm posts, poplar seat and mid-arm back, hickory spindles, white oak arms and crest rail.

the full 200 pounds of weight on the base. Finally, the squirm and the wiggle to settle in! During serving and passing food to others, the weight is constantly shifting back and forth on the different legs of the chair. Now comes the balancing act! 200 pounds are thrown entirely onto the two back legs. Next is the coming down with accumulated speed to an abrupt stop, then the shoving of the chair to the rear with all the weight intact, and the final dragging to a place of rest.

Isn't it a wonder that these chairs have held up as long as they have? Here are the reasons why.

The Legs. Early chairmakers invariably used hard maple. It was easy to come by, but more importantly it is very hard, will resist impression, and does not splinter. Its fine, dense grain makes it easy to turn on the lathe. It also has tremendous resistance to abrasion, a quality especially needed where the legs of a chair meet the floor.

Stretchers. Base stretchers, too, were generally made of maple, only occasionally with white oak or hickory. In those cases I believe the chairmaker took into consideration a possible bending stress on the middle of a stretcher caused by the weight of feet that might be placed there. Whether the amount of stress was enough to put up with the more difficult turning qualities of the woods is debatable. In any event, although the stretchers are not to be considered as important as the legs in terms of abrasion, they too must be of a very hard wood.

The Seat. Here the craftsman's choice was influenced a great deal by the way the seat had to be contoured and shaped. Structurally he could have used a hardwood, but he knew that scooping out a comfortable seat would require at least a two-inch-thick plank to allow for ample depth to receive the legs, back and arm posts. The scooping-out process was done with an adze, a large chisel and shaped scrapers. It was laborious and time-consuming, so in the interest of ease and economy he chose softwoods to make the seat. The craftsman knew that the greater thickness of softwood would allow the legs and spindles to be deeply seated and, at the same time, weigh less, so he chose either pine or poplar, and only quite rarely a hardwood.

The Back. There were many types of chair backs, but for this discussion let me make two categories: the low back and the tall back. The low-back chair is called a "captain's chair," the type I referred to in the incident with the restaurant owner. This chair is very comfortable because of the large rolled and contoured shape which forms the back and the substantial arms. I have seen no exception to the use of either pine or poplar for this purpose. However, the short-turned spindles were always of either hard maple, oak or ash. The great dimension of the softwood back and arms allowed the hardwood spindles deep penetration.

The earliest type of low back was a Windsor chair which used pine or poplar for the back rail only, and here again it was thick enough to allow deep penetration of the spindles. The arms, which were thinner and therefore did not allow the spindles to be deeply seated, were either of white oak or maple.

The tall-back plank-seated chairs which have spindles that run from the seat to the top or crest are almost always of split-out hickory (wood split rather than ripped to rough size to ensure straight grain). A wood is needed that allows for movement—a wood that will give and spring back. Because of the small diameter of the spindles, the wood must have resiliency and an ability to resist fracture. Hickory is the only wood I know of which combines all these qualities.

When there is a thin, bent piece of wood incorporated into the back structure, it is almost always of split-out white oak, a wood which can be steamed and bent to rather small radii without fracturing. It also has great resiliency and hardness. Bent mid-arm rails, cresting rails and backs are invariable made of split-out steam-bent white oak.

The decision regarding what woods to use for a specific chair part was to some degree made easier for the earlier craftsman because most of his chairs were painted. Or perhaps they were painted because the craftsman used various woods. In any event, craftsmen today may want to use other woods than those used by the earlier craftsmen for esthetic considerations. There's no reason why not as long as one follows these guidelines:

- Use hardwoods where there will be shocks and abrasions.
- Use softwoods only in great thicknesses.
- Never join softwood to softwood.

In other words, do not use a wood for a purpose for which it is unsuited. Following is a list of some available woods and the purposes to which they are suited, in my opinion. Others may disagree on specific points. For instance, hickory could be used to make a chair seat and structurally it would stand up. However, its density and hardness make it extremely difficult to sculpt to shape, and its weight would be a disadvantage.

Walnut, Cherry: Good for all parts but has limited steam bendability.

Birch: Good for most parts, but very hard to sculpt.

Beech: Same as for birch, but fractures too easily when making thin spindles.

Sycamore: Great grain for seats, but has a tendency to warp. All right for legs and stretchers, but not for spindles.

Red Oak: Has a very coarse, unattractive grain, but may be used for most parts.

White Oak: Perfect for steam-bent parts, good for spindles and other parts. Too hard and heavy for seat.

Maple: Perfect for legs, stretchers and posts, but too hard and heavy for seats. Can be used if desired.

Poplar, Pine: For seats in two-inch thicknesses or better and for heavy back and arm sections. Do not use for any other parts!

Ash, Hickory: All parts except seats.

Mahogany: Great for most cabinet furniture, but really not suited for plank-seated chairs except as pine and poplar are used.

Spruce, Fir: No use.

Exotic Woods

Observations of a master turner

by Bob Stocksdale

[*Editor's note:* Early this summer, veteran woodturner Bob Stocksdale had an exhibit of some 120 bowls at Richard Kagan's gallery in Philadelphia. We were so taken by his extensive use of exotic woods that we asked him to tell us a little about some of those woods, as well as how he works. The bowls speak for themselves.]

I have three lathes—two Delta 12-inchers and a homemade big one that is built of steel I-beams and swings 31 inches inside the headstock. One of the Deltas has the headstock blocked up 3 inches so I can turn up to an 18-inch diameter inside. I do 90 percent of my turning on it as I have an exhaust fan just back of it to solve the dust problem. All three lathes have jackshafts for better speed selection. They also have reversing switches to aid in sanding.

Almost all of the decorative bowls, trays and smaller salad bowls are started on a single center screw or 6-inch faceplate. I use several different methods to do the inside job, sometimes even the single center screw, but more usually, for footed bowls, the three-jaw geared chuck. Trays usually have a block glued on the bottom, with newsprint between for easy removal.

I do most of my turning with two gouges, 1-inch and 1/2-inch standard tools of the kind also used for spindle work. The corners are ground back a long way so the tip is really a half-oval shape. I use a shearing cut. I never use the deep, long-and-strong style of gouge, because I don't need all that metal, and there's very little strain on the tool. In fact, I'd like to get some gouges made of steel that is only 1/8-inch thick, the ones I have are about 3/16.

Many, perhaps most of the deeper bowls have been roughed out first, dried in a heated room for about a month, then finished. The room is about 90 degrees, and I usually put a bowl on the floor for a week and then move it up onto the shelves for three weeks and it's dry. I have very little cracking and checking. When cracking does occur, I rough-sand the

Stocksdale

bowl and then repair it with a mixture of liquid epoxy and sawdust, as much sawdust as the epoxy will take. It sets overnight and you can turn right through it.

When the bowl is dry and back on the lathe, I finish the turning inside and out and then sand. I use a rubber disc sander on the outside with the lathe at its slowest speed, around 500 or 600 rpm. I start with 60 grit and move up through 100, 150 and 220. I go to a finer grit on some very hard woods, and occasionally use intermediate grits. The insides are sanded with the same grit sequence, after a final shearing cut with the small gouge from the rim as far as possible toward the bottom, a very light cut of 1/16-inch or less. This leaves the wood smooth. That disc sander is a real time-saver. On a large bowl, I sometimes use it with the lathe stationary to take all the tool marks off the inside.

Sometimes I oil bowls; some woods, like boxwood are better with no finish at all. But most of the decorative bowls have three coats of DuPont bar-top nitrocellulose lacquer, two coats of gloss, and after a little sanding, a flat satin coat.

I have a one-man shop and expect to keep it that way. I average about five bowls a day, fewer with difficult woods, up to 12 in walnut. It depends on the wood. My efficiency drops to about 50 percent when someone else is in the shop. I work a 35-hour week, 10 months a year.

I have about 20 tons of wood on hand to select from so I seldom make more than one or two of any particular wood at one time. I have many sources of supply. A lot of the exotic woods I get in log form from suppliers in London. I get teak from a source in Bangkok. When I get a new wood, I rough out a bowl and sit it on the bench and watch it. If it cracks, I put it in a plastic bag to slow it down for a few days then take it out again. I get to know what it will do by leaving it on the bench as long as I need to. I'm in no big rush to finish a bowl.

Canafistoula, Brazil, pinkish brown, 14-in. dia., $35

Canafistoula—I purchased several boards of this wood at White Bros. in Oakland. Unfortunately the boards were only 1 inch thick. It makes nice trays but I think it would look nice in a bowl too.

Wenge—This wood (photo opposite page) is fairly common in Europe. I know of two hotels that used it in their lobbies. Very little comes to this country. I got this from Penberthy. Rather hard to turn as the very coarse grain tears easily. The unusual grain pattern is so nice in some pieces that I do not use any finish as it would tend to kill the contrast.

Olivewood, Italy, cream and brown, 7-1/2-in., $50

Olivewood—Another log from a dealer in London. Mediterranean olive is far superior to California olive for grain and workability. I enjoy the odor of the wood as I work it and it turns and sands very easily. The log is badly cracked but large enough to get some final bowls anyhow.

Paldoa, Philippines, brown and black, 8-in., $40

Paldoa—One of the more beautiful woods to come from the Philippines. It is a little harder than walnut but in sanding it gets unusually smooth and silky to the touch. It must have silica in it.

Shedua, Africa, olive green, 15-1/2-in., $50

Shedua—I got this wood from Penberthy and have had pieces much larger. The plank was 16 inches wide and 16 feet long. I have had some 30 inches wide and 24 feet long. It is harder than walnut and tends to tear a bit, but is very stable so I have no warping problem on large trays. It makes a good furniture wood and is readily available here.

Para Kingwood, Brazil, purple, 6-in., $85

Para Kingwood—A friend found this wood in London for me and I think it the most beautiful wood I have worked. I promptly ordered the rest of the supply—five logs about eight feet long. Forest Products Lab says it is no different from regular kingwood but the grain and color are far superior. Being in the rosewood family, it turns beautifully and is so easy to finish.

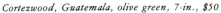

Cortezwood, Guatemala, olive green, 7-in., $50

Cortezwood—This is the hardest wood I have come across, with the possible exception of African blackwood. I feel sure it would turn the edge of any carbon steel gouge. It is sometimes sold to novices as lignum. It is sometimes called "bastard lignum vitae". It is easy to sand but hard to turn smooth as it tends to chip and tear.

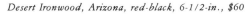

Desert Ironwood, Arizona, red-black, 6-1/2-in., $60

Desert Ironwood—Some hippies got me almost a ton of this wood from the Arizona desert. There are great quantities of scraps and trimmings because the logs are so irregular and full of flaws. These have been dead for years and many cracks are full of sand, so it is not a wood to make a big profit on. It is almost as hard as lignum but sands well as it is not stringy or oily.

Pernambuco, Brazil, red, 9-in., $100

Pernambuco—I got the wood for this piece from a log purchased in London. It is the wood used for violin bows and the shavings make a brilliant red dye for wool. I spend extra time collecting the shavings and sell them for $3.00 a pound. It is not an easy wood to work because it takes care to get all the sanding marks out.

Black Yokewood, Africa, brown, 6-in., $40

Black Yokewood—This is from another huge log that I bought on speculation in London. The dealer said it was quite similar to African blackwood but he does not know his woods very well. Forest Products Lab says it is related to shedua, which is available at several dealers here. I am fascinated by the black line between the sap and heartwood. I am afraid this is another one that will darken quickly. This was the first bowl off the log so I don't know.

Padauk, Africa, red, 8-1/2-in., $40

Padauk—Padauk is another dye wood but I do not work it very much because of the rapid change of color that most pieces go through. I bought several pieces in London but this one came from a wood collector in Louisiana. Easy to work, but like rosewood it should not be oiled as oiling hastens the darkening.

Boxwood, Cambodia, white, 6-in., $40

Boxwood—Penberthy Lumber Co. supplies me with boxwood. It is one of the nicest woods to work because it cuts so cleanly and has a sheen from the tools before it is sanded. It reminds me of an eggshell and I have not found a finish for it that doesn't kill the beauty of the wood so I leave it bare, knowing that people with oily hands and peanuts will leave marks on it.

Silkwood, Australia, light brown, 11-1/2-in., $100

Silkwood—A wood collector in Australia sent me this piece of wood. It is the most lustrous wood I have had. It is in the maple family but is not very common. This piece is from near the stump. It works nicely but the highly figured area does not cut smoothly so my gouges have to be sharpened several times.

Canalete, Venezuela, brown, 8-1/2-in., $45

Canalete—This is a very oily wood of the cordia family and is quite common in Mexico. It goes by many different names. For some reason it is very hard to get. I got this piece from a wood collector. It is easy to work, does not clog up sandpaper, and has a strong, pleasant odor.

Tulipwood, Brazil, red, 6-1/2-in., $50

Tulipwood—Here is another wood used by the French in their old furniture for decorative bandings and veneers. It is another member of the rosewood family and not available in this country. It's easy to work but the logs are badly checked so a lot of repairs are necessary to get a good bowl.

Goncalo Alves, Brazil, reddish tan and deep brown, 11-1/4-in., $50

Goncalo Alves—This fine turning wood is another that has an unusual silky feel as it is sanded. Very easy to turn but many of the planks and boards twist and contort in the dry kiln and many surface checks show up. Recently I was offered a huge log that is in Le Havre, France. It weighs a couple of tons and would cost around 50 cents a pound. Too much to buy sight unseen.

Laurel, India, brown, black, 12-1/2-in., $37.50

Laurel—Most Indian Laurel that I have is not exciting enough to work but this is a dog board from a veneer company and it has almost a bee's wing pattern. So I had to make a tray from it even though it was only 5/8-inch thick when I got it.

Blackwood Acacia, California, light brown, 7-1/2-in., $75

Blackwood Acacia—This bowl is made of local acacia and did not cost me anything. It is a difficult wood to work because the sanding and tool marks are hard to remove. This shape is a hard one to do too. When I roughed it out the top of the bowl followed the curvature of the log, as it does now. I enjoy the final result because the wood has so much luster and depth.

Coralline, India, red, 11-1/2-in., $100

Coralline—I bought this log (15 inches in diameter, 17 feet long) on pure speculation. It grew in India and I selected it in London, but had never heard of the wood and the dealer was no help at all and charged extra because I would not take four logs. It is very difficult to work and takes a long time to sand as it is tough and stringy. The end result is worth the effort and after I had used 80% of the log I found it a very good dye wood—now I save all the shavings.

Ebony, Nigeria, black, 10-in., $200

Ebony—This exceptional piece of Nigerian ebony came to me from Penberthy Lumber Co. in Los Angeles. It is not easy to come by such a fine example of this wood as much of it has lots of flaws. The log was sort of diamond-shaped on cross section so I cut it in two with a big bandsaw and got two bowls out of each section. This one was near the center of the tree and had much nicer grain than the other. This ebony is not real hard and it turns and sands without problems. Any cracks that might be in the wood can be repaired with epoxy and lampblack and they will not show at all.

Kingwood, Brazil, purple, 5-in., $60

Kingwood—This is the only bowl in those photographed that is turned on end grain so the center of the log is in the bottom of the bowl. The logs of this wood are quite small and round so it lends itself nicely to this shape and style. This wood was used for inlay bandings on old French Provincial furniture.

Cocobolo, Nicaragua, orange, red, black, brown, cream, 10-in., $350

Cocobolo—This ranks among the top five pieces that I have made. It must be a freak piece of cocobolo because it does not change color like all the other cocobolo I have had. Most of it will change overnight and gradually darken until the grain patterns disappear. This piece did not change with two months exposure near a window. I designed it to get a few touches of sapwood and as much as possible of the fantastic grain patterns that appeared just under the sapwood. An easy wood to work in spite of its hardness. Many people are allergic to it but luckily I am not one of them.

Textbook Mistakes

Somebody forgot that wood always moves

by Tage Frid

Looking through several textbooks about wood and woodworking, I have found that, especially for the beginning craftsman, there is quite a bit of misguidance or, in my opinion, mistakes that are very common. It seems as though someone wrote a book once who forgot that wood always moves, and all those who followed continued with the same errors.

Before going any further, I think we should set down a few facts about the material we work with: how it reacts after it is cut, dried and made into wood products, and what happens to it after many years of use. I expect anything I design and make to be used for many years after I am gone, so I feel it is very important that whoever designs and makes furniture doesn't make the mistakes that books advise. What they advise in some cases is more difficult, more work and sometimes creates a time bomb that guarantees the wood will eventually split.

I don't think I have to explain about the birds and the bees. We all know that the seed gets into the ground and the sapling gets started and each year puts a new year ring on. A tree grows from the inside out, which means that the closer you get to the center, the older the wood. I don't want to go into a big thesis about wood, just enough to show where the books are wrong. We know that the center of the tree is the oldest and the outside the youngest,

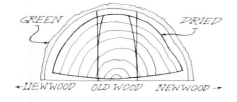
GREEN DRIED
←NEWWOOD OLD WOOD NEWWOOD→

which means the pores or cells on the outside are more open than the center ones, so the outside will shrink more than the inside. This tells how the

wood moves after is is cut and dried.

The reason that this is important is that after the wood is dried and made into a piece of furniture, the wood will continue to expand and shrink every year with the seasons. How much it moves depends on how dry our houses get in winter, and how damp in summer.

Just as the new, outside wood shrinks more when it dries, so it expands more when the humidity rises. This means that when joining boards together — say, for a tabletop, or whatever — the boards should be chosen and placed such that new wood should be joined to new wood, old wood to old wood.

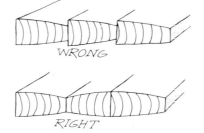
WRONG
RIGHT

Otherwise, no matter how well you plane and sand the boards after joining them, the different rates of expansion and contraction will guarantee an uneven joint as soon as the humidity changes.

Another thing most books tell you is to alternate the wood to compensate for the cupping caused by shrinkage. This would be fine if you wanted to design a washboard. But if you want to use your wood, for example, for a tabletop, it will take a lot of screws to hold it down, plus every second board will usually have a lot of sapwood, especially today with the shortage and high cost of wood, where every piece must be used. But, if we don't alternate the wood, it will work together and form an arch that will be very easy to hold down with a few screws. Also, we will have the center of the wood facing up, meaning

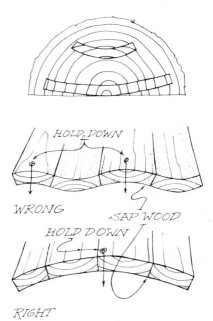
HOLD DOWN
WRONG SAP WOOD
HOLD DOWN
RIGHT

less sapwood, better color, harder and usually fewer knots.

Maybe the greatest mistake found in books concerns gluing boards together long grain to long grain. It is suggested you strengthen the joint by putting in dowels. It is also suggested that you leave a space of 1/8-inch at both ends of the dowel. I don't know how they expect to stop a dowel exactly 1/8-inch out on both ends. Even if this were pos-

CUT AWAY VIEW

sible, the joint would be filled with glue so we would have a piece of wood going across the grain. The dowel is, say, four inches long and will stay like that, but the board it's in will not continue to be four inches. As time goes on it will shrink, and even if there is no glue in the dowel joint (an impossibility), the result will be a split board. Whenever I see old tables with a split near a joint, I would bet there are dowel joints hidden in there.

The right way to join boards long grain to long grain is without dowels. Run the edges over the jointer slowly, or even better, just use a hand jointer plane, and get a slight concave surface.

CONCAVE SURFACE

Then glue the boards together. This puts a slight pressure on the ends. When the wood dries and gives off moisture at the ends first, the pressure is released and the ends will not split. At the same time, we can use fewer clamps.

If wood is glued together using this method and we try to break it apart, generally it will break somewhere other than in the joints. If it did break in the joints, it would take wood from both pieces, which proves we have a joint that is as strong as the material itself. This means there is no reason for what the books suggest — putting a spline or tongue and groove in the joint to get more glue surface. Furniture factories like to use tongue and groove because it allows machines to line up boards. But for individual craftsmen it's a waste of time.

Another piece of bad information in the books is the suggestion to put a tongue on the ends of tabletops and to glue a piece on each end with the grain running in the opposite direction to keep the tabletop straight. It's correct to use the end piece, but don't glue it as they suggest. That will not give the wood the freedom to move, which it will. The end boards will stay constant in length, the center boards will contract and expand in width. There is no glue that is capable of holding them, so the result is that they are going to split. The tongue and groove should be glued (or better yet, pinned)

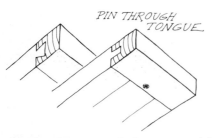

PIN THROUGH TONGUE

only in the center inch or so, which gives the wood the freedom to move. When cutting these end boards, joint

or plane a slight concavity on the inside edge so that the ends will continue to exert pressure after the center is forced in. The best (and most difficult) way is to use a sliding dovetail joint to hold the end boards in.

Most books highly recommend doweled joints, which are not very strong. I would never use a doweled joint myself, for example, in a chair. In mass production it is considerably easier to use dowels, especially because all the joints can be put together in a split second. So naturally the factories recommend doweled joints highly. But for individual craftsmen this is wrong.

As we all know, you cannot glue end grain to end grain or end grain to long grain, because there is no strength in end grain. We can depend only on gluing long grain to long grain. That is the reason the mortise and tenon are much stronger than dowel joints. With dowel joints there is only 1/8-inch or so where we have long grain to long grain. The rest of the joint is end grain.

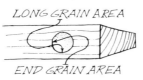

LONG GRAIN AREA

END GRAIN AREA

A dowel joint is good only if joining two boards end grain to end grain, because then the whole dowel will be surrounded by long grain. (In another article I will write about a dovetail dowel when I have perfected the tool which will make the joint.)

Another mistake mentioned in the books is that when making hand dovetails, it doesn't make any difference if you make the pin or the tail first. There is a difference. The easiest and most correct way is always to make the pin first, the tail last. How well the joint fits is determined by how

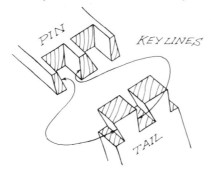

PIN   KEY LINES

TAIL

accurately we follow the "key line" that transfers the pin's shape to the tail (or the tail's shape to the pin). If the tail is made first, when we cut on the

"key line" drawn from the tail, we destroy that important line with the very first saw cut. But if the tail is made last, we have several strokes with the saw before we completely destroy the line we are "splitting."

In the last issue of *Fine Woodworking,* the article about checkered bowls shows a good example of not allowing wood to move. If the technique shown is used, it is sure that the bowl is going to split sooner or later. First the walnut will split, and later the teak, which moves much more slowly because of its natural oils. With long grain running in a complete circle in the checkered ring, that ring will keep the same diameter forever, but the walnut and teak are going to move and shrink, splitting the bowl. The same bowl could be made by segmenting the walnut and teak on the sides, and offsetting where the joints meet, as in a brick wall. For the bottom, I would resaw and cross-laminate the teak in a three-ply construction and inset it into the side.

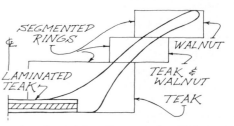

SEGMENTED RINGS   WALNUT

LAMINATED TEAK   TEAK & WALNUT   TEAK

Another thing I never do if I am going to glue pieces together is to use a sander. Sandpaper always removes the wood from the edges faster than the center, with the result that the joints will be tight in the center and open along the edges. I would use a sharp circular saw blade or, if I have to do any correcting, I would use a hand plane, which would make the surface perfectly flat and give a much better glued surface.

These are just a few things I have found by looking through some of the textbooks available. There are a lot of books about woodworking but very few are worth buying. So far I have not found any I can recommend. I think the best one available today is *The Encyclopedia of Furniture Making* by Ernest Joyce.

[Editor's note: *The Encyclopedia of Furniture Making* can be purchased for $14.95 at local bookstores, or directly from Drake Publishers, Ltd., 801 Second Avenue, New York, NY 10017.]

Dry Kiln

A design to season 500 board feet

by William W. Rice

A number of years ago in a small New England town I met a man drying oak flooring. He cut the oak into 1 x 3-1/2-in. random-length strips while it was green. These were carefully stacked in his garage on sticks until the garage was full, except for a 3-foot space to the wall on one side and about 4 or 5 feet on the other. The lumber reached from the back wall to the doors. A thin partition extending down from the ceiling to the top of the load contained three 18-in. window fans spaced along the length of the lumber pile. On the wall hung two thermometers, one with a piece of wicking surrounding the bulb and dangling into a pan of water.

This man had a dry kiln. When he fired up his wood stove, he could heat the garage to about 100 degrees. The fans circulated the hot air through the lumber pile; when the humidity got too low he misted the pile with the garden hose. After a month, his flooring was flat, check-free and at a low moisture content.

The operation succeeded because the man knew what he was doing as he manipulated the heat and humidity to produce flooring that would machine, finish and perform well in service. For those of us who need small quantities of dry wood, a homemade kiln may be the answer.

Wood is a cellular material (*Fine Woodworking*, Summer '76 and Fall '76) that in the tree, log or freshly sawn board contains two forms of water. Free water is located in the cell cavities in a liquid state and can move by capillary action from cell to cell. Bound water is held in the cell walls by molecular attraction and moves by diffusion. During drying, the loss of free water does not change the dimensions of the cells and the effect can be likened to emptying a coffee cup. However, as bound water is released from the cell walls, the cellulosic strands move closer together and the wood shrinks. In very small pieces of wood, the free water leaves the wood first, followed by the bound water. But larger pieces dry from the surface towards the center and bound water evaporates at the surface while free water is still traveling from the interior. This creates moisture gradients in the wood, which cause drying stresses, and the result is checks, splits and warp.

The three factors to be controlled in drying wood are temperature, humidity and air movement through the pile. In that New England garage, the wood stove undoubtedly produced erratic temperatures. Control of humidity was probably minimal—the moisture evaporating from the wood maintained the necessary relative humidity, occasionally supplemented by the garden hose. Only the air circulation was con-

stant throughout the kiln run. How fast the load dried depended on the way the man handled these factors, plus the characteristics of the species.

In general the higher the temperature, the faster the drying. Heating the wood also heats the water and water vapor it contains and reduces the molecular forces bonding the water to the wood. Thus water moves more easily through the wood to the surface where it can evaporate. Temperatures below 70° F do not promote drying; temperatures above 212° F are likely to cause structural damage, especially in hardwoods. High temperatures over periods longer than three days can reduce the strength of wood and make it brittle.

Most kilns operate between 100° and 180° F. The normal sequence is to maintain low to moderate temperatures (100° to 140° F) until the free water has been removed and then to raise the temperature to accelerate the process. As the wood becomes drier, it takes more energy to break the bound water loose from the cell walls.

In large commercial kilns the usual heat source is steam generated in a boiler and distributed by finned pipe similar to home baseboard convectors. While steam has proven to be the most economical, hot water, electricity, radio frequency and solar energy will also work. A steam system has the added advantage of easily furnishing vapor for humidification. An electric heating system is usually lower in initial cost and easy to control, but expensive to operate.

Relative humidity is the amount of moisture air contains, expressed as a percentage of the maximum amount it could contain at that temperature. Air at low relative humidity can absorb large amounts of water vapor before becoming saturated. Air at high humidity has little capacity for additional moisture. Heating air without admitting additional moisture reduces its relative humidity; cooling the air will reverse the process and increase the relative humidity. By manipulating the relative humidity of the air, we can control the drying of wood.

The hygroscopic property of wood allows us to predict how it will react to various combinations of temperature and relative humidity. A piece of wood will release or absorb moisture until its moisture content is in balance with that of the surrounding air. This is called equilibrium moisture content (EMC) and it is expressed as a percentage.

Thin pieces of wood arrive at equilibrium with the atmosphere in minutes and react quickly to fluctuations in relative humidity. The surfaces of thicker pieces of wood also arrive at equilibrium quickly. However it takes a long time, even years, for lumber to reach equilibrium throughout its mass. This "reaction time" results in moisture gradients during

William Rice, a former kiln operator, teaches wood science and technology at the University of Massachusetts.

drying. Wet wood subjected to a low relative humidity (and therefore a low EMC) will dry quickly because the moisture gradient is steep. The differential between internal moisture content and surface moisture content causes water vapor to flow to the drier zone. The larger the differential, the faster the rate. The kiln operator adjusts the temperature and relative humidity to control the drying rate without excessive stress formation and consequent degrade.

Humidity is easily increased in the kiln by spraying steam into the chamber through a perforated pipe. Small kilns can be humidified by steam released from open, shallow water tanks equipped with immersion heaters. A third, and very economical, way of controlling humidity is to use the moisture evaporated from the wood by not venting it from the building. This sometimes retards drying since the exact humidity called for in the schedule may not be achieved, but it saves fuel because less outside air must be warmed and humidified. A skillful kiln operator can do an excellent job of drying and never use the steam spray until the end of the run, when it is needed for stress relief.

Air circulation is necessary to carry the evaporated moisture away from the lumber surface and to heat the lumber to accelerate evaporation. The air circulation system also vents wet air from the kiln and brings in fresh, dry air to aid in humidity control. The air is moved by fans. In modern kilns, velocities of 500 feet per minute through the load are desirable, although speeds as low as 200 fpm can be effective. Whatever the air speed, it is essential that the air move uniformly through the stack so that the lumber dries evenly. Thus baffles are used.

With regard to species characteristics, low-density woods give up moisture faster and with less stress development than do the high-density species. Part of the difference is due to the thickness of the cell walls and the resulting volume of free water. Structural characteristics that affect the permeability of wood, such as the formation of tyloses or other deposits within the cell, slow down the drying rate and increase the risk of degrade. This is why white oak takes longer to dry than red.

How a kiln operates

Briefly, a lumber dry kiln is operated as follows: The boards are carefully stacked in the kiln chamber with uniformly thick stickers between the layers. Stickers should be spaced on 16-in. or 24-in. centers along the pile and vertically aligned in successive courses of lumber. The ends of the boards should be supported because even a 10 or 12-inch overhang will droop during drying. Good stacking is critical to obtaining flat, dry lumber.

As the lumber is stacked, the operator selects and sets aside several boards that represent the wettest and the driest material in the load. He may be guided by a moisture meter, by weight (heavy generally means wet), or by other knowledge about the initial wetness of the load. A commercial kiln operator takes four to eight samples in 20,000 to 50,000 board-foot loads. Even with loads as small as 500 BF, two or more samples should be taken to ensure control.

The operator cuts sections about 30 inches long from the centers of the sample boards, to avoid being misled by previ-

From wet-bulb and dry-bulb readings, operator uses large chart to find relative humidity (above diagonal line) and equilibrium moisture content. Chart below left gives typical kiln schedules; chart at right determines EMC values for stress relief at end of kiln run.

Final desired average moisture content	Moisture content to which driest sample should be dried	Equilibrium moisture content at which charge should be equalized	Desired moisture content of wettest sample at end of equalizing	Equilibrium moisture content values for conditioning treatment	
				Softwoods	Hardwoods
5%	3%	3%	5%	7- 8%	8- 9%
6	4	4	6	8- 9	9-10
7	5	5	7	9-10	10-11
8	6	6	8	10-11	11-12
9	7	7	9	11-12	12-13
10	8	8	10	12-13	13-14
11	9	9	11	13-14	14-15

CHERRY 4/4, 5/4 and 6/4

Moisture Content	DB	Dep.	WB	RH	EMC
Initial to 35%	130°	7°	123°	81%	14.0%
35 to 30	130	10	120	73	12.1
30 to 25	140	15	125	64	9.6
25 to 20	150	25	125	48	6.9
20 to 15	160	40	120	31	4.3
15 to Final	180	50	130	26	3.3

CHERRY 8/4

Moisture Content	DB	Dep.	WB	RH	EMC
Initial to 35%	120°	5°	115°	85%	16.2%
35 to 30	120	7	113	80	14.1
30 to 25	130	11	119	71	11.5
25 to 20	140	19	121	56	8.4
20 to 15	150	35	115	35	5.0
15 to Final	160	50	110	21	3.2

WALNUT (Black) 4/4, 5/4 and 6/4

Moisture Content	DB	Dep.	WB	RH	EMC
Initial to 50%	120°	7°	113°	80%	14.1%
50 to 40	120	10	110	72	12.1
40 to 35	120	15	105	60	9.7
35 to 30	120	25	95	40	6.6
30 to 25	130	40	90	21	3.8
25 to 20	140	50	90	14	2.6
20 to 15	150	50	100	18	2.9
15 to Final	180	50	130	26	3.3

WALNUT (Black) 8/4

Moisture Content	DB	Dep.	WB	RH	EMC
Initial to 50%	110°	5°	105°	84%	16.2%
50 to 40	110	7	103	78	14.1
40 to 35	110	11	99	67	11.4
35 to 30	110	19	91	48	8.1
30 to 25	120	35	85	23	4.4
25 to 20	130	50	80	10	2.0
20 to 15	140	50	90	14	2.6
15 to Final	160	50	110	21	3.2

WET-BULB DEPRESSION (°F.) — Each cell shows relative humidity (top) over equilibrium moisture content (bottom).

Temp. Dry Bulb (°F)	2	4	6	8	10	12	14	16	18	20	22	24	26	28	30	32	34	36	38	40	45	50	Temp. Dry Bulb (°F)
30	78/15.9	57/10.8	36/7.4	17/3.9																			30
40	83/17.6	68/12.9	52/9.9	37/7.4	22/5.0	8/1.9																	40
50	86/19.0	74/14.4	62/11.5	50/9.4	38/7.5	27/5.7	16/3.9	5/1.5															50
60	88/19.3	78/15.6	68/12.7	58/10.7	48/8.9	39/7.6	30/6.3	21/4.9	13/3.2	5/1.3													60
70	90/20.6	81/16.5	72/13.7	64/11.6	55/10.1	48/8.8	41/7.7	33/6.6	25/5.5	19/4.3	12/2.9	6/1.5											70
80	91/21.0	83/17.0	75/14.3	68/12.3	61/10.9	54/9.7	47/8.6	41/7.7	35/6.8	29/5.8	23/5.0	18/4.0	12/3.0	7/1.8	3/0.5								80
90	92/21.3	85/17.3	78/14.7	71/12.8	65/11.4	58/10.2	52/9.1	47/8.4	41/7.6	36/6.8	31/6.1	26/5.3	21/4.6	17/3.8	13/2.8	9/2.1	5/1.3	1/0.4					90
100	93/	87/	80/	73/	66/	60/	55/	51/	45/	41/	37/	32/	28/	24/	20/	17/	13/	10/	7/	4/			100
110	93/	87/	81/	75/	70/	64/	60/	55/	51/	47/	42/	38/	35/	31/	28/	25/	20/	17/	15/	11/	5/		110
120	94/	88/	82/	77/	72/	67/	62/	58/	54/	49/	45/	42/	39/	34/	31/	28/	26/	22/	19/	15/	10/	5/	120
130	94/	89/	83/	78/	73/	69/	64/	60/	56/	52/	48/	45/	42/	38/	35/	33/	29/	26/	24/	21/	15/	10/	130
140	95/	89/	84/	79/	75/	70/	66/	62/	58/	54/	51/	46/	44/	41/	38/	35/	32/	30/	27/	24/	19/	14/	140
150	95/	90/	85/	80/	76/	72/	68/	64/	60/	57/	53/	49/	47/	43/	41/	38/	35/	33/	30/	28/	22/	18/	150
160	95/	90/	86/	81/	77/	73/	69/	65/	62/	58/	55/	52/	49/	46/	43/	41/	38/	36/	33/	31/	26/	21/	160
170	95/	91/	86/	82/	78/	74/	71/	67/	64/	60/	57/	54/	51/	48/	46/	43/	41/	38/	36/	34/	28/	24/	170
180	96/	91/	87/	83/	79/	76/	72/	68/	66/	62/	59/	56/	53/	51/	48/	45/	43/	41/	38/	36/	30/	26/	180
190	96/	92/	87/	83/	80/	76/	73/	69/	66/	63/	60/	57/	55/	52/	49/	47/	45/	42/	40/	38/	33/	28/	190
200	96/	92/	88/	84/	80/	77/	74/	70/	67/	64/	61/	59/	56/	53/	51/	49/	46/	44/	42/	39/	34/	30/	200
210	96/	92/	88/	85/	81/	78/	75/	71/	68/	65/	63/	60/	57/	55/	52/	50/	48/	46/	44/	41/	36/	32/	210

ous end drying. Then he cuts 1-in. wafers from the ends of each sample, immediately weighs them, and dries them in an oven at 220° F until they stop losing weight. He calculates the moisture content of the wafers from the formula:

$$\text{moisture content (MC)} = \frac{\text{original wt.} - \text{oven-dry wt.}}{\text{oven-dry weight}} \times 100$$

While the wafers are drying he weighs each sample board to .01 lb. and seals the ends with paint or glue. The sample boards are assumed to contain the same percentage of moisture as did the oven-dried wafers. The boards go back into the kiln and stay there, to be retrieved periodically and weighed to gauge the progress of the drying. Based on these control samples, the operator manipulates temperature and humidity to dry the lumber as rapidly as possible with a minimum of degrade.

By calculation, the oven-dry weight of the sample board can be found. This value is used to determine current moisture content of the sample as the load dries. The formulas:

$$\text{calculated oven-dry wt.} = \frac{\text{original sample wt.}}{100 + MC} \times 100$$

$$\text{current MC of sample} = \frac{\text{current wt.} - \text{calc. oven-dry wt.}}{\text{calculated oven-dry weight}} \times 100$$

Research and experience in the drying of various woods have resulted in kiln drying schedules which guide the operator in applying the right combinations of temperature and humidity. But only with a great deal of experience can a kiln be run on a rigid schedule. More information about kiln operation can be found in the *Dry Kiln Operator's Manual*. This manual also presents a wealth of information about wood-moisture relationships, degrade and storage.

The kiln load is started at the temperature and humidity corresponding to the moisture content as determined by sampling. It is held there, and the sample checked daily, until the moisture content has dropped to the next line on the schedule, when the kiln is adjusted accordingly.

All kiln schedules start with low temperature and moderate to high relative humidity, and become hotter and drier as the wood moisture content drops. Generally, hardwoods for furniture and other interior uses are dried to 6% to 8% MC. Softwoods such as white pine should also be dried to this level for furniture, although often softwood millwork is only dried to 10% MC.

At the end of the drying period the wood will contain drying stress (often misnomered as casehardening). This stress is normal but it should be relieved before the wood is machined, by raising the humidity in the kiln until moisture enters the surface fibers, swelling them slightly and relaxing the stresses. This is called equalizing and conditioning.

Total drying time in the kiln varies with the initial moisture content, species, thickness, and final moisture content. Low-density species dry quickly. Thick, dense woods dry slowly. Examples of comparative drying times from green to 7% MC are:

4/4 white pine	8- 9 days
4/4 red oak	21-28 days
8/4 white pine	25-30 days
8/4 red oak	56-72 days

While kiln drying green lumber has the advantage of placing the drying process under control from start to finish, thereby reducing degrade, it does cost more in terms of capital investment and energy consumption. Commercial operators much prefer to kiln dry most species after they have been air dried as low as possible. This cuts the kiln residence time in half.

Properly air-dried stock (well stickered, good pile foundation, roofed) can be started in the kiln at its current moisture content, partway through the drying schedule. The higher temperatures and lower humidities safely accelerate drying since the danger of checking was passed during air drying. A combination of air and kiln drying is especially desirable when seasoning 8/4 and thicker lumber.

Dry kiln construction

Basically, a dry kiln is a well-insulated box equipped with devices to control the environment inside. Size depends on how much lumber is to be dried in one charge and may range from a unit about the size of a garden shed to one 50 feet square by 30 feet high or larger. Kilns are usually sized by their holding capacity of 4/4 lumber, expressed in board feet. A 20,000-BF kiln would be about 15 feet wide by 50 feet long.

Kiln length to width ratio is often determined by the length of the lumber or by combinations of lengths. In small kilns, the length of the unit must be carefully considered. A kiln designed to hold 12-foot boards cannot accommodate 16-foot boards. On the other hand, a compartment designed for 16-foot stock and then operated most of the time with shorter lengths will be inefficient and, because air cannot circulate evenly, drying quality may be poor. In a well-loaded and properly run kiln, the drying time will not vary significantly with the volume of lumber.

Craftsmen using less than 5,000 BF at a time find it prohibitively expensive or impossible to obtain space in commercial kilns. But a craftsman can build and operate his own small kiln. The plan offered here is for a kiln of 500-BF capacity, in 8 ft.-2 in. lengths. This kiln should be sheltered inside a barn, garage or shop; if it is to be used in a small area such as the basement of a house, it should be vented to the outside like a clothes dryer.

Kiln structure

It is important that the kiln be well insulated to minimize heat loss, with a good vapor barrier on the inside of the insulation. This is to prevent the high humidity generated in the kiln from penetrating the insulation and destroying its effectiveness. The roof is especially vulnerable to moisture penetration. Wherever wires or pipes pass through the kiln wall or roof, they should be in a conduit that can be sealed. In this design the conduits pass through framing members rather than stud spaces and insulation. Doors and vents should fit snugly with gaskets to prevent leaks.

If masonry construction is used, the interior walls should be sealed with an asphalt-base sealer. Two coats of aluminum paint are also advisable for both a moisture barrier and reflective insulation. Our plan calls for conventional frame construction with studs and joists 16 in. on center. It is assumed that the unit will be located on a level floor and that the bottom plate will be sealed to the floor with caulking. A few anchor bolts tying the plates to the floor will ensure that the kiln stays put, but they are not essential. If a floor is poured specifically for the kiln, an inch of Styrofoam insulation under the concrete will reduce heat losses. It is also useful to install a floor drain for those times when the kiln is extra wet.

31

The units should have a temperature range of about 80° to 200° F. Bulb capillary length of 5 ft. is sufficient. These thermostats do not indicate temperature except at the setting device. If the operator wants to see the actual temperature, we lem of finding wood. Dry it yourself.

[Author's note: The *Dry Kiln Operator's Manual* by E. F. Rasmussen (Ag. Hdbk. No. 188) is available at $2.65 from the Superintendent of Documents, U. S. Govt. Printing Office, Washington, D.C. 20402.]

Apply kraft-backed or foil-backed fiberglass insulation to the framing with the backing to the inside of the kiln. Then install a continuous film of 6-mil plastic to the inside framing, to line the walls and ceiling completely. Fold the plastic in the fan wall. These internal bearing mounts must be braced to the fan deck and ceiling so they remain fixed. Install the fans so they blow in the same direction; the fans needn't be reversible because the load is small.

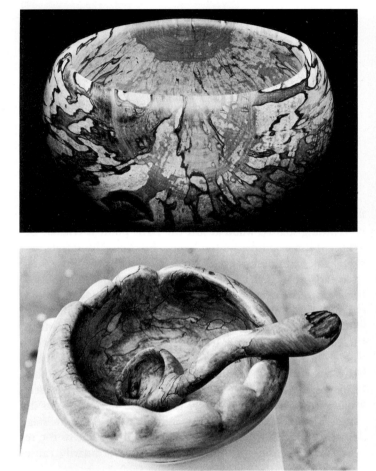

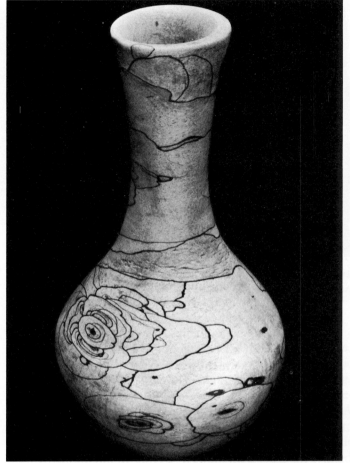

Spalted maple bowl with ladle, 10-in. dia., $375; spalted yellow birch fruit bowl, 12-in. dia., $250. Both bowls were made and priced for museum collections. Maple rosebud vase, right, 2-1/2 x 6 in., about $50, is by Melvin Lindquist, author's father.

the slowest of all the birches because it is the hardest; however, when it spalts it is very beautiful, and if caught at the right point will work easily and still remain hard. Birches tend to spalt regularly and predictably with the grain because of the straightness of the tree's normal growth.

Beeches also spalt predictably with the grain, but the wood is often unstable and checks easily. Spalting occurs after two years in most cases. Elm spalts rather quickly, also within two years. However, it frequently lacks character and often looks anemic. But if it's found at just the right time, and the wood has good figure in it, some beautiful pieces may result. Apple spalts, but oh boy does it crack! Oak may spalt, but it tends to rot from the outside in. Occasionally, though, oak will provide a splendid, magnificent piece of spalted wood.

But the best of all spalted woods are the maples, especially old New England sugar maples. Old sugar maples contain infinite grain configurations with fantastic and beautiful patterns. The old-time makers of fine furniture and musical instruments coveted the beautifully grained maple wood that someone's grandfather had stored for generations to come. There are names for the recurring grain configurations, although today it's difficult to get such wood, and the cost is unbelievable. There are tiger maple, fiddleback maple, bird's-eye maple, blister maple, curly maple and burly maple, to mention a few. Because of all these various grain patterns and because of the hardness of the wood, old sugar maple trees can contain remarkable patterns, designs, and even pictures of recognizable objects.

Soft maple will spalt in anywhere from two to four years.

Rock maple, or sugar maple, starts to spalt after two to five years, and once the process is working, there is a point at which it quickly speeds up and the tree goes rotten all the way. Just before that is the time to get it. I once found an old sugar maple, full of maple sugar taps, on the side of a dirt road, and I estimated the tree had begun to grow two hundred years ago. It was full of tiger, curly, and blister configurations, all magnificently spalted. The lines were so intricate that it looked as though an ancient Chinese calligrapher had deliberately penned his designs within the wood. The wood itself was still very hard; its texture was sensuously creamy, and the color of the aged wood was rich and golden. I was amazed at the beauty that was hidden within the old rotting hulk of a tree. The farmer must have thought I was crazy to touch it, but he didn't say anything for fear that he might scare me away and the blasted mess would stay there forever. There were maps of the world, animals, birds, fish, mountains, even a detailed "painting" of a rose, all done in fine lines like a pen and ink drawing. The most amazing thing was that the wood between the dark lines changed color from area to area, so that it seemed to be a carefully executed design of the most sophisticated combination of lamination and marquetry.

By far the most exquisite of spalted woods, and in my opinion better than the rarest exotic, is a piece of choice, aged, pictorial-figured, spalted sugar maple. The pictures within such wood seem to be a record of the tree's history: the storms, the sunny days, the cool moonlit nights, the wars that happened during its time, the sunsets, the pain and cold

Block cut from spalted maple log, above, shows fungal zone lines extending throughout the wood, a three-dimensional lattice. Dark area at center is completely decomposed. Downed rock maple tree, left, shows spalted end grain. Mushrooms growing on end of maple log, below, are reliable clue to spalting inside.

of the ever-changing New England weather. There is mystery locked inside, and infinite beauty—a worthless old tree making a last attempt to display its glory.

Think of the availability of the material: the cost is your time. Quality depends upon your perseverance and faith that the right piece is there, free for the taking. The process of working spalted wood begins with finding the material—in essence, found art. Finding spalted wood is very simple once you know what to look for. All I do is go out in the woods and look for fallen or dead standing trees. Maples are the best, because they take longer to spalt. Birches are often disappointing because the bark almost always looks intact, but the inside of the tree may be rotten to the point of mush. But no matter what you look for, you'll never know what's inside the log until you cut it. A lot of it is guesswork, a lot is based on experience and keys or signs to look for. The best source for exceptional spalted wood is the dead, fallen tree that has been lying around and looks as if it's not worth the powder to blow it to oblivion. Check the soil that the tree is resting on. If it is rich dark earth, or mossy, or covered with rotting leaves, that's a good sign. If the end or side of the log is covered with mushrooms it is a good bet that spalting will lie within. Many times you can see spalting on outer layers of the wood, where the bark has come off the tree. After a while you acquire X-ray vision and can guess what is going on inside the log. But there is no substitute for cutting into the wood to find out what's there. Most of the time, it's a surprise.

Normally I approach the end of the log that has been exposed to the weather, and cautiously crosscut off about three inches of the end. This usually takes out the end checks and the "mock spalting" that often occurs on the surface. Having exposed the face of the log at that point, I usually make a second cut about 16 inches down the log because I work with relatively small sections that are easy to carry out of the woods, and happen to be the length of the bar on my lightweight saw. If the figure or picture is good, I rip six-inch thick sections working around the center, cutting through any faults, cracks or spots that might check later. Stay away from the center or pith because it's a sure thing that it will check. The other possibility at this point is to take the log or butt to a mill (they may not saw it, fearing metal or doubting its worth) and have it cut into boards. It's difficult to work it this way because you never know what you'll run into.

Cutting spalted wood is theoretically similar to cutting gems and lapidary work. As in cutting picture jasper, the object is to get the greatest possible amount of picture from the piece at hand. The wood must be carefully studied and observed before cutting, to ensure the best picture within the chunk, relative to the bowl being turned. So this introduces the sculptural theory of the object being contained within the mass, which it is the artisan's function to release.

Spalting has characteristics too numerous to list, but among them are some that govern cutting methods to produce the best figures. The end grain of a log gives a clue to what is inside. The picture will often be very beautiful and full, if the log is well spalted, and it can be worked, providing the entire crosscut disc is not used (because it will definitely crack). So the best use of spalted wood, allowing the most control, is side grain or ripped stock. The lines forming the picture in the end grain will normally travel parallel, lengthwise with the log. So if the figure is double-lined, making swirly star-shaped patterns in the end grain, the log may be crosscut several times, like slicing ham. That same picture will occur several times, with slight variations, for a considerable distance until the pattern shifts because of a limb or irregular growth. The lines that make end-grain patterns also make side-grain patterns. Birches, which spalt more regularly, have fairly straight, predictable lines, sometimes close together, traveling the entire length of the log. The side-grain figure will resemble zebrawood, but the color will be far brighter. The end-grain picture will be a network of fine black lines.

If a good spalted log is found at just the right point, the markings may be consistent and predictable throughout, and thus easy to cut, because the broken-down, partially rotten wood is very soft and cuts nicely. Deciding where to cut is the real problem. You must learn to see the wood, the finished object, in your mind's eye, and then balance that against your observations of the log, its faults and patterns. In essence, you must flow and harmonize with the wood and the wonder of the graphics and design within. A wrong move will spoil the picture; the right move will unfold unbelievable beauty.

Here is an opportunity to cut the wood with the same care that later will make the object. The tree was carefully grown, and your object must be carefully made simply because of the nature of the material. So the harvesting or gathering of the wood must be equally special. It really is like a crop. The tree dies and begins to decay; when it spalts just right, harvest.

After the wood is cut, I usually paint the ends of my chunks with an inexpensive white glue and water solution, applied liberally, to keep the ends from drying too quickly. I use epoxy to seal the very best pieces, because they come only once in a lifetime. I see them as uncut diamonds, so the expense is worth it. After sealing I stack the wood in an open-air shed, making sure to sticker between the pieces for air circulation. I leave the blocks in the shed for a year, and then bring them into an indoor shed. The indoor shed is closed with less air circulation, but it freezes in the winter and heats up during the summer. I do not sticker the blocks indoors, but merely pile them on top of each other. After a few years, they are dry enough to turn. The thinner the block the quicker the drying. The usual green bowl methods (*Fine Woodworking*, Summer '76) may be used, but the risk of splitting may be large, depending upon the piece. I'm three years ahead of myself on wood, so I let it age and mellow by itself. A climate-controlled room would be effective, I'm sure, but nature will do the job given the chance.

Spalted wood has always been around; it might be right in your own back yard. Recognizing the potential, and the limitations of the material, anyone can have free access to wood so rich and alive with color and character that it transcends the nature of the wood it was before its metamorphosis. Realize the wood has made a transition, a long journey from one life to another, and catch it, discover it, at just the right moment. Your woodworking will enter a new phase unlike any other you've experienced.

Fresh-cut end of spalted maple log shows advanced decay and highest degree of spalting in rainbow colors, a rare find. Covered jar made of spalted tiger maple, 6-in. dia., is production work to retail in the $50 to $100 range in craft galleries.

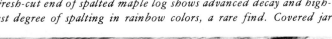

SEE PAGE 149

TOOLS

Work Bench

A design for holding the work

by Tage Frid

There are many workbenches available on the market today. Aside from obvious reasons of economics, why make my bench? I can convince my students and myself easily enough, but to convince you I should explain the benefits of this design and how I arrived at these specifics.

When I came to this country in 1948 I was given a tour of the school where I was to teach. I was guided to a large room and introduced to the teacher with whom I was to work. We talked for a while, or rather he did the talking because my vocabulary didn't go much beyond yes and no. By using arms and legs I finally conveyed to him that I wanted to see the woodshop. When I was told I was standing in it I just about passed out. In the room was a huge thickness planer I think Columbus' father must have brought over, and a few small power tools. I was really flabbergasted when I saw the student "workbenches." These were large tables for two persons with a vise in each end. Most of the time the students were holding down their work with one hand and working with the other. Some had taken much time to make special contraptions to hold their work so they could use both hands, which I'm sure was the Lord's intention when he designed us with two. (Of course the Japanese use their feet to secure their work, leaving both hands free.)

After being in school for a few months I realized that the bench I wanted did not, to my knowledge, exist in this country. So I designed my first workbench, which was quite similar to the one I was taught on. Later we made one for each student. Since then we have been making workbenches every two or three years so that the students have their own when they graduate. I find it a good exercise in which they learn

how to set up the machines for mass production and work together as a production team. It takes us three days from rough lumber to have all the parts ready to fit and assemble, and to have the bench top glued up. This year each bench cost us about $100, half for wood and half for hardware.

Over the years, having made the bench so many times and having had numerous people using and criticizing them, I have arrived at this design and these dimensions as best suited for a cabinetmaker. With its two vises and accessory side clamps there are five possibilities for holding the work—two in the right vise, one in the left vise, one between the bench dogs and one between the side clamps. Both vises are the type with only one screw and no guide pins to interfere with the work. A piece can be clamped all the way to the floor if necessary, and the vise can hold irregularly shaped objects. With only six bolts, the bench is easy to assemble and disassemble, and takes minimum storage space. The only glued parts are the bench top, the right vise and the leg sections. Everything else bolts together so that any damaged pieces are easy to replace.

This bench is almost six feet long, but if you wish to lengthen the bench you can easily do so by extending the bench top at the center and the two leg crosspieces (#18 on the plan) the same amount. You can shorten it in the same way. I would advise keeping all dimensional changes in five-inch increments so that the distance between the bench dogs remains the same. The bench is designed as a right-handed bench but could be converted to a left-handed one by reversing the plans. If additional storage space is needed, I suggest attaching a piece of plywood between the

Vise closeup shows top spline construction. Dowel jig helps support long boards in other vise.

leg crosspieces and inserting two end pieces to form a large storage compartment. If you wish you can add a piece behind the bench to hold gouges, chisels, screwdrivers, etc. But I find it more a bother than a help because if you are working on pieces larger than the bench top surface you have to remove the tools so that they don't interfere.

If you are working on long boards or panels you can make a simple device to support the weight of the board. Take a good heavy piece of wood (a 2x4 or 4x4 will do), and drill holes of at least 1/2-inch diameter in a straight line down the length of the piece about one inch apart. By clamping this into the right vise and moving a dowel to the hole just under the work you can easily add support to a long piece.

Before beginning, get your hardware. That way, if you wish to make a substitution or if something isn't readily available, you can make all your dimensional changes before any wood is cut. We could not find a 14-inch bolt so we make our own by brazing a nut to the end of some 3/8-inch threaded rod which we have cut to the right length. We got bench screws and dogs at Woodcraft Supply in Woburn, Mass., but I understand Garrett Wade in New York and others also may have them.

When choosing the wood, make sure you select a dense hardwood and be sure the wood is properly dried. We use maple because it is extremely hard and durable and is the least expensive in this area (it takes about 60 board feet). When cutting up the stock be sure to cut the longest pieces first. Cut them all one inch longer than the final dimension. It is best to purchase rough lumber, joint and thickness-plane

it rough, and then final thickness-plane the whole top together after it is glued. If a thickness planer isn't available, buy the lumber planed and align carefully during gluing. I suggest not using pieces wider than four inches in the top because of possible warpage problems. We use 8/4 stock for everything except pieces #18 and #8, which are 5/4 stock. For the heavier pieces which finish 2-3/4 by 4 inches, we glue up two pieces of 8/4 because in this area it is just about impossible to find properly dried lumber of that thickness. If necessary, you can bricklay or stack these pieces if you are short on lumber. We use Titebond yellow glue for all the glued sections.

Base parts are wedged and glued.

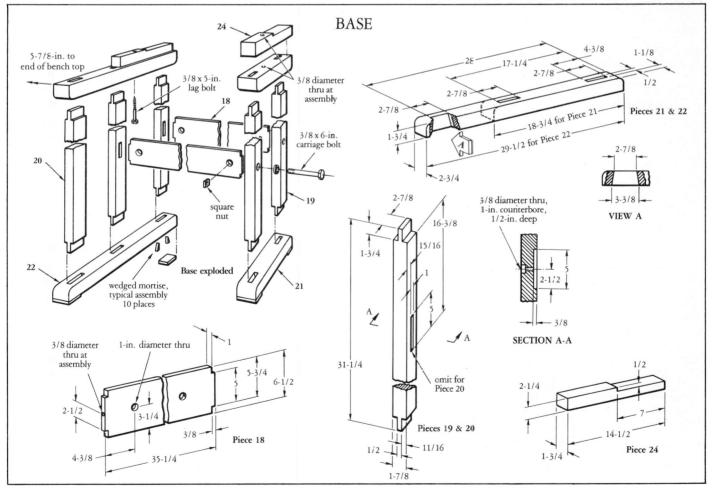

At top, plywood board is used to square three vise parts when gluing them together. Middle vertical board is bench-top end (Piece 5). After gluing, other parts of vise are fitted together with the vise in place on the top. Other photos show bottom and rear views of vise.

shoulder of the right-angled hole, pulling the bolt in tight. In our benches we insert the vise hardware brackets flush, but this certainly isn't crucial.

Now comes the most difficult part of assembly—the right-hand vise. It is advisable to make the tongues on the pieces all slightly oversized and carefully fit them with their grooves. It is essential that every part of the vise be completely square. We use finger joints in the corners but dovetails would probably be faster if you are only making one bench. In gluing the vise pieces together it is helpful to cut a piece of plywood to the exact dimension of the inside rectangle of the vise. If you clamp the vise pieces around this piece, the vise will have to end up square. The plywood also provides an edge to clamp against on the open side.

The vise should be glued and fitted and all the holes drilled for the hardware before cover piece #14 is added. The hole for the vise is drilled in piece #11, and from there guided into piece #5, with #5 bolted in place. It might be necessary to chisel a little notch into the bench top to make room for the vise bracket, but such a notch is invisible. The bench is flipped upside down for the fitting of the guides. The notches should be scribed off the runner pieces and carefully routed or chiseled out by hand. Countersink all the screws so that they don't interfere with the vise travel. Piece #17 should be screwed down first and then the other guides set in place. Take the time to make all of these fit right. Fitting the vise will drive you crazy at times, but be patient and worry about one section at a time and eventually it will all fit just right. When the vise is working properly, piece #14 is added. It is set into pieces #11 and 12 so these pieces must be chiseled out. If you want to get a little fancy you can undercut the edges so that the effect is almost like one large dovetail. A complimentary angle is cut on the edges of #14 and the piece is glued. You must glue only to the moving parts of the vise and not to any of the stationary parts of the bench top. Drill up from the bottom through the bench dog slots to locate the tops of the slots and finish chiseling them out.

Piece #8 is screwed onto the back of the bench after it receives a groove to support the plywood for the tool trough. The plywood is screwed directly to the underside of the bench top and is further supported by the filler pieces which secure the top to the legs. The filler pieces #24 stabilize the top and connect it to the base. The two corner blocks are screwed in from the bottom. Their only function is to make the trough easy to sweep out. Piece #23 is used to prevent direct clamping onto the work you are holding. A piece of plywood would function equally well here.

After the bench is completed, the top should be hand planed and belt sanded level. All the edges should be eased off slightly, or "broken," to minimize chipping out when something hits against an edge.

All of the places on the underside of the right-hand vise where wood is running against wood should be coated with melted paraffin thinned slightly with turpentine—say a tablespoon or two to a block of paraffin. The paraffin is first melted in a can or pot, and the turpentine is added with the container removed from the heat source. The mixture is liberally painted on in its liquid state to protect the pieces and help them to function smoothly. No oil is used on any of these pieces.

At completion, the rest of the bench and especially the work surface should be completely penetrated with raw linseed oil. This will take several hearty coats. At least once a year the bench top should be resurfaced. This is done by scraping it down, releveling it, and again penetrating it with oil.

Four small pieces should be added under the legs so that the bench rests on four points. The thickness of these pieces can serve as an adjustment for the final bench height.

Now your bench is completely finished and looks so beautiful you hate to use it. If you take good care of it, working *on* it and not *into* it, it should stay like that for years and years.

[*Author's note:* Material for this bench includes 50 board feet of 8/4 maple; 10 board feet of 5/4 maple; one piece of 1/2-in. Baltic birch plywood 8 x 60; two 1-1/4-in. diameter bench screws, one 18-in. overall length, the other 13-3/4 long with a swivel end; 1 pair 7-in. bench dogs with heavy spring, 1 x 5/8 knurled face, 7/8 x 5/8 shank (we used Ulmias); two 3/8 x 8 bolts; four 3/8 x 6 bolts; one 3/8 x 14 bolt (or threaded rod); two 3/8 x 5 lag screws.

[*Editor's note:* Blueprints of this bench are available for $6. The prints do not give any additional information, but some readers may find the orthographic projections drawn to a scale of 1-1/2 and 3 inches to the foot convenient to work with. Send check to The Taunton Press, Box 355, Newtown, CT 06470. Connecticut residents add 7% sales tax.]

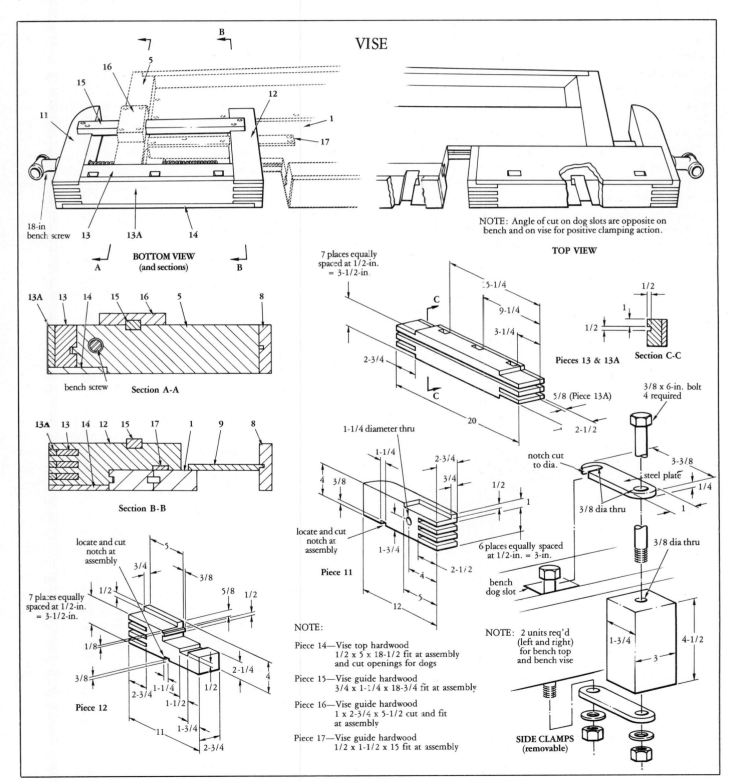

Hand Planes

The care and making of a misunderstood tool

by Timothy E. Ellsworth

A plane is one of the most essential tools used by wood-workers and one of the most misunderstood. A simple examination of most modern planes on the hardware store shelf will be proof of this. The bottom will probably be warped and out of true by as much as 1/16th of an inch. There will be rounded edges around the throat or opening, and the chipbreaker will be very coarsely made.

The result is that a significant amount of remedial work is necessary to make the plane function. If the manufacturers don't understand planes or don't care about these potentially precision instruments, then how can the woodworker be expected to understand?

For those woodworkers who have been frustrated by planes or who have given them up completely, the following discussion might help. I am assuming some degree of familiarity with planes to the reader, but recommend *Planecraft,* published by C.P.J. Hampton, Ltd., Sheffield, England, for fundamental reading, as well as the booklet, *Planes,* published by Stanley Tools.

Let me begin by describing the qualities of a good metal

A partially disassembled smooth plane. The all-important adjustable frog is between the iron and the plane body. In a block plane, there is no frog; the iron rests on the plane body and a moveable toe plate adjusts the blade opening.

plane, because that is what most people are familiar with. The bottom must be flat, really flat: no warp, no dips or hollows. There must be some provision for varying the opening, either by means of an adjustable throat (used in block planes) or a moveable frog (used in bench planes). The bearing surface for the iron must be flat and free of burrs and irregularities. There must be a cap iron or chipbreaker, except in the case of block planes. Adjusting knobs and lateral adjusting levers are normal on all but the cheapest planes. The steel in the iron must be of high quality, but this is rarely a problem.

Most of the planes that you will find in hardware stores will have uneven bottoms. There was a time when plane bottoms were precision surface ground, but cost cutting by manufac-turers has, for the most part, eliminated this expensive process. The common practice now is to surface plane bottoms on abrasive belts. The result is a less-than-true bottom.

Truing and tuning your metal plane

The surface you are planing can be no truer than the bottom of your plane. You have two options in truing up the bottom. One would be to take the plane to a machine shop and have it surface ground. This might cost about $20 to $30. The second option is to lap it yourself. This process is very simple and requires a perfectly flat piece of 1/8 or 1/4-inch glass at least 12 by 12 inches and some fine abrasive powder such as silicon carbide which can be found at many auto-body shops or art suppliers. Get both 400 grit and 600 grit.

About one-half teaspoon of the 400-grit powder is sprinkled on the glass with about one teaspoon of water. The plane bottom is placed on the glass and a figure eight grinding motion is used, keeping even pressure on the plane all the while. Use the entire surface of the glass to keep the wear even. In a short while the abrasive will become worn out and it will be necessary to rinse the plane and the glass in water and start again.

After repeating the process several times, inspect the bottom of the plane. The dips and hollows will show up as shiny spots not yet touched by the lapping. Continue lapping until they are eliminated and the entire plane bottom is uniformly grey. At the same time the plane bottom is being ground, so is the glass. So try to grind the glass uniformly to avoid making it hollow.

If the glass was flat to begin with and the lapping uniform, your plane should be perfectly flat and true. At this point it is a good idea to lap once or twice more with 600 grit to bring

Once you've made your first plane, there's no limit to the different ones you can make. Here's a sample of those made by the author.

up a fine finish. Although it is not necessary, you can polish the bottom with jeweler's tripoli polishing compound. After this step, scrub off the tripoli residue with soap and water. I like to use a touch of parafin to lubricate the bottom as I plane, but this may cause problems later if you plan to use a water stain on the planed surface.

Sometimes the surface of the frog on which the iron rests will be very rough. In this situation lapping can be used to make it flat and help prevent the iron from chattering while planing hard woods.

While I am talking about plane bottoms, I might mention the other maintenance which you can do from time to time. Quite often the plane bottom will get nicked, especially on the edges. File or lap off any of the burrs resulting from these nicks. They will show up as lines, even grooves, in planed surfaces.

With the plane bottom now perfect, you will need to set the opening, a most important step usually overlooked. With the iron sharpened, honed and set in the plane, adjust the iron to the maximum depth of cut you expect to make. The

properly seated on the plane iron. First make sure that the flat side of the iron is just that: flat. There is a tendency when honing the flat side to round it over slightly at the edges. This will cause trouble. Once the iron is flat the chipbreaker should seat on it perfectly when tightened. If you hold it up to the light there should be no light coming through the joint. At the same time the chipbreaker should be sharp right to the point of contact with the iron so that no shavings can get caught or wedged up under it. It will probably be necessary to grind the chipbreaker on your oil stone to make it meet the iron properly.

The chipbreaker should be set back 1/64 to 1/16 inch from the cutting edge of the iron. The closer setting would be used for the very fine shavings on finish work and for hard-to-plane woods. Setting the chipbreaker back 1/32 to 1/16 inch would be for rough work and large shavings. The combined effect of the narrow opening in the plane bottom and the close setting of the chipbreaker causes the shaving to make such a sharp bend that it has no chance of propagating a tear-out ahead of the iron, and leaving a rough surface.

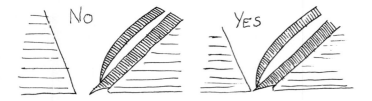

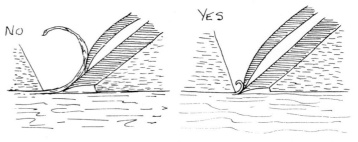

resulting opening in front of the iron should be barely enough to let the shavings through easily. If necessary, remove the iron, loosen the frog screws and adjust the frog. Check the opening again. This opening will be especially critical for very fine cutting in hard woods, curly grain, and for final finish work. Let me repeat that the opening should be as small as possible, but yet let the shavings through easily.

The next concern is the chipbreaker or cap iron. It must be

The problems associated with a block plane are not much different than those of bench planes. Because the block plane is used mainly for end grain, the iron is set at a lower angle and is flipped over so that the bevel is up. There is no breaker. The opening is not adjusted by moving the frog, but rather part of the plane bottom at the toe moves backward and forward. The bottom can be ground in the same fashion as the larger planes. One is then concerned only with sharpening the iron, setting the depth, and adjusting the toe plate to close up the opening, as was done for the bench planes.

The uses of planes

To describe the uses of the various planes requires some generalization as there is not much consistency between which planes different craftsmen use for different tasks.

The block plane has two main uses. One is planing end

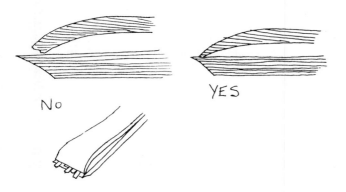

grain. The other is any planing job requiring one-handed operation. With a low iron angle and the lack of a chipbreaker, the block plane has limited use on long grain because it tends to cause tear-outs.

There is much less consensus on what the specific uses of the various sizes of bench plane should be. There are four common sizes: smooth, jack, fore, and jointer, ranging in size from the smooth (as short as six inches) to the long jointer (24 inches and up). I would venture the following statement: The longer the plane, the less it tends to be affected by local hollows and high points and the easier it is to get a true surface. On the other hand, because of its size and weight, the longer plane tends to be somewhat unwieldy and tiring to use. For larger and longer surfaces it has its advantages. I have seen jointer planes used effectively for everything from six-foot edge joints to three-inch end grain surfaces.

As you might expect, the smaller bench planes such as the smooth plane are much lighter and easier to control, but affected more by the irregularities in the rough wood. Many craftsmen use them, as the name implies, to smooth the marks left by the larger planes. Some might argue that there is really no reason why the larger planes should not leave a smooth surface. In the long run, the individual will find his own preference. The best advice to a potential buyer of a first plane would be to get one of the mid-sized ones, the jack or fore, which are in the 12 to 18-inch range.

A final note on planes and hand tools in general deserves to be made. They are getting harder and harder to find. We have become so dependent on machines that the hand skills are fast disappearing. The manufacturers are responding by dropping many lines. The lines they keep are cheapened since they know that the unskilled public will likely not know the difference. It is sad.

What about wooden planes?

It is fulfilling to make objects of craft or art. To make the tools with which you manufacture the objects is exhilarating. This is the case with wooden planes. They are simply made and can enliven the planing process. As to function, handmade wooden planes can achieve results equal to the finest metal planes—some would say better. They can be made to fit the job: long, short, wide, narrow, curved, flat, or any number of specialized shapes. The plane body can be made to fit your hand and your way of planing. For those who like to work with wood, there is a joy in using a tool also made out of wood.

Are wooden planes better than metal planes? Just about the only factual thing that can be said is that the sole of a wooden plane is less likely to mar the wood being planed. But a wooden plane can't take abuse, so that one's first plane, which does tend to get abused, should probably be of metal. Conversely, a metal plane must be kept tuned to perform right, so that the choice between metal and wood turns out to be mainly subjective.

Materials for making wooden planes

The materials needed to make wooden planes are relatively easy to find. In fact, it is probable that most of what you need can be found in your own shop.

The wood used needs to be a hard, dense wood. We are

aiming for a solid blank to make the plane out of, but in most cases this will have to be glued up from whatever is available to you. Hard maple works quite well, as does beech. In fact, many of the old planes were of beech. Oak is hard enough,

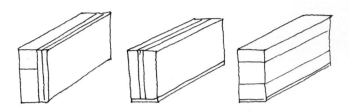

but a little too coarse. Other native woods such as apple, pear, dogwood, iron wood and hickory are excellent, if you can find them. The best yet would be to use some of the extremely dense exotic woods to make a thin bottom to glue onto the main body of the plane. Lignum vitae, cocobola, bubinga, and tulipwood are excellent, but as with all good things, they are hard to find and expensive.

You will also need some 1/2 or 3/4-inch dowels, depending on the size plane to be made, as well as some 1/4-inch dowels.

For the plane iron and chipbreaker, there are a number of options. You can borrow one from your metal bench plane or you can find old ones at flea markets, junk dealers and garage sales. You can also get replacement irons for metal planes at some hardware stores or from the manufacturers. In some cases you might find irons without breakers, in which case it is possible, with a little ingenuity, to make the breaker.

I should note here that you may not have access to the machines mentioned in this project. In this event, planemaking will be a challenge, but still quite possible. You may have to adjust the dimensions and use your ingenuity to compensate for the lack of machines. I have made planes entirely with hand tools, but of course it required a lot of patience, bordering on endurance.

Making the plane blank

Measure the width of the iron to be used and add 1-1/2 inches. That will be the width needed for the blank. Much of the extra material will be lost in subsequent machining operations.

Determine how long a plane you want, add at least four inches (more if possible), and that will give you the length of the blank. In no case should the blank be less than ten inches or it will be awkward and dangerous to machine.

For larger planes the blank should be four to five inches high, and for smaller ones, three to four inches. It is best to err in the direction of making the blank too high. (For purposes of this article, dimensions have been standardized. Needless to say, innumerable variations are possible.)

Dimension the blank. In most cases it will have to be fabricated from two or more pieces of solid wood glued together. Once the glue has cured, the bottom should be run over the power jointer to clean up the bottom and to square it to the sides.

If a special hardwood bottom or sole is to be added, do it now. There is no limit to how thick the bottom can be as long as it is over 1/4 inch. Make it oversize in length and width.

Glue the piece on, let the glue cure, and then plane off the overlapping edges.

With or without the special bottom piece, you should end up with a block that is surfaced and square in all dimensions.

Laying out the blank

Lay the blank on its side and make a mark on the bottom edge where the iron should come through. This should be 1/3 of the distance from the front. Draw a line from this point at 45 degrees toward the rear of the plane. Also mark in a clearance angle. This can be either a straight line at about 60 degrees to the bottom, or a curved line. It should intersect the 45-degree line at the plane bottom.

The center point for the wedge pin must be located, 23/32 inches back of the intersection of the 45-degree line and

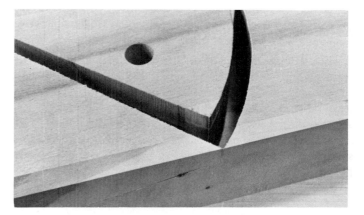

After the plane blank is glued up and the holes are drilled, the two cheeks are bandsawed off.

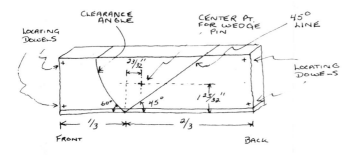

clearance angle, and 1-25/32 inches above the bottom of the blank. Also mark the position of the four locating dowels somewhere near the four corners of the blank.

Machining the blank

With the plane blank still on its side, drill 1/4-inch holes through the blank where the four locating pins go, and a 1/2-inch hole where the wedge pin goes.

At this point you should have a blank with five holes going all the way through it, and the 45-degree line and clearance angle lines drawn on it. I would transfer these marks onto the top and bottom of the plane so as not to lose them in subsequent operations.

With the plane blank resting on its bottom on the bandsaw table, bandsaw or resaw a 1/2-inch piece off each side. These

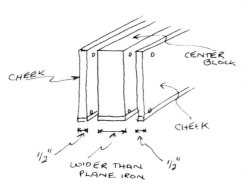

two 1/2-inch pieces are called the cheeks. This operation should leave a center block somewhat wider than your plane iron.

Thickness plane or joint to an even thickness the two cheeks to get out the unevenness left by the bandsaw.

Run one side of the center block over the jointer to get out

When bandsawing out the section of the center block, make sure you leave a feather of wood.

the bandsaw marks, and thickness plane the other side until the center block is 1/16 inch wider than your iron.

From the lines that you transferred onto the top and bottom of the blank, redraw the 45-degree angle line and clearance angle on the center block.

The next operation is to bandsaw out the section of center block between the 45-degree angle line and the clearance-angle line. This middle piece (with the 1/2-inch hole in it) is the waste piece, and so the bandsawing must be on the waste side of the line. *Do not bandsaw through the bottom.* Rather, have the two bandsaw cuts meet exactly at the junction of the two lines, leaving a feather of wood connecting the two pieces which can be hinged and severed to separate the clearance-angle block from the 45-degree angle block.

If this is done properly, when the two cheeks are put back on and the locating pins put in, the resulting opening should be less than 1/32 inch. Also note not to discard the middle piece with the 1/2-inch hole. This will become the wedge.

At this point you can use any means at your disposal to clean up the surfaces of the 45-degree angle and the clearance angle. I prefer using a disk sander for the 45-degree angle, with the table set carefully at 90 degrees and a mitre gauge set at 45 degrees. To clean up a curved clearance angle, some kind of drum sander is helpful. Be careful to take away a minimum of material to prevent the opening from getting any wider than necessary.

A groove or slot must be made in the face of the 45-degree angle to allow for the cap screw on the chipbreaker. To

Micro Bevels

Getting a better edge

by R. Bruce Hoadley

Sometimes the most basic and obvious principles escape our attention. A good example is microsharpening, a concept that can be used to advantage by every woodworker on a wide array of woodworking tools. The basic idea is simply to add a very narrow microbevel in the final sharpening, thereby producing a more durable edge.

When tools are sharpened, they are ground down to form a usually specified sharpness angle. The smaller the angle, the sharper the tool will be, but also the more fragile the edge and the quicker it will dull. Increasing this angle increases the durability of the edge but also increases the cutting force required to push the edge through the wood. The force may also be compounded by the clearance angle — the angle the bottom of the tool makes with the wood. With hand tools, the clearance angle can be virtually zero, but with power tools frictional heating requires a positive clearance angle. (With dull tools, the clearance angle actually becomes negative.)

So there is a trade-off involved — to decrease the cutting force required without decreasing the tool's sharpness angle to the point of making the edge too fragile. Adding a microbevel gives us a compromise. It increases the effective sharpness angle of the tool, but doesn't affect chip formation because the bevel is so narrow.

In carving chisels, as typified by the common gouge, a microbevel of about 0.005-inch on the concave face increases the effective sharpness angle to about 25-35 degrees (from 15 degrees) and will make a world of difference in longer edge wear. After the conventional sharpening is completed, the microbevel can be applied by light strokes of a round hard Arkansas pencil or round-edge slip on the concave face. This leaves the flatness of the clearance face undisturbed to ensure the edge will "bite" but modifies the sharpness angle. Determining the correct width of the microbevel may be aided at first by using a magnifying glass and hair for comparison. Eventually, the bright reflection of the microbevel can be gauged by eye, or the necessary number of strokes of the stone may become standardized.

The common bench-type hand plane can also be microsharpened to advantage. But to avoid interfering with chip formation, the microbevel should be added to the already ground bevel forming the under face. Keeping the microbevel to only about a 40-degree sharpness angle will ensure that a slight positive clearance angle still remains. This is the "honing angle" often recommended in plane sharpening.

With boring bits, microbevels can be added to the lips and to the inner edge of the spurs.

Instructions for sharpening planers, jointers and other machines having multiple-knife cutterheads usually recommend leaving a hairline of jointed surface on each knife. This jointed edge is in reality a microbevel.

Finally, a new jackknife, as it comes from the factory, usually has a "sharp" edge formed by double-bevel grinding which creates a negative clearance angle when held in the customary draw-grip position used in whittling. The knife merely rides along the wood surface without cutting. The blade must be reground to locate the edge along the lower face to give edge contact with the wood. Adding a microbevel on the face away from the work will improve edge life.

Microbevel is bright vertical edge along greyish sharpened chisel face. Hair gives sense of scale. Arkansas pencil is used to put a microbevel on a gouge. Putting it on wrong side merely dulls the tool. Drawings show right way.

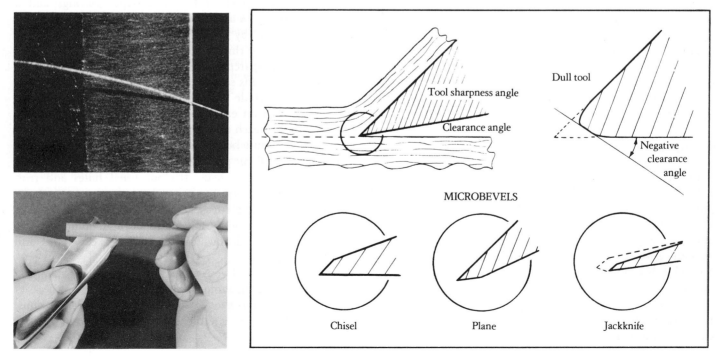

The Scraper

A most versatile tool

by Tage Frid

The scraper is one of the most important and versatile tools for wood sculptors and cabinetmakers. It is available as a simple, rectangular piece of steel, called the scraper blade and as a blade mounted in a handle that looks like a large spokeshave called the cabinet scraper.

Sharpening and maintaining the scraper are simple, but do take practice to learn. Many people get frustrated and give up, but once you can maintain the proper edges you will wonder how you ever did without it. Whenever I lecture, people want me to demonstrate the care and use of the scraper because few are able to learn this on their own.

The same scraper blade can be used for crude and fine work, to scrape glue or to produce a high-gloss finish with lacquer or shellac. It is better than steel wool between coats of finish because it doesn't leave tiny shreds of metal embedded in the pores of the wood. And when an old scraper gets too narrow to use it can become a tool for making half-blind or hidden dovetails.

The cabinet scraper has many uses too. It can remove old finishes without the use of solvents. It is excellent for removing paper after veneering and, like the scraper blade, it removes excess glue. If sharpened correctly it will put a fine finish on burl woods or delicate veneers.

The working edge of a scraping tool is the burr which does the actual cutting. Magnified, the burr resembles a small hook running the length of the edge. The scraper blade is sharpened by first filing the edges square. Then a medium stone removes the file marks. I prefer a wet/dry carborundum stone without oil. Then I use a honing stone, and here I prefer a Belgian clay water-stone, used with water. I hate to use oil because it mixes with particles from the stone and gets on my hands and the bench. Before I know it, the work too gets oily. The edge a water-stone produces is just as good as with an oilstone and it cuts the metal much faster. And if the stone wears hollow you can redress it yourself with sandpaper, by hand or machine.

After the edges are honed square the scraper is ready to have its cutting edge or burr put on. This is done by stroking the edge with a burnisher held at an angle of 85° to the face of the blade. A burnisher is a piece of steel that is harder than a scraper blade. The back of a chisel works just as well—I think even better—and I

Tage Frid teaches furniture design and cabinetmaking at Rhode Island School of Design. He's been a professional woodworker for close to 50 years.

don't have to buy another unnecessary tool. The whole sharpening procedure is explained in the photographs on the following pages. The biggest mistake people usually make is to get too excited and burnish too hard. The resulting big hook, which digs too far into the wood, is fine for rough work like glue scraping. But for fine finishing you need a light touch when burnishing the cutting edge. It is just like when you had your first date and touched the other person's hand for the first time—but this time you don't have to blush.

When the blade gets dull, you can burnish the old burr down and pull it back again five or six times before you must file and stone.

For rough work I simple file the edges and don't stone it. I keep the burr left by the filing, burnish it out flat, and pull it back again. This edge will cut as well as if it were stoned, but it will have microscopic nicks that won't matter much for rough work.

The cabinet scraper is sharpened almost the same way, except its blade has a bevel and the burr is slightly larger, so it is burnished at a slightly steeper angle. As you file it, knock the corners off the blade so they don't dig into the wood.

A scraper will cut sanding and finishing time in half, and the end result will be considerably better than if only sandpaper were used. Since the rate of tree growth depends on the season, some parts of a board are harder than others. Sandpaper will remove the softer wood more quickly and the result will be a very uneven surface—which may not become apparent until the finish is applied. I never use an orbital sander because it has a flexible rubber or felt pad that will make the surface even more uneven. The best finish surface is obtained by first using a smoothing plane or cabinet scraper, then a flat scraper blade which will keep the surface flat and remove the wood quickly and efficiently. Then sandpaper.

If the first steps have been done correctly, very little sanding will be required. I use only 80-grit and 120-grit paper before applying the finish. I feel that often too much time is wasted by going any further. I always use a piece of cork for a sanding block. It is rigid, but not too hard, and it is very inexpensive. And I save the sanding dust to mix with either shellac or lacquer, depending on the finish I am using. (For an oil finish I use shellac.) This makes an excellent paste for filling small imperfections. If stain is to be applied I mix sanding dust with half Titebond glue and half water. The sanding dust will fade and shade with the wood, and is better and cheaper than any plastic preparation.

A swan neck (also called a goose neck) scraper blade is sharpened and handled the same way as the straight scraper. It is used in curved places—mostly for carvings, moldings, sculpture or sculptured furniture.

You can buy scrapers for about $2. But I always use a Sandvik #475, which costs about $4 and is worth every penny. Its polished edges and high-quality steel produce a much cleaner burr without imperfections. You can look at various scrapers on the market and see the difference in the quality of the steel. Since most people buy only one or two blades in a lifetime, it is a good investment to buy the best.

After reading this and trying to sharpen a scraper several times, you might be the most frustrated person in the world. But don't give up. All of a sudden it will work out right, if you don't get too excited. Remember the light touch.

[Cork sanding blocks are available for $.75 from George Gordon, Box 144, Pittsford, N.Y. 14534, Sandvik scrapers from Woodcraft Supply.]

Sharpening the scraper blade

The first step in sharpening a scraper blade is to file the edges square. Clamp the blade in the vise; curl the fingers around the file for control.

Hold the file square to the edge and draw it along in long, even strokes.

Remove file marks with a medium stone.

Then hone with a fine stone held askew to avoid wearing a groove in its face. The edge of the blade must remain flat and square—don't rock the stone.

Finally, wipe the stone along both faces of the scraper to remove any remaining burr.

Put a drop of honing oil on all four edges of the blade to prevent the chatter of steel on steel and place the scraper on the bench with its edge extending over the side.

Use the back of a chisel as a burnisher. Hold it at an angle of about 85° to the face of the scraper and draw it back and forth until a small, even burr forms.

Two or three passes should do it, with light pressure (about four ounces).

Check the burr with a fingertip and repeat on all four long edges of the blade.

When the scraper gets dull you don't have to go through the whole process of filing and stoning. Lay the blade flat on the bench, add a drop of oil and slowly lay down the burr with the back of the chisel until you can't feel it on the top surface.

Lift one edge of the chisel to make sure you burnish the whole length of each edge and guide your finger along the bench to keep the chisel from slicing into your other hand. Then burnish to raise the burr as before.

When an old, much-sharpened scraper blade gets too narrow to use, it can become a tool for continuing the saw cut in half-blind and hidden dovetails. Set it in the kerf and tap it with the hammer. It saves a lot of chiseling.

Using scrapers, sharpening cabinet scrapers

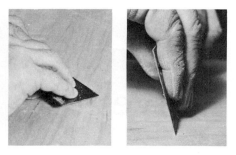

Now the scraper is ready to test on the top of the bench. Curl your fingers around its ends and bow it slightly with thumb pressure. Start with the blade vertical and tilt it until it just bites the wood, about a 70° angle, and push. If it is sharp it will make fine shavings, not dust. ⟶

The scraper can also be pulled toward you—it will cut better and more evenly if it is held askew to the grain direction, but moved parallel to the grain. Don't scrape away at one spot; reverse direction and work the whole surface so it stays smooth and even.

It won't cut properly and the blade will get dull quickly if you hold it at too shallow an angle. The correct angle is at right. If the corners dig in, press harder at the center of the blade to bow it more.

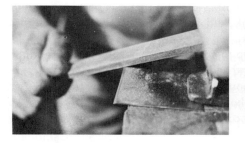

To sharpen the cabinet scraper, clamp the blade to the bench with the bevel upward and overhanging the edge. Hold the file in both hands and draw it along the bevel, maintaining an angle of 25° to 30° so the bevel is twice the thickness of the blade.

File until there is a burr on the back, then stone the edge and back on carborundum and hone with a fine stone until the burr is gone. The cabinet scraper is sharpened on both long edges—use a stick with a saw kerf as a holder so you don't cut yourself.

Then burnish the same way as the scraper blade but at a steeper angle, resulting in a slightly bigger burr. To set the cabinet scraper in its handle, remove the wing screw on the back of the handle and the two knurled screws on the front.

Place a piece of paper under the front of the sole to gauge the depth (double the paper for a deeper cut) and drop in the blade so it rests on the bench, with bevel facing upward and burr frontward. Hold the blade in place and tighten the knurled screws.

Set the wing screw until it just touches the blade and test the cut. For a deeper cut tighten the wing screw against the blade, making it bow. Always push the cabinet scraper with the blade leaning away from you. It, too, should make fine shavings.

To remove a finish, set a large burr on the cabinet scraper and tighten the wing screw so it bites between the finish and the wood. Scrape across the grain.

A scraper blade is the perfect tool for leveling a lacquer finish between coats. Just go lightly over the whole surface to remove bumps and dust. Start with the ends because they are the most difficult places.

After the pores are sealed, use the scraper to remove as much lacquer as possible without cutting through the surface. The change in color tells you you have gone too far. Work across and with the grain; be sure you don't miss any place, or the finish will streak.

After final scraping, for a glossy surface mix a pumice-and-oil paste and rub it on with a felt block. For a really high shine use rottenstone and oil. Then rub on sanding dust to absorb the oil. For a matte finish apply dry pumice with a shoe brush.

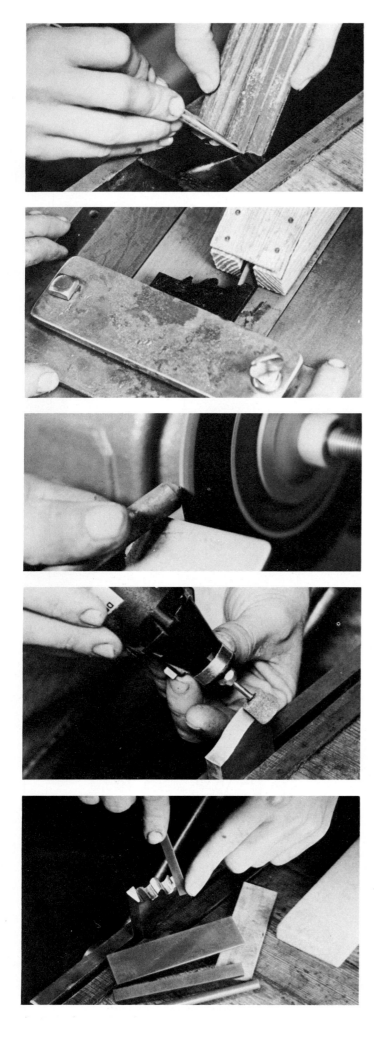

radii will require special grinding operations and here an abrasive cutoff wheel about 1/8 inch thick is most useful. Normally cutoff wheels are used on special industrial machinery with elaborate guards, but they do excellent work mounted on a bench grinder or on the arbor of a table saw. They cannot withstand lateral stress and you must be careful to cut directly into the wheel and avoid binding or pinching. Stay well under the maximum safe r.p.m. printed on the wheel, and guard it as much as possible, exposing only the cutting edge. On a table saw, simply raise the arbor until the wheel meets the table at the proper bevel angle, and carefully remove all sawdust to prevent a fire. I also use cutoff wheels on the table saw to cut knife blanks from 24-inch bars of shaper steel.

A jig to hold knives for grinding can be made from two pieces of scrap steel about 1/4 inch thick. Drill both pieces, tap the holes in the bottom one to accept bolts and sandwich the blank between them. A valuable aid is the diamond wheel-dressing tool. It looks like a Phillips screwdriver with diamond impregnated in the tip and can be used to shape and dress a grinding wheel to any profile.

High-speed rotary grinders, such as the Dremel, can be used with small diameter wheels to grind sharp curves. Mounted wheels for such tools can also be chucked in the drill press, with the table tilted to the correct bevel.

After the knife has been ground to the desired profile, it must be sharpened. First, remove the burrs by whetting the face of the knife on a fine stone such as hard Arkansas. Then whet the ground edge with a regular bench stone for straight or bevel cutters, and a slip stone, moon stick or Arkansas file set for curved cutters. When properly sharpened the knife should shave.

Before mounting the knives, make sure the collars are free of dirt, grease and chips. Set the bottom collar on the spindle and place the knives in its slots, allowing them to extend about the distance of the required cut. Be sure the knives are long enough to reach at least the centerline of the collar. Place the top collar over the knives, engaging the slots, and make sure the lock-edge notches fit properly. Adjust the knives to the desired cut by turning the Allen screws on the bottom collar, and hand tighten the spindle nut. Now lock the spindle and snug the nut. It is wise to place a heavy board in front of the knives when the machine is turned on, just in case.

Finally, a few cautions: Never run the spindle clockwise as this would loosen the spindle nut. Cut from the bottom whenever possible, as the knives are less exposed and there is no risk of binding. Avoid kickback by keeping the knives sharp and using hold-down fixtures. Keep the cutterhead well balanced and investigate any undue vibration.

[*Author's note:* Shaper collars and knives can be obtained from the following sources: Wisconsin Knife Works, Inc., 2710 Prairie Ave., Beloit, WI 53511; Forest City Tool Company, Box 788, Hickory, NC 28601; Charles G. G. Schmidt & Co., Inc., 301 West Grand Avenue, Montvale, NJ 07645; Woodworkers Tool Works, 222 S. Jefferson Street, Chicago, IL 60606].

At top, existing molding mitered to the attack angle of the knife can be used as layout template for an exact reproduction. Below, a cut-off wheel mounted on table saw arbor refines the contour that has been roughed out on a bench grinder. For safety, cut-off wheel should be used with a knife holder and guard. A diamond wheel dresser shapes grinding wheel to reverse profile of the desired cut. High-speed grinder sharpens difficult contour. At bottom Arkansas file set is used to hone knife.

Bench Stones

The variables that produce the better edge

The woodworker planning to acquire new sharpening stones for chisels, plane irons, and the like has quite a variety to choose from, and might well ask about the differences among them.

A talk with Jack Heath, an amateur cabinetmaker, and also product manager of abrasive stones for the Norton Company, brings out the key differences.

As Heath sees it, the purpose of the bench stone in woodworking is to remove the ragged burr of metal resulting from the grinding process, and to leave the edge as smooth as possible. Butchers like the sharp, ragged burr because that's what makes a knife cut through meat best, but for woodworkers, the burr merely picks up heat, tears off and leaves an even worse edge. Looked at another way, for

hardwoods the smoothness of the edge is more important than the so-called sharpness. Equally important, the finer the edge, the longer it will stay sharp.

So the key properties that a woodworker looks for in a bench stone are the fineness of the edge produced and the resistance of the stone itself to wear. A third property might be the speed with which material is removed—how fast the stone cuts.

These properties are the result of three variables: the size of the particles (or grit) that do the sharpening, the hardness of the particles, and the bonding strength of the stone, that is, how tightly the particles are held together. Particle hardness and bonding strength together determine the hardness of the stone.

Generally, the harder the stone, the

slower it will cut, the slower it will wear, and the better edge it will produce, given the same grit size. Of course, the finer the grit size, the finer the edge produced, for a given stone hardness.

There are two broad categories of stones to choose from: first, natural ones like hard and soft Arkansas (pronounced Ar*kan*sas in the trade) and Washita, a coarser form of Arkansas; secondly, man-made ones of silicon carbide (a black stone sold under the trade names of Crystolon and Carborundum) and of aluminum oxide (a brown stone sold under the trade names of India and Aloxite).

The man-made stones have the hardest particles, but the natural silica stones have finer particles and a higher bonding strength. This combination of finer particles more densely compressed is the reason Arkansas stones produce the finer edge.

But the finest cutting stones are not the fastest cutting stones, and vice versa. That's why a compromise stone must be picked, or more commonly, two stones used consecutively.

To Heath, the best combination for a woodworker—if cost is somewhat of a factor—is a medium grit man-made stone and a soft Arkansas. If cost is not a factor, then he would use the hard rather than soft Arkansas. Heath

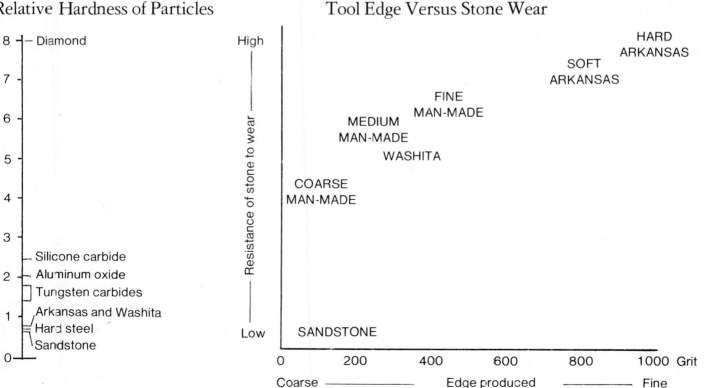

Relative Hardness of Particles

Tool Edge Versus Stone Wear

believes there is a marked difference between the edges produced by fine man-made stones and the natural ones, and would take a blindfold test on it.

He can also differentiate between the hard and soft Arkansas just by feeling them. But he's not sure he could tell the difference in cutting ability of a chisel sharpened by a hard or a soft Arkansas. Where the difference would show up, Heath says, is in how long the chisel would stay sharp.

For the cost-conscious woodworker, Heath doesn't believe the relatively slight difference in edge produced between hard and soft Arkansas is worth the extra cost, not if the woodworker has other tools to buy. A hard Arkansas is two to three times the cost of a soft, and is more suited to surgical and engraving tools.

Heath says Arkansas stones are becoming harder to find and notes that the reason hard Arkansas is so expensive is the higher costs of shaping and the low yield from quarry to shipment—on the order of two percent (for soft it's maybe twice that, but still only four or five percent).

So Heath would recommend a natural stone for the final honing process if it can be afforded, but for initial honing he would go for a medium grade man-made.

As to the choice for woodworkers between silicon carbide and aluminum oxide, that's like ''tweedledum and tweedledee'', because both are standardized in grit size and bonding strength. Where it might make a difference is in particle hardness. The silicon carbide stone will also cut non-metals like glass and ceramics, and tungsten carbide as well. The aluminum oxide will cut these materials, but not as efficiently. So the silicon carbide stone could be more versatile—if that's important.

And of course, for the highly cost-conscious woodworker, who still has many other tools to buy, sticking to a man-made medium/fine combination (half the cost of a soft Arkansas) is the way to go. The main price you pay here is in how often you rehone—not a very great price in the eyes of many woodworkers.

A final note: Heath doesn't recommend a coarse stone at all for fine woodworking tools because he doesn't think anyone should let his edges go so long that they require it.

METHODS OF WORK

Ball plane

I was recently asked to make a double-curved "ball plane" with which to smooth a laminated cherry sphere five feet in diameter.

The wooden sole of the plane is curved throughout its length and width, combining the traditional sole design of the wheelwright's compass plane and the joiner's hollow molding plane. I followed the plane-making methods set out in *Fine Woodworking*, Winter '75 to make the basic plane, which is 10 in. long by 2⅞ in. wide and high. The blade angle is 47 degrees and the iron is 51-mm (2-in.) "Record" tungsten-vanadium iron and cap set.

After making the block, a template was used to trace a section of a five-foot diameter circle on the sole. The sole was then chiseled to within 1/16 in. of true, and a flat scraper was used to finally reach the true line. This operation formed the curve throughout the sole's length. The plane bottom was scraped slightly hollow so it would function like a Japanese smoothing plane, hitting the work at three points only: front, back and cutting iron. This helped level the ball in every direction. A spokeshave and another scraper, ground and shaped to the same 5-ft. arc, were used to curve the sole across its width.

The iron was then roughly ground to the same curved line and finally brought to the exact curve with a sequence of increasingly fine sharpening slips.

I used white beech for the sole and the main part of the block, oak for the top plate and wedge, walnut for the front horn and cherry for the rear palm handle. The handles were shaped to fit the hand whether pulling or pushing. The entire plane weighs only two pounds, an important consideration since many days were spent bringing the sphere to within ¼ in. of a five-foot diameter.

—*Eduardo A. Rumayor, Bronx, N.Y.*

Vee-Block for resawing

I have had only mixed results using a rip fence on a band saw for resawing wood. Unless the blade teeth are perfectly set and sharpened, the blade tends to drift even though the board is firmly held against the fence. This

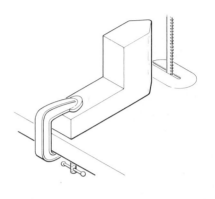

drifting can cause the wood to bind and will leave a wavy surface.

The blade's tendency to drift can be sidestepped by using a vee-edged block attached to the band-saw table, as in the drawing. The block is located so that its rounded point is even with the toothed edge of the blade, and at the desired thickness of the board from the blade. The block must be carefully made so that the radius at the vee is square to the face of the blade.

To use this approach the board to be resawed is scribed along its edge at the desired thickness. The vee-block provides a guide to hold the side of the board parallel to the blade. The board is fed into the blade with the operator free to swing the unsawed end to counter the drift. The surface will still need to be planed before it is of furniture quality, but this setup is much easier, faster and more accurate than using a rip fence.

—*M. G. Rekoff, Jr., Minneapolis, Minn.*

Darkening glue lines

Glue lines of polyvinyl and aliphatic resin glues (white and yellow) can be darkened with tincture of iodine. This turns the glue a dark purple, perfect for walnut and dark mahogany. It should be applied after wet-sanding as it does not penetrate deeply, but it does go through oil nicely. I have also had good results using it under lacquer.

—*Richard S. Newman, Rochester, N.Y.*

SEE PAGE 46

Antique Tools

A buyer's guide to many you can use

by Robert Sutter

The latest tool catalog has come in the mail, so you settle down with the "wishing book" in eager anticipation. But my oh my, those prices: sixteen dollars for a saw, twenty-two for a brace, sixty for a plough plane. It sure puts a damper on your ardor to fill your shop with all those wonderful-looking objects in the pages of that catalog open across your knees.

Well, how do you go about getting your heart's desire while preserving as much of your bank account as possible? One way is to budget a realistic sum of money for your basic tools and then make additions only as the need arises. Buy the best you can get in the way of edge tools and saws. If you must, you can acquire inexpensive yet less soul-satisfying hammers, pliers, screwdrivers, files, etc. at the local hardware store. Beware of special house brands and bargains, though; you only get what you pay for. Shop carefully and compare with your wishing book; you may find that a small price difference will procure a more trustworthy item than the bargain bucket at the local hardware emporium.

Another way to build your journeyman's kit is the antique tool route. There is certainly a big kick to be gotten out of finding a half dozen peachy chisels at the back of the antique shop for just two dollars apiece. That sort of bargain may be easy on the budget, but old isn't necessarily good, and if they turn out to be made of Swiss cheese, you can't exchange them. Realize that when searching for old tools you compete with the tool collector and that chances are he knows a lot more about the tricky business of buying antique tools than you do.

Recognize, too, that sellers of antiques keep informed about trends in their field. They know that competition between collectors for new acquisitions raises prices, and they are aware that old tools have recently been touted as preeminently collectible. Dealers also know the worth of old tools on the current market, so don't expect to find an antique dealer who doesn't know what he has in that box of rusty old tools lying half out of sight under the dropleaf table in the back of the store. He knows, and he put that box where it is on purpose.

Okay, let's assume that in spite of my admonitions you decide you're going to look around for some old tools. What can you expect to find and what will the results of your search cost? I'll try to answer those questions from experience garnered in fifteen years of collecting and over thirty of buying tools for my workshop.

Braces

The first braces were naturally formed tree limbs of the proper shape. Next came factory-shaped wooden braces with brass reinforcement plates. Such items are in the seventy to one-hundred-fifty-dollar class—more if unique. Metal braces with rudimentary screw chucks were in use side by side with wooden ones. Later on in the 19th century, and early in the 20th, braces with universal shell chucks and ratchet sweeps began to be manufactured. Stanley braces from 1900 on can often be found with ten to fifteen-dollar price tags, which, if sound, will function perfectly today. Check the chuck to be sure it closes all the way and is concentric. See that the wooden parts are not split and that the metal is bright under the dirt. If so, you've got a usable tool for a reasonable price.

A word about rusty tools here. A little rust easily scraped away to expose bright metal is okay and can be cleaned up. Discoloration due to use and handling likewise. But eschew the item encrusted with rust. It won't clean satisfactorily no matter the effort, and the metal will bear pit marks and deep-seated rust pockets for evermore. While

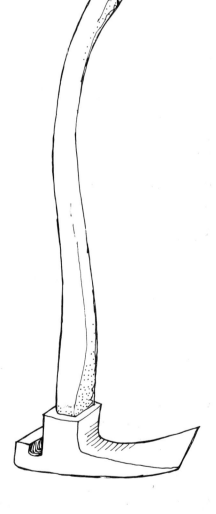

ADZE

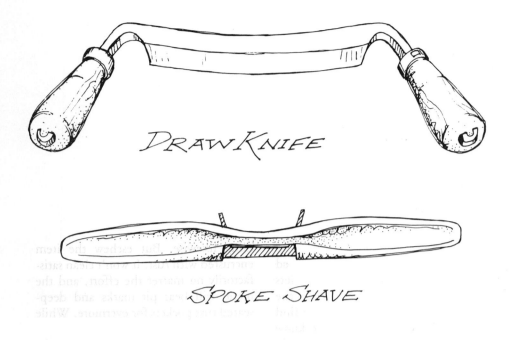

DrawKnife

Spoke Shave

dles, for the only way to sharpen them is to remove the handle. To use an adze requires a very sharp edge on the adze and a very sharp skill on your part. Have someone who knows show you how to use it, and then practice on scrap timber before working on anything important. Watch out for your toes as the tool is swung towards them.

Drawknives, etc.

Another archaic but useful tool is the drawknife. Anyone who has visited one of the restoration villages has undoubtedly seen a drawknife in use or at rest on a shaving bench. For quick shaping of round and curved work, this tool is hard to beat. Since the depth of cut is dependent on how the tool is held relative to the work, some practice is required to cut a long, uniform shaving. There is also an element of risk in pulling a large, sharp knife towards your stomach. Safer and more easily controlled is the spokeshave which operates on the same general principle as the drawknife but has the mechanics of a plane to control the cut. Spokeshaves come in brass, iron or wood bodies with straight, convex, concave, or rounded soles. Sometimes two differently shaped soles, each with its own blade, were mounted side by side in a single handle. New spokeshaves are easily obtained from purveyors of fine tools through their catalogs or as antiques.

merely unsightly in some cases, such pits and pockets on edge tools affect the edge-holding ability of the tool.

Saws

You may find some good, usable old saws, but I doubt it. Old, all-steel saws are often temptingly priced since they are not very popular with collectors, who prefer frame and turning saws. In years gone by, a craftsman bought a saw and used it until it was worn out from repeated sharpening and setting. He replaced broken handles and rivets as they were needed for the steel saw handles. When the saw was past using, it was discarded—for you to pick up. Therefore resist the temptation to buy an old saw even though it costs but three or four dollars. Purchase the highest grade new one you can and take care of it. It will serve you well just as the four-dollar relic served its owner when it was shiny and fresh from the store.

Adzes

The adze is one of the oldest tools in the woodworker's kit. Paleolithic specimens are to be seen in museums, but today the adze turns up more often in crossword puzzles than in real life. For the unfamiliar it is a sort of mashie-niblick axe with an oddly curved handle. An adze is a smoothing and shaping tool used for finishing large areas of wood such as floors and beams as well as for all sorts of chores in shipyards. The adze is no longer a common item on the shelf of hardware stores in

this country, even though still available in most of Europe. Should you decide you can't live without one, you will have to purchase it as an antique. The Collins Axe Company made adzes out of good steel with proper balance until a few years ago. They were japanned black and sold without handles, as were all adzes, since the handle is a matter of individual design. You can often find a good, quite new Collins adze head lying about for perhaps eight to fifteen dollars. Those that have handles and are older will be more expensive. By the way, adze heads are never permanently fixed to their han-

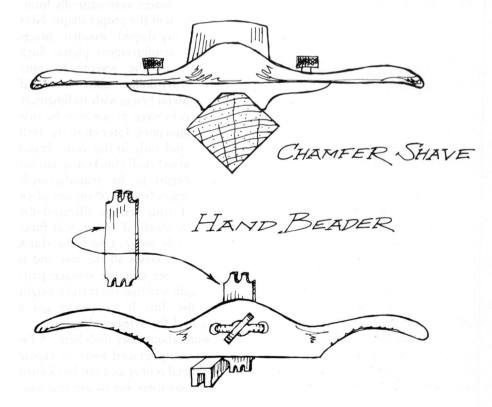

Chamfer Shave

Hand Beader

Prices run from six or seven dollars for a modern spokeshave to twenty dollars for 19th century iron ones. Wooden shaves were commonly made out of beech or box woods, but occasionally you will see ebony or cherry or other fine cabinet woods used. Beware of wooden spokeshaves as the throat wears easily and makes them difficult to set. Because of this deficiency, many wooden specimens have brass or even ivory set into the throat to provide a hard, less easily worn surface. Towards the end of the 19th century, Stanley and others produced a chamfering spokeshave which is most useful and worth some hunting about for.

Another branch of this large and useful family of tools is the scratch stock or universal hand beader. It is really a scraper of sorts with handles like a spokeshave. The hand beader has a thin steel blade with a shaped edge held almost vertically to the plane of the work piece. When pulled, the blade scrapes a bead or other shape out of the wood. A scratch stock will cut moulded edges on curves, and works well regardless of grain direction or complexity. Since it scrapes, there is practically no tendency to tear the wood. Unfortunately, this tool can now be found only as an antique.

Chisels

There are more varieties of chisels than there are herring dishes in Finland. In one catalog I counted twenty flat carving chisels and one hundred and thirty gouge shapes, fishtails, allonge fishtails, spoon, and backbent chisels. In addition there were bevel-edge paring chisels in several grades, long and strong hooped chisels, in-cannel gouges and mortise chisels. Prices ranged from under four dollars to over ten. Antique chisels are available in all the variety of the newer ones plus others long out of production such as slicks, framing, and corner chisels. Except for slicks and corner chisels, not many collectors are interested, so prices vary from under a dollar to ten or twelve dollars, with exceptions running up in the twenty-five to fifty-dollar range.

Framing, corner, and hooped chisels are for pounding on as are mortise chisels. Paring chisels, in-cannel gouges, and slicks are for pushing. The latter will take a razor edge while the former (somewhat softer to withstand the stresses of being pounded) take a little coarser edge. Chisel making is an art. Good steel, well forged and properly heat-treated to be hard at the edge and tough in the body and tang is what you will be seeking, often in vain, in modern tools.

Chisels are really the only case in tool acquiring where I would suggest antique over new because the older handmade tools are more likely to have the qualities required. Of course, shapes and sizes must be found one by one, and often just what you need is unavailable, but seek out the old steel and you'll likely have a winner. Many older chisels have inlaid edges, a piece of very hard, brittle steel for the edge welded onto a softer, tougher steel shank. Buy old chisels with as much intact blade and inlay as possible. Picturesque, well-worn, short-bladed tools are useless because they are probably ground back past the hardened portion at the business end of the blade. Tools by Buck Brothers, Barton, Isaac Greaves, Wm. Butcher, Underhill Edge Tool Co., and many Sheffield, England, companies are pretty sure to be of high quality. Don't let the words "cast steel" confuse you. The blades weren't cast, for cast steel in the 19th-century context refers only to a type of tool steel of high quality.

For those woodworkers who are always looking for the best tool to do the best job, there is an aesthetic quality to tools used by generations of craftsmen before our time which is as satisfying as the keen edge or comfortable fit of a new tool. Perhaps it is justification enough for the search. I often think so.

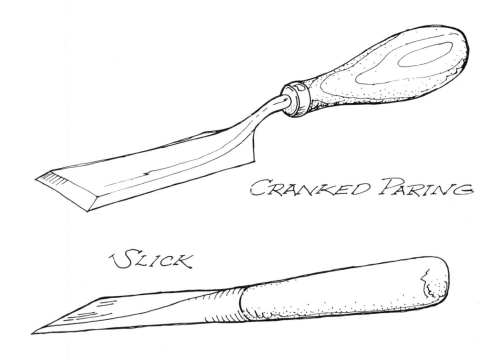

CRANKED PARING

SLICK

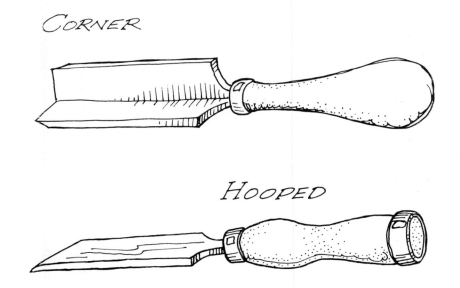

CORNER

HOOPED

Stroke Sander

Building a machine to smooth flat panels

by M.G. Rekoff, Jr.

A hand-stroke belt sander is a wood-working power tool used to smooth large, flat surfaces. Both soft and hard woods can be sanded without gouging, a frequent danger when using portable belt sanders. The author was motivated to design and build the stroke sander when faced with making 38 cabinet doors of 3/4-inch birch plywood edged with solid birch. The stroke sander was a convenient way to sand the edging flush with the ply.

When using the stroke sander, the work is placed on the table and positioned under the moving sanding belt. A sanding block is brought to bear on the sanding belt and is moved back and forth along it while the table is simultaneously moved in and out at right angles to the direction of belt travel.

The area that can be sanded without repositioning the work is limited only by the table length and the range of its travel. This stroke sander can accommodate a 30 by 73-inch workpiece without repositioning. The design can be altered, within reason, to accommodate work of other dimensions. The distance between the sanding belt and the sliding table is adjustable to accom-

Sander has three drums for greater working room, but middle one could be eliminated. Sanding belt moves clockwise.

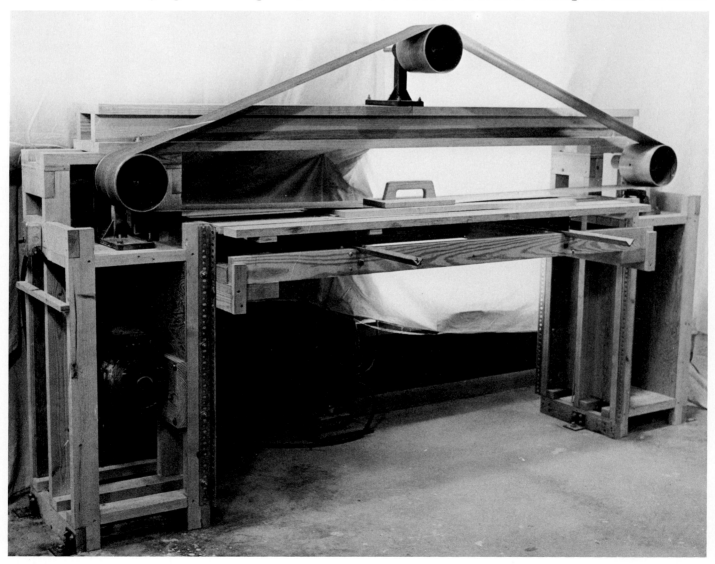

modate work of different thickness.

The least expensive commercially available stroke sander costs about $1500 without the drive motor. The stroke sander described here can be built for under $400 using all new material and including a new motor. The costliest items are the sanding belt drums and the motor; the cost can be further reduced if a used motor can be obtained. A three-drum version was constructed because at the outset it was not clear that two drums would provide enough space for the operator's hand. Since the project has been completed, it appears that a two-drum version could be satisfactory, if used with some care and a low-profile sanding block. The two-drum version would, of course, further reduce the cost of construction.

The drums are made by Mooradian Manufacturing Company (1752 E. 23rd St., Los Angeles, Calif. 90058. Telephone 213-747-6348). They are 7 inches in diameter and 7 inches long, to accommodate a standard 6-inch sanding belt. The two drums mounted

Standard drive drum (left) and reversed (right). Idler drum not shown.

on the pedestals are stock items; one is a drive drum and one is an idler which has mechanisms for adjusting tension and tracking. If a three-drum sander is to be built, the drum on the beam is a drive drum reversed in its stand, and this reversal must be specified when the order is placed.

There is hardly anything more frustrating than an underpowered woodworking tool, particularly a sander. The drum manufacturer recommends a minimum 1-horsepower motor. The

stroke sander described here is powered by a 1-1/2 horsepower, 1750 rpm, single-phase, 220-volt induction motor. The author has not been able to stall the machine using a 100-grit belt. To reach sanding belt design speeds, a motor pulley of 3-1/4-inch diameter and a drum drive pulley of 2-1/2-inch diameter is recommended. The drive vee belt is 1/2 by 60 inches.

The powered pulley is on the left, and the sanding belt travels over the work table from right to left. This con-

Pedestals are 18 inches square, 48 high overall. Top shelf is 9-1/2 inches deep. Two front columns are 39-1/2 inches high. Upper, middle and lower cross members go from front to back to support shelves. Angle irons in insets fasten to floor.

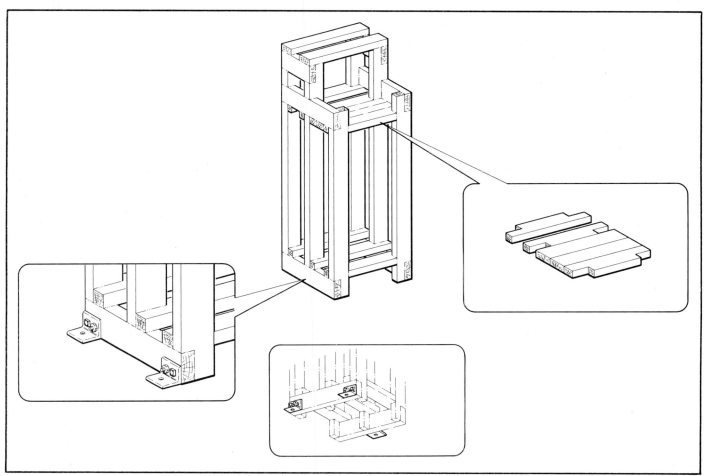

figuration is dictated by the design of the adjustable idler drum.

The machine has seven major parts: two pedestals, a beam, a table, a table support, and two support arms. These are fabricated from standard-dimension lumber and all joints are screwed and glued. The machine should be built and assembled according to the sequence of the instructions that follow.

Pedestals

One pedestal supports the drive drum and one the idler drum. The difference between the two, apart from provisions for mounting the motor, is

that the drive pedestal has a slot in its shelf for the vee belt. The pedestals are made from stud-grade fir 2 by 4's jointed and planed down to 1-3/8 by 3-1/4 inches to ensure sharp corners and square sides. The shelves are made from a harder wood such as yellow pine or oak to provide a firm surface to which the drum stands can be bolted. The pedestal columns, crossmembers and shelves are fastened together with screws (#10 flat heads used throughout). The inside surface of the back side of each pedestal is covered with 3/8 or 1/2-inch plywood from the drum shelf to the floor, to stiffen the structure against side loads.

The shelves were attached to the

underside of the middle crossmembers of the pedestal so that the inboard middle crossmember would act as a dust shield, partially blocking the sanding dust as it comes off the workpiece. The sanding belt clears the upper edge of the middle crossmember by less than one inch.

The motor mount pad is an 18-inch long piece of 2 by 10 fastened to the front and middle columns of the pedestal with four lag screws, with 1/4-inch plywood placed above it to act as a dust shield.

The pedestal supporting the idler drum has a solid shelf and is enclosed with 1/4-inch plywood to provide space to store sanding belts.

To ensure proper belt tension and tracking, each pedestal must be bolted to the floor. Three brackets are used, one on each outboard corner and one centered inboard. The brackets are made from 3-inch lengths of 3/16 by 2-1/2-inch square angle iron, drilled with 7/16-inch holes. Each is bolted to the pedestal with both a lag screw and a carriage bolt.

Beam

The beam supports the third drum and rigidly fixes the top edges of both pedestals with respect to each other. The box construction ensures stiffness for proper belt tension. The beam was made from No. 1 yellow pine to ensure that it would be knot-free. The vertical members are 2 by 4's, and the horizontal members are 2 by 10's. The horizontal members are screwed and glued to the verticals.

In the original design the beam extended over the entire top surface of each pedestal, but lumber of the requisite quality and length was unavailable. The beam on the author's machine is 8 feet long and this provides enough overlap to ensure rigidity.

Table Support

The table support permits the table to move at right angles to the belt. The wooden members are knot-free No. 1 yellow pine 2 by 4's; the wheel rails are 1/8 by 1-1/4-inch square angle iron 48 inches long.

The crossmembers are cut to length, vee-grooved and fastened to the longitudinal members with lag screws. The framework is further stabilized with

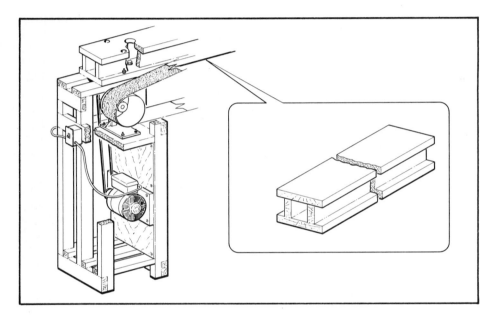

Pedestal (above) holds motor and drive drum. Table support (below) allows table to move at right angles to belt. Longitudinal members are 73 inches long, 22 inches apart. Rails are about 18 inches in from ends.

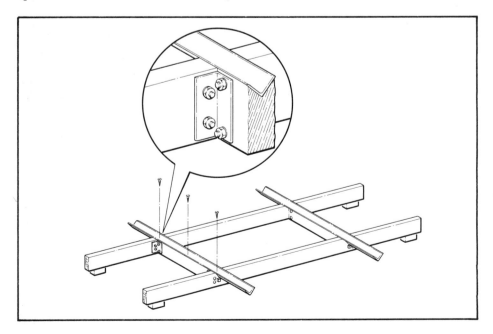

1/8 by 1-1/4-inch square angle iron brackets 3-1/4 inches long. This arrangement keeps the bolts from fouling the lag screws and each other. After the frame is assembled, the longitudinal members must be notched with a handsaw to extend the vee-groove all the way across the table support.

The wheel rails are fastened to the framework with screws, (countersunk to clear the wheels). A 1/4-inch machine bolt is installed in drilled and tapped holes at each end of one rail to prevent the table from inadvertently rolling off.

Wooden blocks 2-1/2 inches square by 4 inches are screwed and glued to the underside of each end of each longitudinal member to prevent motion in the direction of belt travel. To ensure a close fit, these blocks are best attached after the pedestal is bolted to the floor, the support arms are attached, and the table support is in place.

Support Arms

Two support arms are required; one is the mirror image of the other. Each is made from a 30-inch piece of No. 1 yellow pine 2 by 4. A 1-1/2 by 7-inch strip of 3/4-inch plywood is screwed and glued to the front end of the arm. A block 1-1/2 by 2 by 5 inches is screwed and glued to the arm's upper surface, flush with the rear end of the arm.

Two 6-inch pieces of 1/8-inch angle iron 1-1/4-inch square are carriage bolted to each arm 1-1/2 inches away from the front plywood strip and from the rear block. The spaces are to receive the ends of the table support.

The support arm is attached to the pierced angle iron on the pedestal with carriage bolts, but the drilling of these holes is best delayed until the machine

is finally assembled together.

Table

The stroke-sander table is made from 5/4 by 3-1/2-inch lumber (2x4 stud-grade fir planed down). The cleats are made from 3/4 by 2-1/2-inch plywood scraps screwed and glued to the top.

The wheel brackets are made from 24-inch lengths of 3/16 by 2-inch square angle iron, and the four wheels are 5/8 by 2-inch composition roller skate wheels. Any suitable caster wheels would do. The axles are 1/4-inch machine bolts inserted into threaded holes 3/8-inch from the bottom edge of the angle iron and locked into place with a lockwasher and nut tightened against the angle iron.

The wheel brackets are fitted by first cee-clamping them to the table and then placing the table on the table support. The wheel brackets are then adjusted so the table moves freely back and forth on the tracks. When the desired performance has been achieved, the table top and brackets are drilled for carriage bolts, and the heads are countersunk. A door or window lift handle fastened to the underside of the table is convenient.

Assembly

When the various components of the stroke sander are constructed to the extent described above, the machine is ready for assembly.

Bolt Pedestals to Floor. A relatively flat and level surface should be chosen for erecting the stroke sander, considering nearby obstacles that might interfere with table travel. A chalk line is placed on the floor to align the front edges of the pedestals. The drive pedestal should be on the left when

facing the machine from the operator's position.

The pedestals are separated by the length of the longitudinal member of the table support, measured both at the bottom and at the shelf levels of the pedestals. If the floor is not perfectly flat, these distances will differ. Position the pedestals so that the shorter of the two distances is the length of the table support plus 1/8-inch. This permits easy removal of the table support when changing table height. Then mark the floor through the bolt-down brackets and fasten the pedestals to the floor, but use slightly oversize holes in the brackets to allow for adjustments. For subsequent alignment work it is prudent to level both pedestals in the front to back direction (at right angles to the sanding belt), using the drum shelves as the reference.

Attach Beam. The beam is positioned atop the pedestals and centered so that it overlaps each by the same amount. A 3/8-inch hole is drilled through the center of the beam in line with the center of the inboard upper crossmember of each pedestal. The hole in the top element of the beam is enlarged to pass a socket wrench. A 3/8 by 6-inch lag screw, with washer, is passed through the holes, driven into the crossmember, and tightened down. Two 3/8-inch holes

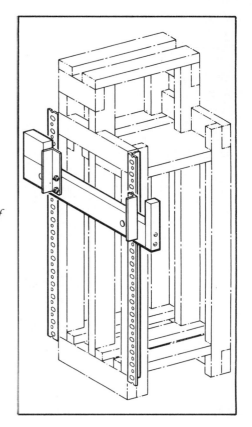

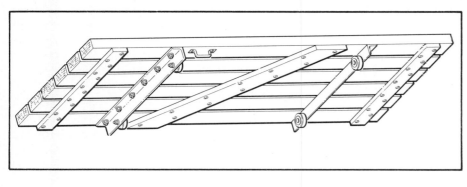

Right-hand rail support is shown at right. Pierced angle irons allow adjustment of rail support height. Table (below) is 25 by 72 inches, rides on rails.

71

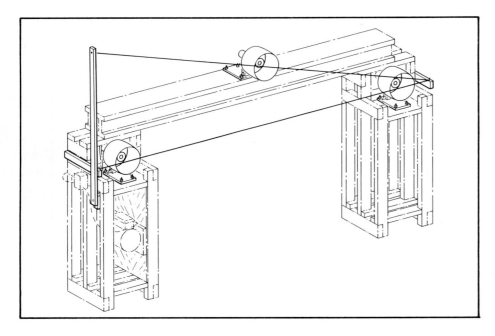

Stick and two strings define vertical plane used in aligning drums.

are drilled in each end of the lower flange, and matching holes are drilled in the pedestal top members. Two carriage bolts (3/8 by 3-1/2 inches) then bolt the beam to the pedestal.

Attach the Pierced Angle Iron. The pierced angle iron is 1-5/8 inches square. It comes with 3/8-inch holes drilled on 1-inch centers, and every other hole is oblong (roughly 3/8 by 3/4 inch). Saw through the center of the round holes to cut four 36-inch lengths. The pierced angle iron is attached to the front and the back inboard columns of the pedestals with four equally spaced 3/8 by 1-3/4-inch carriage bolts in each piece. It is best to bolt through the 3/8-inch round holes. Position the pierced angle iron flush with the inboard edge of the pedestal, with its top edge 5/16 inch below the top edge of the front inboard column. The pierced angle is located on the rear inboard column by using a level to extend a line from the top of the front pierced angle iron across the pedestal's inboard face.

It is prudent to locate the bolts attaching the pierced angle iron to the pedestal in exactly the same place on each piece. This facilitates adjustment of table height because these bolts can be used as references.

Determine Support Arm Spacing. Center each pedestal drum on its respective shelf, with 1/2 to 3/4 inch between the back face of the drum and the front edge of the beam. Align the front edge of each drum parallel with the front edge of its pedestal, and cee-clamp each to its shelf. Be certain that the idler drum, with the adjustable base, has been centered in its adjustable range. Loop a string around the drums and tie off tautly. The string marks the future location of the sanding belt.

Set the table support directly on the floor and position the table on it. Measure the distance from the floor to the top of the table, and call this distance D. The distance D depends on wheel diameter, wheel thickness, and location of holes drilled in the wheel bracket for the axles. These will vary from machine to machine.

If the sanding belt is 1-3/4 inches above the table surface, one can readily sand both 3/4 and 1-1/2-inch stock without adjusting the height of the table because the belt is flexible.

Attach Support Arms. Cee-clamp each support arm to its corresponding pierced angle iron to satisfy the following conditions: a) the support arm is level, b) the support arm is located D + 1-3/4 inches below the lower string tied around the drums, and c) the rear longitudinal member of the table support butts against the rear inboard column of each pedestal. Then mark through the 3/8-inch round hole on each pierced angle iron that is nearest to the center line of the support arm, drill 3/8-inch holes and attach each support arm with two 3/8 by 2-inch carriage bolts.

This position for the support arm is likely to be the one most frequently used. By permanently marking these holes in the pierced angle iron, the table can quickly be restored to the normal position after being moved. The marked holes also will facilitate other setups. For example, if one wishes to sand the top and bottom of a box 18 inches high, one need only count down 18 holes (or measure down 18 inches) from the marked hole and put the carriage bolt through.

With the support arms bolted in place, the string can be removed from the drums.

Install the Table Support. Lift the table support onto the support arms and place the longitudinal members into the slots provided for them. Screw and glue the 1-1/2 by 1-1/2 by 4-inch blocks to the underedge of the longitudinal members. Place the blocks against the support arms to ensure a close fit.

Mount Beam Drum. Locate the beam drum in the center of the beam between the pedestals. The beam width has been specified so that the bolt holes for the drum support will be in the flanges of the beam. With the axis of the drum at right angles to the beam axis, mark the mounting holes. Drill for 5/16 by 3-1/2-inch carriage bolts and bolt the drum stand to the beam.

Before aligning the drums, it is necessary to determine the horizontal distance between the edge of the beam and the front edge of the beam drum. Hang a plumb bob over the front side of the beam drum. Measure the distance between the front edge of the lower beam flange and the plumb bob string, and call this distance S.

Align Drums. Thus far, the two pedestal-mounted drums have been clamped close to their correct positions, and the beam drum has been bolted in place. The procedure for aligning and attaching the pedestal drums is relatively simple; unfortunately, the description is quite involved. The basic task is to establish a vertical reference plane and to locate the drums with respect to this plane. This vertical plane will be described by two strings.

Two horizontal sticks are temporarily attached to the outer edge of each pedestal, with their top edges in line with the drum axles. Stretch and fasten a string over the top of the horizontal sticks a distance S + 1 inches away from the beam. Clamp a vertical stick to the outer edge of one of the pedestals. Stretch another string from the opposite horizontal stick to the top of the vertical stick so that the string passes in front of the beam drum axle. The slanting string is tied off at the same point as the horizontal string. The plane formed by the two strings can be made vertical by adjusting the vertical stick. A level can be used to locate the slant string directly over the horizontal string. Or the slant string can be located S + 1 inches away from the beam

At this point it is prudent to make sure that the rim of the beam drum is one inch away from the slant string at both points on the rim directly opposite the string. If not, loosen the beam drum mounting bolts, twist the drum stand into place and retighten.

With the vertical reference plane established, position each pedestal drum so that each side of its rim is one inch away from the string. Locate and mark the mounting bolt holes.

Only the front two holes for each drum can be drilled because the beam and pedestal top are in the way. The two rear holes can be drilled from the underside of the pedestal shelf by using a sheet metal or Masonite template which matches the drum stand base holes. Attach each pedestal drum with 5/16 by 3-1/2-inch carriage bolts. Recheck the location of the drums with respect to the string before tightening the bolts.

Determining Sanding Belt Size. Position the idler drum at the center of its adjustable range. With a steel measuring tape, measure the distance around the outside of the drums. The sanding belt for the author's machine is 210 inches in circumference. Do not order sanding belts until after making this measurement. Belts are made to order by most woodworking supply houses.

Install Drive Motor. Bolt the drive motor to the pad. Wire the motor so that the drive drum rotates clockwise when viewed from the operating side of the stroke sander.

Adjust Belt Tracking. When the sanding belt is received, install it on the drums so the motor will drive it in the direction specified by its fabricator, but don't start the motor yet. Tighten the tension adjustment on the idler drum. Move the sanding belt by hand and observe how it tracks. The drums are 7

The author's son at work. Third drum gives plenty of working room.

inches long and the sanding belt is 6 inches wide; thus there can be some leeway in the tracking adjustment. The sanding belt should be more or less centered on the drums. Adjust tracking to the best extent possible while moving the sanding belt by hand.

Belt tracking is further checked by "bumping" the motor, that is, switching it on and quickly off before it reaches full speed. If the sanding belt tracks satisfactorily, turn on the motor for a full-speed test. If not, more adjustment is indicated. It is important to establish proper tracking by working up from low to high speeds because it does not take long to ruin a sanding belt when it rubs against a drum stand. If the drum is misaligned so that the belt comes off toward the operator's side at near full speed, one will have a room full of writhing belt.

The tracking adjustment range provided in the idler drum design may be insufficient, making it necessary to twist the drive drum stand slightly. This is done by loosening three of the bolts, twisting the base in the proper direction, and retightening.

Sanding Block

The 6 by 12-inch sanding block, or trowel, is made from glued-up 3/4-inch oak stock. The oak handle is

screwed and glued to the base. For a two-drum machine, a smaller, 2 by 2-inch block screwed and glued to the base would be a more appropriate handle.

Operational Suggestions

Nothing should be stored on the beam while the machine is running. Anything vibrating off the beam onto the belt can be propelled in a random direction with considerable velocity.

When sanding, be sure to hold the sanding block flat. The workpiece will be badly gouged by pressure on the belt with the front or back edge of the sanding block. There is a great temptation to do this to remove a localized blemish, but it will lead to nothing but grief.

The lower part of the idler drum pedestal can be finished off as a storage cabinet for extra sanding belts by adding two shelves and a door.

The selection of sanding belt grit depends upon the intended use of the stroke sander. The author has found that 100 grit (the finest grit available) is the best for most purposes. Since belt sanders in general remove material at a great rate, it is wise to use the finer grits. But for heavier work, such as smoothing edge-glued planks, 60 grit is satisfactory.

Wood Threads

A handmade tap and screwbox

by Richard Starr

"In this remarkable and very simple and efficient tool of unknown antiquity, the great preliminary difficulty of making an original metal screw by hand with a file is escaped and nothing more precise is needed than a spiral saw kerf on a wooden cylinder, a steel point plugged therein, and a piece of sheet iron edged upon a hole."

Ancient Carpenters' Tools:
Henry C. Mercer, 1929

Two tools are needed to make screws and nuts of wood. The screwbox, or die, cuts an outside thread on a dowel that becomes the screw, while the tap cuts a thread inside the hole to be used as a nut. Because the screwbox consists of a vee-shaped gouge cutter positioned ahead of a threaded hole, the tap must be made first. It is then used to thread the inside of the screwbox.

The most common wood taps are similar to the tools for tapping metal and are made on a machinist's lathe or perhaps cut by hand with a file, laboriously. A woodworker without a lathe, or wishing a thread coarser than four turns to the inch (the limit of most lathe lead screws), is left only with commercial taps for wood. But they must be purchased paired with a screwbox, and the sets are expensive, especially in large sizes.

The wooden tap described by Mercer in the quotation above offers a solution. It is a hand tool made with hand tools, of common materials. The design is awkward in diameters under an inch, where an all-metal tap would be better. It is particularly suited to cutting the large screws needed for vises, clamps and presses. Fractional pitches and left-hand threads are no problem, and Mercer cites diameters up to eight inches. The screwbox or die design is good for any size even less than one inch.

The wooden tap consists of a helically grooved cylinder with an adjustable single-tooth cutter, and a guide block that fits behind the nut to be threaded. The sheet metal guide

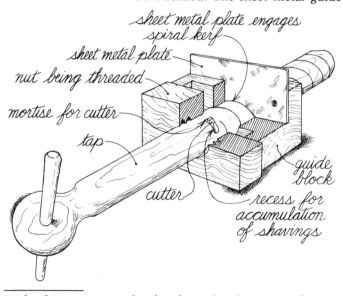

sheet metal plate engages
spiral kerf
sheet metal plate
nut being threaded
mortise for cutter
tap
cutter
guide block
recess for accumulation of shavings

Richard Starr, 33, teaches hand woodworking to grades 6, 7 and 8 at Richmond School in Hanover, N.H. Starting with a clue provided by an old-time craftsman and references in musty books, he rediscovered this technology.

plate engages the helical kerf and draws the rotating tap through the hole. The scraper cutter pushes its shavings ahead of itself, thus requiring several passes before it reaches full depth. Its adjustability, which allows nuts to be threaded slightly oversize or undersize, is essential for a close fit and to compensate for changes in humidity.

To make the cylinder for the tap, choose a square of wood about four times as long as the deepest hole you expect to thread, plus two or three inches for the handle. The material must be a close-grained hardwood that will wear well and resist chipping along the edge of the saw kerf. I have used cherry, yellow birch, and rock maple, but hornbeam might be better. Choose a piece that is straight-grained and well seasoned to minimize changes in dimensions.

The shaft must be turned to the desired minor diameter of the nut. Use a vernier caliper rather than a pincer-type to measure accurately. Make the finish cuts with a large skew chisel, or a large gouge and a shearing cut, to leave the wood smooth and regular without using sandpaper. Sanding would leave grit in the wood, dulling tools used in later operations. A finish of hardening oil such as Watco, then wax, will help the wood wear longer.

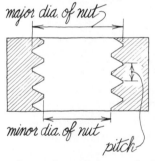

major dia. of nut
minor dia. of nut
pitch

The helix cut into the cylinder determines the rate of advance of the tap, which is equal to the pitch of the screw. The cut must be shallow—around 3/16 in.—so it won't jam the guide plate or weaken the tap, but it should engage the plate snugly lest the tap widen the thread as it is backed out. The cut may be made on the band saw by tilting the table to the helix angle, holding the tap against a fence and rotating it into the blade. Or it may be cut by hand.

To make the kerf with a band saw, first determine the helix angle at the minor diameter of the nut and make a paper

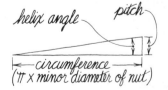

helix angle
pitch
circumference
(π × minor diameter of nut)

template. Choose a scrap board and cut a short kerf, as shown in the drawing. Use the template to lay out and slice off the bottom of the board at the helix angle. The apex of the angle should be at the left for right-hand threads, at the right for left-hand threads.

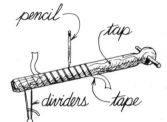

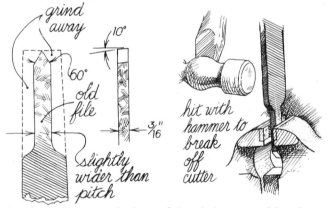

Two-inch tap (left) and die or screwbox (right) can be bootstrapped. Tap is made first, starting with a handmade helical kerf, then used *to make thread inside the screwbox, which is shown here cutting a thread in yellow birch.*

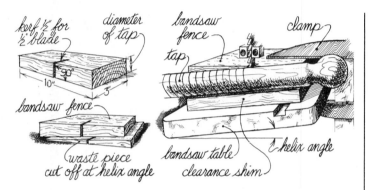

Now lay the cut surface of the board on the table and tilt until the blade lines up with the kerf. Mount the fence atop a shim for clearance, and clamp the assembly in place. Be sure the fence is square with the width of the blade.

For best results use a new, sharp blade, adjust the guide blocks close to the blade and tap, and set the blade tension high. Place the blank tap firmly against the fence and rotate it slowly into the blade. It will advance itself, creating the helical kerf. Make a test cut and measure it to check the pitch. I always make the blank overlong and use the end for the test, cutting it off afterward. If successive turns of the helix are too far apart, the table angle is a little too great, and vice versa. Adjust accordingly.

This is one of those band-saw operations where the wood is unsupported directly below the cut. The blade may grab and draw the wood quickly down toward the table, which would mar the tap or break the blade. Avoid this by holding the tap firmly in both hands and rotating it slowly, allowing the blade to cut at its own speed.

To cut the kerf by hand, prepare a ribbon of paper the width of which is a pencil line's thickness less than the pitch of the thread. Wrap this ribbon tightly around the tap, leaving the width of a pencil line between successive turns, and tape the ends down. Check the helix with dividers before marking it out. Score the pencil line with a chisel and make the 3/16-in. deep cut with a small backsaw or dovetail saw. Depth can be gauged with tape on the saw.

The cutter is ground from the business end of an old file, as shown in the drawings. Cool the metal frequently to preserve its temper. To separate the cutter from the waste, place it

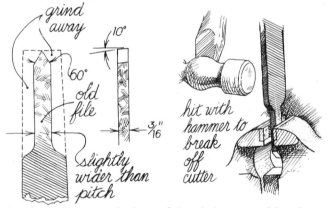

point down in a metal vise and break it away with a heavy hammer. Dub off all the edges except those that will be cutting, and sharpen on India and Arkansas stones.

The cutter sits in a through mortise and is held by a small wedge. Center the mortise hole about a half-inch beyond the end of the kerf, with one edge following a diameter of the tap. This edge will accommodate the working face of the cutter. Lay out the square by marking a line tangent to the drilled hole at right angles to the helix, and chisel it out. Be sure the blade fits snugly.

Cut the wedge an 8° taper from scrap that is just thinner than the width of the cutter, and insert it in the mortise to gauge the amount of wood that must be removed from the back face. When the wedge fits tightly, insert the cutter and mark the wedge where it emerges from the tap. Trim at both

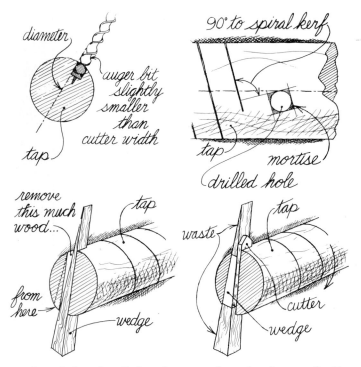

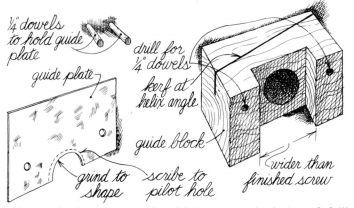

ends and chamfer all the edges to reduce the chance of splintering. Finally, gouge a shallow relief valley ahead of the cutter, to make room for shavings as the tool works.

The guide block has these important features: A pilot hole a hair larger than the tap so the tap will turn freely; a metal plate set in a kerf at the helix angle; a recess in front of the plate to allow shavings to drop out; and enough surface area for clamping to the nut. The notch must be wider than the major diameter of the thread and half again as deep as the pitch, to clear the cutter. For a 2-in. tap I have used a block

about 3 in. by 6 in. by 2 in. thick. Center the hole and drill it; saw and chisel out the notch; then lay out the kerf at the helix angle. Drop perpendiculars on the ends of the block so the kerf will intersect about one-third of the hole, and cut it with a fine backsaw.

Any sturdy sheet of metal will do for the guide plate. I've used old saw blades and an old scraper blade. Drill two 1/4-in. holes in the block, insert the plate and mark it for drilling or punching. Two 1/4-in. pieces of dowel will secure it in place. Now use a pair of dividers to scratch an arc on the metal, gauged from the circumference of the hole to a little less than the depth of the helical kerf on the tap itself. Remove the guide plate and grind away the excess metal. Ease the corners of the arc so it won't catch in the wood, and remove any burrs. With the plate back in the block, the kerf in the tap should engage and turn freely. Drill a hole in the bulge of the tap for a tee handle, and the tool is ready to work.

Choose a sturdy hardwood to test the tap because strength is essential in most applications. Many woods won't take good external threads, but nearly any wood can be tapped as a nut—even pine. Drill a pilot hole in the stock the same size as the hole in the guide block. Clamp the guide block behind this stock, insert the tap and turn it a few times to ensure that

everything is aligned. Adjust the block by tapping it gently with a mallet and draw some witness marks so the guide block can be removed and replaced if necessary.

Up to now the cutter has a sharp vee point and at full depth will cut an ideal vee thread. In practice, the crest and the root of threads should be truncated to create a little flat that avoids sharp, fragile edges and provides clearance for smooth running. The truncation is obtained by dubbing off the point of the cutter, and by not setting it to full depth.

Set the cutter to project about a third of its final depth or about one quarter of the pitch. (At full depth, the cutter will be projecting about two-thirds of the pitch.) Drive the wedge in tight so the strain of cutting can't force it back in its mortise. Make the first pass through the hole and listen for the pleasant grinding sound as the cutter etches its helical path. When it emerges at the chip recess, see that it drops all the shavings before you wind it back. To adjust the cutter for the next pass, set a screwdriver or pin against its back end and gently tap it forward with a hammer. Make sure the wedge is tight after each adjustment.

It's important to take small bites, especially in very hard woods. Otherwise the tap will be difficult to turn, the thread will be rough, and the tap may be damaged. Consider that all the chips must be pushed ahead of the cutter—a 2-in. tap of 3/8-in. pitch, in a 3-in. nut, travels a linear distance of more than three feet. The little recess gouged ahead of the cutter increases chip-carrying capacity, but the tap can easily become overloaded and jam. Some roughness in the threads is normal, especially on the end-grain portions of the helix, and will occur with an all-metal tap too. Such tearing can usually be polished away by running the nut over a screw a few times with a little linseed oil or wax. I've tried to ease the cutting with beeswax or oil, but have found that any lubricant just glues the shavings together, jamming the cutter. The cutter functions as a scraper, and scrapers are most efficient on hard, dry wood. As the cutter emerges it is liable to cause some splitting and roughness, just as an auger bit would. A piece of scrap with the pilot hole drilled in it and sandwiched between the stock and the guide block will prevent this.

The screwbox cuts threads on the outside of a wooden cylinder. It consists of a vee-gouge positioned in front of a threaded hole, and the first real job of the wooden tap is to thread this hole. When the box is rotated onto a dowel, the cutter makes a notch that immediately catches the threads, drawing the cutter around in a helical path.

The tool is usually made in two parts, although in smaller sizes it can be cut from a single block. The top half contains the threaded hole and the cutter; the bottom contains the

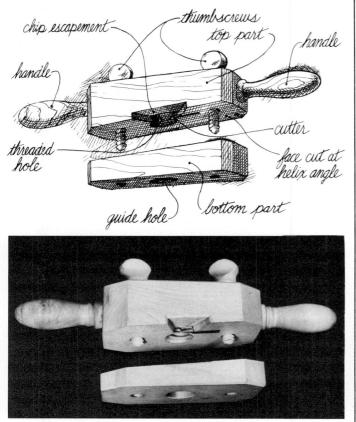

guide hole. The two halves meet at the helix angle of the screw (to be determined) and the cutter fits tightly into a mortise. This simplifies positioning the cutter and eliminates metal hold-downs for it. Metal bolts with wing nuts or wooden thumbscrews hold the two halves together. Once the thread is started the screwbox will cut with its bottom half removed, if a clamp is introduced to hold the cutter. This allows threading up flush to a shoulder.

The proportions of the screwbox aren't critical as long as the top contains at least four turns of thread, and provision is made for the handles and thumbscrews to clear the finished screw. The handles may be made separately and mortised in, or turned in one piece with the top half of the box.

Choose a dense hardwood that has been well seasoned. I have used cherry, maple and yellow birch. Square both pieces on all four sides, align them carefully and clamp them to scrap atop the bench. Locate and drill holes for the bolts through the two halves into the scrap and fasten the halves together. (If you are using wooden thumbscrews, drill and tap a pilot hole in the bottom half of the box.)

Now turn the box over and drill a hole the size of the major diameter of the screw (which for clearance is a tad less than the major diameter of the nut) through the guide plate, setting the depth gauge so the hole intrudes slightly into the screwbox itself. Reset the bit to the minor diameter of the screw and drill through.

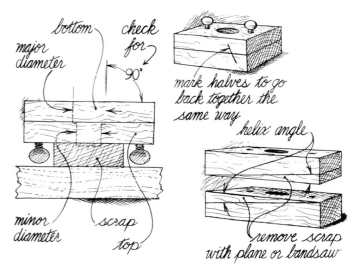

Mark the two halves so they will go back together the same way (there are four possibilities at this point), unclamp the assembly and tap the hole in the top half of the tool. Calculate the helix angle at the pitch diameter (the average of the major and minor diameters). Make a paper template and lay it out. You can plane away the waste or use the band saw, but in either case the surfaces must finish smooth and flat. The two halves should go back together with all the holes aligned and the top and bottom surfaces still parallel. I prefer to finish the surfaces by running them over a long jointer plane held upside down in the vise and set very fine.

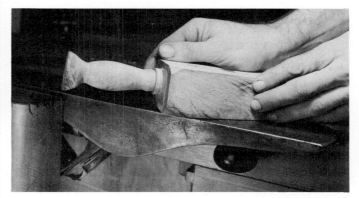

You may prefer, especially in small sizes, to make the screwbox from a single block of wood. Drill the holes and cut it apart at the helix angle. If you plan to turn integral handles, cut the box apart and saw away the excess wood before mounting it in the lathe. The turning axis should be rather close to the top surface, well clear of the angled cut.

The screwbox cutter makes a 60° thread, but because of its position with respect to the minor diameter of the screw it is ground at an outside angle of only 57-1/2°. You can visualize this foreshortening by drawing a vee and squinting at it while tilting the paper. When your eye is at the plane of the page, the vee will appear to flatten out. The front of the cutter is

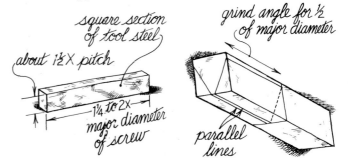

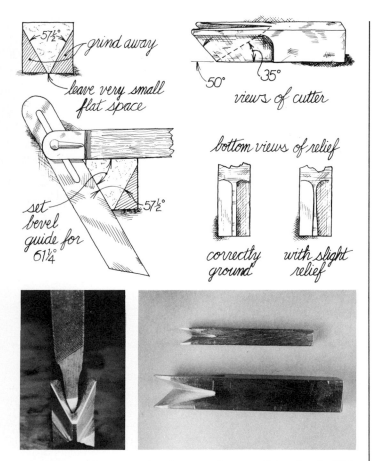

views of cutter

bottom views of relief

correctly ground

with slight relief

Grind the rake and hacksaw or file the inside notch. The length of the notch isn't critical; the idea is to make a sharp cutting edge without leaving the walls so fragile that they break. The notch is cleaned out with a narrow chisel made from the end of a triangular file. First grind two surfaces of the file to an angle sharper than the interior angle of the cutter, then rake the tip back about 70°. The sharp point that results is the chisel. Tap the file handle with a light hammer to pare metal from the bottom of the notch. Finally, grind the top of the cutter down to the filed facets, and harden and temper the steel ("Heat Treating," Fall '76).

Sharpen the inside bevels of the cutter with a narrow India slipstone until you can feel a burr on the outside. Stone off the burr, but do not allow any outside bevel to form. Finish with an Arkansas slip.

The position of the cutter on the inside face of the top half of the screwbox is critical. It must be at the helix angle of the screw; its apex must rest on, and in fact establishes, the minor diameter of the screw; its bottom edge must be parallel to the side of the box and on a line that is almost, but not quite, tangent to the minor diameter. (Set it too high and it lifts out of the work, too low and it digs in.)

Having said all this, the cutter can best be positioned by eye. Draw lines tangent to the major diameter of the threaded

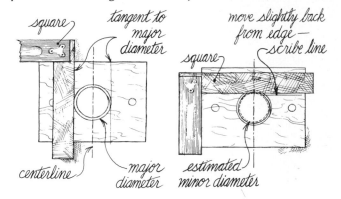

raked forward at an angle of 50° to the top of the shank. This allows the crest of the thread to be cut in advance of the root and prevents the wood from tearing.

Select a square section of tool steel and lay out the angle as shown, leaving a small flat at the apex. Grind to shape, dipping frequently to avoid burning the steel. Leave the surfaces a bit fat and clean off with a file, then file a slight relief behind the cutting edge. This allows the tool to cut smoothly.

A small tap of metal

by Trevor Robinson

With access to a screw-cutting lathe, it's rather easy to make a small metal tap for threading wood. The tap is made from a piece of steel rod six to eight inches long and the major diameter of the nut to be threaded. For occasional use cold-rolled steel will take a sharp enough edge; a much-used tool would be made of tool steel or high-carbon steel. Common sizes are 3/4 in., 1 in. and 1-1/4 in. For all of these diameters six threads per inch is a satisfactory pitch, and a sharp 60° thread is cut for a distance of 1-1/2 in. or 2 in. from one end of the rod. From the same end about 1/2 in. of thread is then removed, just down to the minor diameter. The end is bored to a depth of 3/4 in. at a diameter sufficient to leave a wall thickness of about 1/16 in. The rod is then reversed in the lathe and turned down to the minor diameter from the far end to the start of the thread.

Trevor Robinson, author of The Amateur Wind Instrument Maker, *is a biochemist at the University of Massachusetts.*

When this lathe work is done, a hole is drilled at the top end to take a tight-fitting tee handle, then the actual cutting edge is made by filing or grinding off the bottom end of the thread to make a face that is radial to the rod. Just in front of this face a 5/32-in. hole is drilled through into the cavity. The hole can be filed to make a triangular gouge at the end of the thread, with a sharp, inside bevel. This will direct the shavings into the cavity as the tool is twisted into the nut.

If very hard wood is to be tapped, it should be done in two steps with a starting and a finishing tap. Both have the same minor diameter, but the major diameter of the starting tap is about equal to the pitch diameter of the finished thread, or the average of the major and minor diameters. The starting tap is made with a flat-root thread, cut with a 60° bit whose end has been ground straight across for half the length of its vee. In using the two taps it is obviously essential to start the finishing tap exactly in the cut made by the starting tap.

SEE PAGE 82

hole on the angled face of the screwbox. The major diameter is the circle that was scored by the drill as it completed the pilot hole in the guide block. Measure midway between the lines, and square a center line across the hole.

The minor diameter of the nut was established when the hole was tapped, and the minor diameter of the screw is a tad smaller for clearance. Lay a rule parallel to the edge of the screwbox at the minor diameter of the tapped hole and move the rule a little farther into the hole, to the estimated minor diameter of the screw. Scribe the line with a sharp knife. Set the cutter on the line so that the section of its edge between

the apex and the major diameter is cut in half by the center line, and scribe closely around the shank.

Lay out and cut the chip escape channel as in the photo, making sure it clears the notch on top of the cutter, to a depth that equals the thickness of the cutter. Score the scribe marks for the cutter mortise and chop it to the same depth. Now the cutter must be sunk into the screwbox until the groove it will cut catches the threads in the screwbox. The little Stanley #271 hand router will do the job, but make sure its blade is

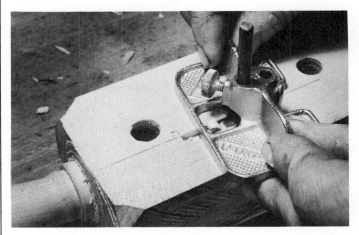

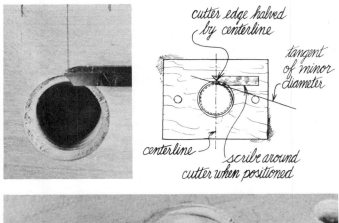

sharp and square to the sole before you begin. Work the mortise and chip channel together, frequently testing the cutter to make sure the fit remains snug.

Use a narrow strip of cardboard as a depth gauge. Along its edge lay out four marks exactly a pitch distance apart. Align three of the marks with the crests of the thread inside the box, and rout until the flat on the cutter exactly centers on the fourth mark. When the depth is correct, the bottom of the cutter may appear to be higher than the last ridge of thread. This is a result of the peculiar helical geometry of screws.

Finally, use the upside-down jointer to plane the surface of the box until the cutter is again flush. Since the bottom of the

Expansion bits

The expansion bit is the wooden screwmaker's cup of tea. It's an inexpensive tool that is continuously adjustable from an inch to more than three inches in diameter. Normal auger bits come in 1/16-inch increments and aren't commonly available larger than an inch and a half. Expansion bits are made for use in the drill press or the hand brace.

The most popular bits for hand use are the Irwin "Microdial" and "Lockhead." The adjustment on the "Lockhead" cannot be tightened enough to hold its setting in hardwood; the more expensive "Microdial" locks more securely. Even so, it sometimes slips to a larger size. I find it necessary to grip the drill head in a vise and bear down hard on the screwdriver.

These drills have a spur that tends to bend outward as the drilling progresses. This enlarges the hole and makes it hard to turn the brace. The cure is to file the spur to about half its original length. After the spur has been shortened it must be filed on the inside surface to reduce its thickness and to re-establish a sharp cutting edge at the top. Auger bits seldom arrive sharp enough to make a clean cut in hardwood. It pays to dress the cutter edges with a fine India stone, then an Arkansas slip.

The little scale printed on the drill is much too coarse for accuracy. I always test the setting in scrap wood, and may adjust it four or five times before arriving at the exact setting.

Auger bits will leave a rough exit hole unless you clamp a piece of scrap behind the stock and drill through into it. I like to clamp a piece of paper between the woods. When paper shavings emerge, the hole is through the stock.   —R.S.

box is also surfaced at the helix angle, it may be used as a gauge. Then remove one shaving more so that when the box is closed tight the bottom plate bears upon the cutter shank and locks it in place. Use a small gouge or knife to pare away the threads in advance of the cutter right out to the major diameter, so the dowel can enter the box.

The dowel to be threaded must be sized to fit snugly but turn freely in the guide hole. Taper or chamfer the end for an easy start and dip the whole dowel in mineral or linseed oil for lubrication because this is now a cutting, rather than a scraping, operation. Set the dowel upright in the vise and start the box with some downward pressure. Once the cut is begun, no downward pressure is needed. The box should turn easily and cut a clean thread.

Most problems result from an improperly set cutter and can be corrected by enlarging the mortise and adding shims. If it won't cut at all, the cutter is probably riding too high on the thread and the mortise will have to be widened to relocate it. If it produces a screw but is difficult to turn, check the minor diameter—a deeper cut may be indicated. If the cutter is misaligned with the thread, it will be difficult to turn the tool and one flank of the thread will bind inside the box and emerge polished. If the bottom surface is polished, deepen the mortise; if the top is polished, add shims to raise the cutter. Such misalignments affect the pitch of the finished screw. A shallow mortise rushes the thread through and lengthens the pitch; when it is too deep it compresses the pitch. The accuracy of the pitch may be checked by comparing the thread with a sliced nut.

It isn't easy to describe the quality needed in a wood to help it accept the helix of a screw with grace and strength. The wood must be strong and hard, and resistant to the shearing forces that would separate the thread from the core of the screw. Yet it still must cut cleanly across the grain.

The most common problem of wood being cut into a screw is that chunks of thread break away. In extreme cases, the screwbox leaves a shaggy, undersized dowel with no threads at all. Chips usually fall from the same position on successive turns, indicating weakness along the length of the grain. I recently cut a large screw in green elm. It had sapwood for about a quarter of its circumference. Chips fell exactly at the boundary between heart and sap along its entire length.

The only consistently fine wood I know for making screws is yellow birch (or red birch, the older heartwood of the same tree). It drips long, continuous shavings from the screwbox. Hornbeam (also called ironwood, leverwood or remin) makes a beautiful, bone-hard screw. Dogwood, juneberry (shadbush or sugarplum) and some of the fruitwoods (especially apple) also work well. Exotics such as boxwood and lignum vitae should be excellent. Oak, ash, cherry and the white birches are sometimes very good and sometimes awful.

Woods that should not be considered for screws include walnut, butternut and beech. Many commercial dowels are beech. Look for the telltale ray flecks and avoid them.

The same characteristics that make green wood cut so well on the lathe make it easy to cut in the screwbox. This is especially important when making large screws with a single-cutter tool. But green wood may check as it dries, and it will shrink. Polyethylene glycol (PEG) treatment may be an answer. But I prefer to rough out an oversize dowel and let it dry slowly until it is about half seasoned. Checking is minimized by avoiding the heart of the tree. Then turn it to size and cut the threads. Build an oversize screwbox or tap the nut undersize, and learn from experience what will work.

Sizing threads

The dimensions of threads in wood can be figured from the same basic relationships as threads in metal. However wood is not worked in increments of .001 in. and such calculations can yield only ballpark figures. For smooth running there must be slop.

In metal threads the tolerances are precise: Truncation is one-eighth of sharp thread height, and clearance is one-sixth of basic thread height. In wood, the amount of clearance also depends on the dryness. As the wood gains and loses moisture circles will become ovals and the pitch of the nut will actually change. The threads in the photo are an inch in diameter. One is a tight fit, the other is a loose, but still good, fit.

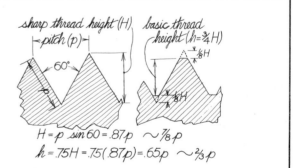

$$H = p \sin 60 = .87p \sim \tfrac{7}{8}p$$
$$h = .75H = .75(.87p) = .65p \sim \tfrac{2}{3}p$$

The maker of threading tools is likely to start with a bit with which he plans to drill pilot holes to be tapped for nuts. He chooses the pitch of the screw and calculates from there. Or he could start with some dowels which he plans to thread for screws, and calculate backward.

For example, starting from a 2-in. drill bit and pitch of 3/8 in.: The drill establishes the minor diameter of the nut. The shank of the tap is turned just a hair smaller so that it will work freely, and the cutter is set, step by step, until it protrudes about two-thirds of the pitch, or 1/4-in., from its mortise. The tool should then tap a nut with flats at crest and root.

The maker scribes this setting on the cutter and slices the test nut in half. He measures its actual major diameter to confirm that it is in the region of the minor diameter plus twice the basic thread height, or 2-1/2 in.

The major diameter of the screw, and thus of the dowel to be threaded, will be smaller than the measured major diameter of the nut by at least one-third of the basic thread height—in this example, more than 1/16 in. and less than 1/8 in.

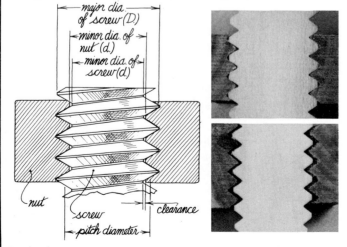

Two Tools

Push-stick; duckbill scriber

In ripping lumber on the table saw, the operator protects his fingers by using a saw guard and a push-stick. A push-stick feeds the stock forward and provides lateral force to guide the board firmly against the fence as well as hold-down force to keep the lumber on the saw table. The traditional push-stick is simply a stick with a notch in one end. This dangerous device has serious disadvantages. Boards (especially at the forward end) cannot be held firmly enough against the fence for accurate ripping. There is little control over the upward thrust of the lumber that results from the friction of the board against the rear edge of the saw blade. These shortcomings tempt the operator to use his free hand to help guide the board, to discard the push-stick entirely, or to decide that the saw guard is in the way and remove it. Here the guard has been removed to take photographs.

Careful analysis of the ripping requirements—feed, guide and hold-

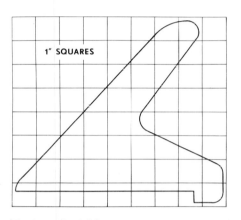

Basic push-stick pattern

down—produces a safe, single-handed push-stick. This improved design applies force at a point well forward on the board to provide enough leverage for firm hold-down. The rear overhang ensures forward feed. The grip of the long bottom surface is enhanced by a covering of thin rubber, rubberized fabric, rug underlayment or abrasive paper, fastened with an adhesive such as silicone rubber or contact cement.

Although the improved push-stick will handle most routine ripping, no single push-stick design will cover all sawing situations, and therefore details of shape and size should be modified to suit the job at hand. Narrow models should be made for ripping narrow strips; wide ones provide greater lateral stability. A double-footed pusher offers maximum control; its two feet may straddle the saw blade and carry narrow cuts safely beyond. This style also is a perfect accessory for the jointer.

It is best to make push-sticks of hardwood plywood, because it resists splitting. I don't recommend softwoods and low-density hardwoods, except for wider models. One-piece push-sticks can be bandsawn to shape from plywood sheets by simply tracing or sketching the pattern on the stock.

—*R. Bruce Hoadley*

The duckbill scriber is easy to make and doesn't require a lot of tools or skill. It is used for scribing frames, moldings or anything that has to fit to an uneven surface such as plaster walls or anything else out of plumb. And I guarantee you, every house has some wall out of plumb. The tool is also handy when leveling the legs of a chair or table.

The only things needed are a piece of hardwood (preferably maple) 1-1/4 in. x 1-1/2 in. x 4-1/2 in., a piece of brass or steel 1/16 in. x 3/8 in. x 1-1/4 in. with two countersunk holes, two 3/8-in. No. 2 flathead screws, and one bolt at least 1/8 in. x 1-1/2 in. with a wing nut to fit.

First shape the block, drill the holes for the bolt and pencil, and cut the groove in the bottom for the metal plate. Then cut off the two outside pieces at 1/4-in. thick and remove the half-round chunk from them.

To assemble it, bolt the three pieces together, then screw the metal plate to the two outside pieces. Be sure to drill pilot holes for the screws and put soap or wax on them before you insert them. File the plate until it is flush.

To scribe a cabinet to a wall, stand it in place or a little bit out. Place the brass plate side of the duckbill against the wall along the line the cabinet is to fit, and open it so the pencil touches the work. Tighten the wing nut. Now you merely run the duckbill along the wall, and the pencil reproduces all its hills and valleys. To level a chair, stand it on a flat surface and block up the legs until the seat is the way you want it and it doesn't wobble. Then lay the duckbill on the table and circle each leg, and you have your cutting lines.

—*Tage Frid*

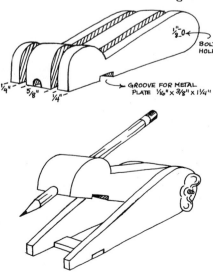

Improved push-sticks are safer.

Heat Treating

Making (or fixing) your tools

by Gordon S. Harrison

Cutting edges made of unalloyed, high-carbon steel are essential to the woodworker's craft. Chisels, plane irons, axes, adzes, gouges, saws, knives, shaves, scrapers, rasps, and bits are simply different configurations of a sharpened, carbon steel blade. The cutting edges of steel woodworking tools must be heat treated to give them the proper combination of hardness and toughness. It may become necessary for you to heat treat a cutting edge in your own shop. You may have spoiled the temper of a chisel by grinding; the factory temper of a gouge may not suit you because the cutting edge is either too soft or too hard; you may want to dress the edge of a large tool such as an ax or adze that is too hard to grind, in which case you must soften the steel by annealing to work it, and then re-harden it; or you may want to make a tool from an old file or leaf spring. Even if you have no occasion to heat treat a tool yourself, you should know how to tell if a cutting edge has been spoiled by overheating. In sum, a knowledge of heat treating is important to a self-reliant woodworker.

There are three steps to heat treating an unalloyed carbon steel cutting tool: annealing, hardening and tempering. Annealing is done by heating the steel to full cherry red and then cooling it very slowly by burying it in an insulating bed of lime or ashes. This softens the steel and prepares its grain structure for hardening. Hardening is done by heating the piece of annealed steel to a full cherry red and then quenching it suddenly in an oil, brine, or water bath. This makes the steel extremely hard and also extremely brittle. Tempering is done by heating the hardened steel to about 500° F. This reduces somewhat the hardness of the steel so it can be hand honed, as well as the brittleness so the tool will not break in use.

The photographs show the hardening and tempering of a drawknife I recently forged from a salvaged automobile leaf spring. First I annealed the entire forging blank overnight in the ashes of a dying fire in my woodburning shop stove.

Annealing eliminates the effects of previous heat treatment on the internal crystalline structure of the steel. Annealed steel has a fine grain structure and is soft, tough, ductile, and easily worked cold with files, hacksaws and abrasives.

A good portion of your tool, from the tip of the cutting edge back toward the handle, should be annealed. Even though it will only be necessary to harden and temper the tip of the tool, you want as much as possible of the remainder of the steel to be soft and tough so that it will not break in service. If you are working with a gouge, anneal at least 4 inches up from the cutting edge. If the gouge is a commercial product, the stem and tang are probably well softened already, but you should anneal the 4 inches anyway because you do not know how much of the tool was hardened at the factory. If you are starting to fashion a file or piece of spring steel into a tool, anneal the entire piece of stock.

To anneal a piece of high-carbon steel, you must thoroughly heat it to between 50°F and 75°F above its critical temperature and then cool it very slowly. When the critical temperature of a piece of carbon steel is reached, its crystalline structure is fundamentally transformed. The critical temperature, also known as the transformation point, depends upon the precise carbon content of the steel. However, the critical temperatures (or the transformation range) of the carbon steels you are likely to be working with are in a narrow range, from about 1350°F to 1400°F. Thus, 1450°F is hot enough to anneal carbon steel, and also to harden it.

There are several precautions to observe as you heat the steel to 1450° F. Heat it slowly so that the temperature rises gradually and evenly over the entire section to be annealed. Heat it thoroughly so the heat penetrates uniformly through its entire thickness. Do not greatly overheat the steel, for even if you do not destroy the steel by burning it (around 2200° F) you may seriously coarsen the grain, which will impair subsequent hardening and tempering. Most carbon steels will go to

Once forged and ground, the draw knife is heated with an oxyacetylene torch to a bright cherry red, or about 1,450 degrees. As soon as the steel is heated to cherry red, it is hardened by quenching rapidly in a bath of used crankcase oil (5-30 SAE).

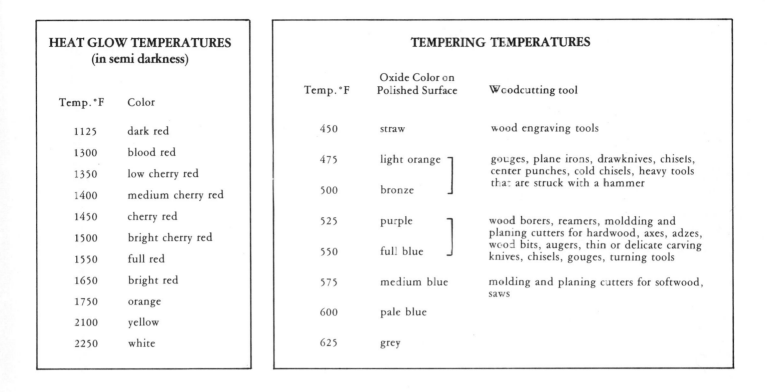

HEAT GLOW TEMPERATURES (in semi darkness)	
Temp.°F	Color
1125	dark red
1300	blood red
1350	low cherry red
1400	medium cherry red
1450	cherry red
1500	bright cherry red
1550	full red
1650	bright red
1750	orange
2100	yellow
2250	white

TEMPERING TEMPERATURES

Temp.°F	Oxide Color on Polished Surface	Woodcutting tool
450	straw	wood engraving tools
475	light orange	gouges, plane irons, drawknives, chisels, center punches, cold chisels, heavy tools that are struck with a hammer
500	bronze	
525	purple	wood borers, reamers, moldding and planing cutters for hardwood, axes, adzes, wood bits, augers, thin or delicate carving knives, chisels, gouges, turning tools
550	full blue	
575	medium blue	molding and planing cutters for softwood, saws
600	pale blue	
625	grey	

1700°F or more before grain coarsening damage begins. Do not direct the flame directly onto the bevel of the cutting edge. Rather, allow heat to penetrate this delicate area of the blade from the thicker adjacent material.

Use a torch for heat. It is possible to bring a small, thin piece of steel to its transformation temperature with a standard propane torch. However, you will have trouble sweeping a propane torch across an object of any size, because there is not enough heat in the flame to evenly raise the temperature of the steel. In this case the heat dissipates too fast, partly because the unheated adjacent steel acts as a heat sink. Thus, a tool about the size of my drawknife, needs an acetylene flame from a Turbo Torch, Prest-O-Lite torch, or oxy-acetylene torch. Use a neutral flame. Make the torch stationary and hold the work in both hands.

How do you determine that the temperature of the steel has reached 1450° F or thereabouts? The traditional method, used by blacksmiths for centuries, is observing the color of the heated steel in semi-darkness. Carbon steel reaches its transformation point when it glows a full cherry red. By the time it has become bright red it is well beyond the transformation point, and when it is orange it is near 1800°F.

Another way to determine temperature is with commercial temperature indicating crayons, such as Tempilsticks. Below its temperature rating, the crayon leaves a dry opaque mark; when its temperature is reached, the mark turns to a liquid smear. I have found Tempilsticks to be invaluable in tempering hardened steel. In the higher heat ranges, 1400°F to 1500°F which we are discussing here, the crayons are more difficult to use, and it is easier to rely on the color of the glowing steel. It is imperative to view the heated steel in a partially darkened room, because brightness will dull the color and you are sure to overheat the work.

When the steel has been heated to a full cherry red, it must be cooled very slowly. Bury it immediately in a bed of dry lime. If lime is not available, dry fine ashes may be used as a

The hardened knife shows oxidation rings, where the curve begins. Temperature-indicating crayon for 500° F is applied to the entire bevel and the blade is ready to temper with a propane torch (right).

The finished drawknife with walnut handles.

substitute. A small piece of steel may take several hours to reach room temperature. A stouter piece may take ten or twelve.

When the steel has cooled it is fully annealed. It is suitable for grinding, filing, and other cold working, and after that you are ready to harden the cutting edge. To harden plain carbon steel, you must heat it slightly above its critical temperature just as you did to anneal it, but instead of cooling it slowly, you must cool it rapidly. Plunge it into a quenching bath of water, brine, or oil. The quench stabilizes the molecular structure of the steel in a condition known to metallurgists as martensite. This particular structure imparts maximum hardness.

Only the portion of the steel that has reached the transformation point will harden when quenched. It is only necessary to harden the cutting bevel and an inch or so back from it. Observe the same precautions as when heating the steel for annealing: heat slowly and evenly; heat thoroughly; do not overheat; let the heat seep into the bevel from adjacent metal.

I prefer, and recommend, used crankcase oil for a quench. It is not as severe as water or brine and the relatively slower quench minimizes the risk of fracturing or distorting the steel. Plunge the heated steel into the bath absolutely vertically, blade first. Distortion will occur if the sides of the blade are quenched differently. There is a danger of igniting the entire bath of quenching oil only if the workpiece is large and contains a great deal of heat and the container of oil is small. This combination should be avoided in any case because it will not properly quench the workpiece.

When withdrawn from the quench, the cutting edge is extremely hard and brittle. It is still not ready to use because it is too difficult to sharpen and is liable to break or crack. The blade must be tempered.

Tempering softens the metal slightly from its state of maximum hardness, restoring a measure of toughness and ductility. To temper a piece of hardened carbon steel you simply heat it to a predetermined temperature below approximately 1000°F. The higher you heat it (below 1000°F), the softer and tougher it becomes. You can temper your tool to the degree of hardness that suits your tastes or needs. The harder the temper, the longer the blade will hold an edge but the more difficult it will be to hone; the softer the temper, the keener an edge the blade will take and the

to hone, but the quicker it loses its sharpness.

Most kitchen ovens will heat to 550°F, which makes them a convenient place to temper your hardened workpiece. Let the piece soak thoroughly in the oven heat for 15 or 20 minutes after it has reached the proper temperature. The rate at which it cools after tempering does not alter its properties, so you may quench it or let it air cool.

It is also possible to temper with a torch. The danger is getting the cutting edge too hot before the heat has thoroughly and evenly penetrated the entire hardened portion of the workpiece. Therefore I use propane flame to temper because the steel heats more slowly than it does in an acetylene flame. Also, I use a Tempilstik to tell me when the selected temper has been attained. Apply the crayon to the entire bevel. When the dry crayon material turns liquid across the width of the bevel, quench the heated portion of the tool to prevent more heat from running into the bevel and ruining the temper.

It also is possible to judge the temperature of the steel visually as it is being heated. The clues are not the glow but a spectrum of colors caused by oxides that form on the polished surface. Each color of the spectrum indicates a specific temperature.

As you apply heat well back from the cutting edge, the oxidation colors will begin to run in both directions away from that point. Just as the color that matches the selected temper reaches the cutting edge, quench the tool.

I do not recommend this method of tempering. It is too difficult to control, especially on long blades. Your kitchen oven or a temperature indicating crayon will give a more accurate result. However, you should learn the colors of the oxidation rainbow, for it they suddenly appear on the edge of a chisel that you are grinding, or on the teeth of a table saw blade that overheats in a piece of hardwood, the steel has lost its temper. A pale blue or grey would indicate significant softening of the blade.

Heat treating always leaves a ring of oxidation colors on the surface of the steel. These can be removed with emery cloth or a buffing wheel and emery compound. If they are obstinate, you can pickle the steel in a bath of sulphuric acid. I use battery acid just as it comes from the service station (called electrolyte, it is sulphuric acid that is about 64 percent distilled water by weight). Rinse in cold water and buff.

Before you set out to heat treat your favorite tool, practice with an old file or spring. Mild steel, of course, will not harden; you must use an unalloyed, high-carbon steel such as is used in files and springs. Be sure you can recognize the transformation point of the steel from its heat glow. Heat and quench a test piece at various shades of red, and attempt to file the steel after each test. If a file does not cut the steel, hardening occurred, which means the transformation point was reached; if it cuts, hardening did not occur and the transformation point was not reached.

[*Authors' note:* Tempilstiks are made by the Tempil Division, Big Three Industries, Inc., 2901 Hamilton Blvd., South Plainfield, NJ 07080. These crayons are calibrated to melt at systematically spaced temperatures from 100°F to 2500°F. They cost about $3.00 each. Tempilstiks are available in the transformation range of carbon steel at 1350, 1400, 1425, 1450, 1480, and 1500°F, and in the tempering range at 450, 463, 475, 488, 500, 525, 550, and 575°F.]

JOINERY

Glues and Gluing

Woodworking adhesives, used correctly, are stronger than wood

by R. Bruce Hoadley

The general term "adhesive" covers any substance that can hold two materials together by surface attachment. Those most commonly used for wood are called "glues," although materials described as "resins," "cements" and "mastics" are equally important in the assembly of wood products. Today's woodworkers use adhesives in a number of ways: to make pieces larger than available stock (such as carving blocks or laminated beams), to create combinations or composites for physical or esthetic improvement (such as plywood, overlays or marquetry) and to join parts to create a final product (as in furniture, sporting goods or structures). Certain basic considerations which may be overlooked or misunderstood are too often the cause of serious gluing problems and are worthy of systematic review.

A logical starting point is to wonder why glue sticks at all. It is sometimes assumed that adhesion results from the interlocking of minute tentacles of hardened adhesive into the fine porous cell structure of the wood surface. However scientific research has shown that such **mechanical adhesion** is insignificant compared to the chemical attachment due to molecular forces between the adhesive and the wood surface, or **specific adhesion.** The assembled joint, or bond, is often discussed in terms of five intergrading phases, each of which can be thought of as a link in a chain. The weakest phase determines the success of the joint. Phases 1 and 5 are the pieces of wood, or adherends, being joined. Phases 2 and 4 are the interpenetrating areas of wood and adhesive, where the glue must "wet" the wood to establish molecular closeness for specific adhesion. Phase 3 is the adhesive itself, which holds together by **cohesion.**

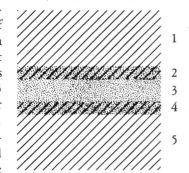

Fundamentally, then, gluing involves machining the two mating surfaces, applying an adhesive in a form which can flow onto and into the wood surface and wet the cell structure, and then applying pressure to spread the adhesive uniformly thin and hold the assembly undisturbed while the adhesive solidifies. The typical adhesive is obtained or mixed as a liquid but sets to form a strong glue layer, either by loss of solvent, which brings the adhesive molecules together and allows them to attach to one another, or by a chemical reaction that develops a rigid structure of more complex molecules.

A wide and sometimes confusing array of adhesive products confronts the woodworker. A common pitfall is the dangerous belief that some glues are "better" than others; the notion that simply acquiring "the best" will ensure success tempts disastrous carelessness in using it. With certain qualifications, it can generally be assumed that all commercially available adhesives will perform satisfactorily if chosen and used within their specified limitations. An important corollary is that no adhesive will perform satisfactorily if not used properly. Within the specified limitations, most woodworking adhesives are capable of developing a joint as strong as the weaker of the woods being joined; that is, the wood, rather than the glue or its bond, is the weak link in the chain.

Wood

Wood is a complicated material. Due to the cellular arrangement within the wood and, in turn, the reactive cellulose within the cell, adhesive bonding is maximum at side-grain surfaces, and minimum at end-grain surfaces. This is especially important to realize in view of the large longitudinal-to-transverse strength ratio we are accustomed to in solid wood. Thus end-grain attachment should be considered only in conjunction with appropriate joints or mechanical fastenings. With side-to-side grain combinations, lamination of pieces with parallel grain arrangement is most successful. With cross-ply orientation, the relative thicknesses of adjacent layers must be considered in relation to the dimensional changes the composite will have to restrain.

Different woods have different gluing properties. In general, less dense, more permeable woods are easier to glue; for example, chestnut, poplar, alder, basswood, butternut, sweetgum and elm. Moderately dense woods such as ash, cherry, soft maple, oak, pecan and walnut glue well under good conditions. Hard and dense woods, including beech, birch, hickory, maple, osage orange and persimmon, require close control of glue and gluing conditions to obtain a satisfactory bond. Most softwoods glue well, although in uneven-grained species, earlywood bonds more easily than denser latewood. Extractives, resins or natural oils may introduce gluing problems by inhibiting bonding, as with teak and rosewood, or by causing stain with certain glues, as with oaks and mahogany.

Since most adhesives will not form satisfactory bonds with wood that is green or of high moisture content, wood should at least be well air-dried. Ideally wood should be conditioned

R. Bruce Hoadley, 44, is associate professor of wood science and technology at the University of Massachusetts in Amherst. He is writing a book about wood science from the cabinetmaker's point of view, to be published next year.

to a moisture content slightly below that desired for the finished product, to allow for the adsorption of whatever moisture might come from the adhesive. For furniture, a moisture content of 5% to 7% is about right. For thin veneers, which take up a proportionately greater amount of moisture, an initial moisture content below 5% might be appropriate.

Machining is especially critical. In some cases, especially for multiple laminations, uniform thickness is necessary for uniform pressure. Flatness is required to allow surfaces to be brought into close proximity. The surfaces to be glued should have cleanly severed cells, free of loose fibers. Accurate hand planing is excellent if the entire surface, such as board edges, can be surfaced in one pass. On wide surfaces, peripheral milling (planing, jointing) routinely produces adequate surfaces. Twelve to twenty-five knife marks per inch produce an optimum surface. Fewer may give an irregular or chipped surface; too many may glaze the surface excessively.

Dull knives that pound, heat and glaze the surfaces can render the wood physically and chemically unsuited for proper adhesion even though it is smooth and flat. Planing saws are capable of producing gluable surfaces, but in general (with exceptions, like epoxies) sawn surfaces are not as good as planed or jointed ones.

Surface cleanliness must not be overlooked. Oil, grease, dirt, dust and even polluted air can contaminate wood surface and prevent proper adhesion. Industry production standards usually call for "same-day" machining and gluing. Freshly machining surfaces just before gluing is especially important for species high in resinous or oily extractives. Where this is not possible, washing surfaces with acetone or carbon tetrachloride is sometimes recommended. One should not expect a board machined months or years ago to have surfaces of suitable chemical purity. If lumber is flat and smooth, but obviously dirty, a careful light sanding with 240-grit or finer abrasive backed with a flat block, followed by thorough dusting, can restore a chemically reactive surface without seriously changing flatness. Coarse sanding, sometimes thought to be helpful by "roughening" the surface, is actually harmful because it leaves loose bits. In summary, wood should be surfaced immediately prior to gluing, for cleanliness and to minimize warp, and should be kept free of contamination to ensure a gluable surface.

Time

Shelf life is the period of time an adhesive remains usable after distribution by the manufacturer. Unlike photographic films, adhesives are not expiration dated. Beware the container which has been on the dealer's shelf too long. Out-dated package styles are an obvious tip-off. It is wise to mark a bottle or can with your date of purchase. It is amazing how fast time can pass while glue sits idle in your workshop.

The adage, "when all else fails, read the instructions," all too often applies to glue. It is unfortunate that instructions are so incomplete on retail glue containers. Manufacturers usually have fairly elaborate technical specification sheets but supply them only to quantity consumers. Too often, many critical factors are left to the user's guesswork or judgment. Mixing proportions and sequence are usually given clearly; obviously they should be carefully followed.

Glues with a pH above 7 (alkaline), notably casein resins, will absorb iron from a container and react with certain woods such as oak, walnut, cherry, and mahogany to form a dark stain. Coffee cans or other ferrous containers can contribute to this contamination. Nonmetallic mixing containers such as plastic cups or the bottoms of clean plastic bleach jugs work out nicely.

Once glue is mixed, the pot life, or working life, must be regarded. Most adhesives have ample working life to handle routine jobs. The period between the beginning of spreading the glue and placing the surfaces together is called open assembly time; closed assembly time indicates the interval between joint closure and the development of full clamping pressure. Allowable closed assembly time is usually two or three times open assembly time. With many ready-to-use adhesives, there is no minimum open assembly time; spreading and closure as soon as possible is recommended, especially in single spreading, to ensure transfer and wetting of the other surface. If the joint is open too long, the glue may precure before adequate pressure is applied. The result is called a dried joint. In general, assembly time must be shorter if the wood is porous, the mixture viscous, the wood at a low moisture content, or the temperature above normal. With some adhesives, such as resorcinol, a minimum open assembly may be specified for dense woods and surfaces of low porosity, to allow thickening of the adhesive and prevent excessive squeeze-out.

Whereas commercial operations usually have routine procedures for clamping, the nemesis of the amateur is not having his clamps and cauls ready. In the scramble to adjust screws or find extra clamps, parts may be shifted and assembly time exceeded. It is worthwhile to clamp up an assembly dry to make sure everything is ready before spreading the glue.

Spreading

Glue should be spread as evenly as possible, even though some degree of self-distribution will of course result when pressure is applied. Brush application works well with thinner formulations. A spatula, painter's palette knife or even a flat stick can be used as a spreader. A small rubber roller for inking print blocks does a great job in spreading glue quickly and evenly. Paint rollers and paint trays can be used with some adhesives.

Proper spread is difficult to control. Too little glue results in a starved joint and a poor bond. A little overage can be tolerated, but too much results in wasteful and messy squeeze-out. With experience the spread can be eyeballed, and it is useful to obtain some commercial specifications and conduct an experiment to see just what they mean. Spreads are usually given in terms of pounds of glue per thousand square feet of single glue line, or MSGL. A cabinetmaker will find it more convenient to convert to grams per square foot, by dividing lbs./MSGL by 2.2. Thus a recommended spread of 50 lbs./MSGL, typical of a resorcinol glue, is about 23 grams per square foot. Spread it evenly onto a square foot of veneer for a fair visual estimate of the minimum that should be used. Usually, the recommended spread appears rather meager.

Double spreading, or applying adhesive to each of the mating surfaces, is recommended where feasible. This ensures full wetting of both surfaces, without relying on pressure and flatness to transfer the glue and wet the opposite surface. With double spreading, a greater amount of glue per glue line is necessary, perhaps a third more.

Clamping

The object of clamping a joint is to press the glue line into a continuous, uniformly thin film, and to bring the wood surfaces into intimate contact with the glue and hold them undisturbed until setting or cure is complete. Since loss of solvent causes some glue shrinkage, an internal stress often develops in the glue line during setting. This stress becomes intolerably high if glue lines are too thick. Glue lines should be not more than a few thousandths of an inch thick.

If mating surfaces were perfect in terms of machining and spread, pressure wouldn't be necessary. The "rubbed joint," skillfully done, attests to this. But unevenness of spread and irregularity of surface usually require considerable external force to press properly. The novice commonly blunders on pressure, both in magnitude and uniformity.

Clamping pressure should be adjusted according to the density of the wood. For domestic species with a specific gravity of 0.3 to 0.7, pressures should range from 100 psi to 250 psi. Denser tropical species may require up to 300 psi. In bonding composites, the required pressure should be determined by the lowest-density layer. In gluing woods with a specific gravity of about 0.6, such as maple or birch, 200 psi is appropriate. Thus gluing up one square foot of maple requires pressure of (12 in. x 12 in. x 200 psi) 28,800 pounds. Over 14 tons! This would require, for an optimal glue line, 15 or 20 cee-clamps, or about 50 quick-set clamps. Conversely, the most powerful cee-clamp can press only 10 or 11 square inches of glue line in maple. Jackscrews and hydraulic presses can apply loads measured in tons. But since clamping pressure in the small shop is commonly on the low side, one can see the importance of good machining and uniform spread.

But pressure can be overdone, too. Especially with low-viscosity adhesives and porous woods, too much pressure may force too much adhesive into the cell structure of the wood or out at the edges, resulting in an insufficient amount remaining at the glue line, a condition termed a starved joint. Some squeeze-out is normal at the edges of an assembly. However, if spread is well controlled, excessive squeeze-out indicates too much pressure; if pressure is well controlled, undue squeeze-out suggests too much glue. Successful glue joints depend on the right correlation of glue consistency and clamping pressure. Excessive pressure is no substitute for good machining. Panels pressed at lower pressures have less tendency to warp than those pressed at higher pressures. Additionally, excessive gluing pressure will cause extreme compression of the wood structure. When pressure is released, the cells spring back and add an extra component of stress to the glue line.

The second troublesome aspect of clamping is uniformity, usually a version of what I call "the sponge effect." Lay a sponge on a table and press it down in the center; note how the edges lift up. Similarly, the force of one clamp located in

To find out just how much pressure typical woodworking clamps could apply, Hoadley attached open steel frames to the crossheads of a universal timber-testing machine. With a clamp positioned to draw the frames together, the load applied was indicated directly.

The clamps are described in the table, with the last column giving the average of three trials by average-sized Hoadley, tightening as if he were trying to get maximum pressure in a gluing job. The quick-set clamp listed first in the table was used to calibrate the setup: A secretary squeezed 330 lbs., a hockey player squeezed 640 lbs., and Hoadley squeezed 550 lbs. Repeated trials by each person yielded readings that agreed to within 10%. An asterisk indicates that the clamp began to bend and the test was stopped at the value listed.

Brand, size, handle style	Screw dia., thread type	Load, pounds
Lust, 5-in. jaw, straight handle	.645 in., square	550
Hartford, 4-in. jaw, straight handle	.370 in., square	400
Jorgenson, 4-in. jaw, straight handle	.375 in., V	420
Stanley, 6 in., T-bar handle	.375 in., V	355*
S.H. Co. bar, crank handle	.625 in., square	2060
Sears 3/4-in. pipe, butterfly crank	.625 in., square	1120*
Jorgenson, 4 in., T-bar handle	.610 in., square	2110
Jorgenson 8 in., butterfly handle	.750 in., square	1100
Pony, 8 in.	spring	25
Craftsman, 10 in., straight handle	.435 in., square	920
Unknown C-clamp 2-in. jaw, T-bar	.310 in., V	560

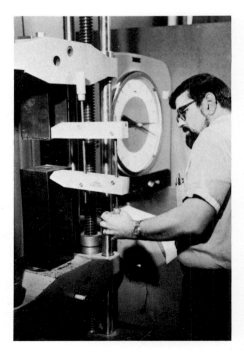

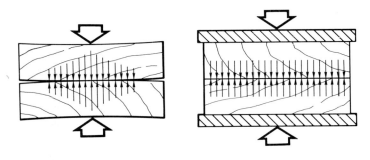

the middle of a flat board will not be evenly transmitted to its edges. It is therefore essential to use heavy wooden cover boards or rigid metal cauls to ensure proper distribution of pressure.

Clamp time must be long enough to allow the glue to set well enough so that the joint will not be disturbed by clamp removal. Full cure time, that is, for development of full bond strength, is considerably longer. If the joint will be under immediate stress, the clamp time should be extended. Manufacturer's specified clamp times are established for optimum or recommended shelf life, temperature, wood moisture content, etc. If any of these factors is less than optimum, cure rate may be prolonged. It's best to leave assemblies overnight.

Most glue specifications are based on "room temperature" (70° F). Shelf life is shortened by storage at above-normal temperature, but may be extended by cold storage. Normal working life of three to four hours at 70° F may be reduced to less than one hour at 90° F. Closed assembly at 90° F is 20 minutes, against 50 minutes at 70° F. A curing period of 10 hours at 70° F can be accelerated to 3-1/2 hours by heating to 90° F.

Finally, cured joints need conditioning periods to allow moisture added at the glue line to be distributed evenly through the wood. Ignoring this can result in sunken joints. When edge-gluing pieces to make panels, moisture is added to the glue lines (1), especially at the panel surfaces where squeeze-out contributes extra moisture. If the panel is surfaced while the glue line is still swollen (2, 3), when the moisture is finally distributed the glue line will shrink (4), leaving the sunken joint effect.

Adhesives

No truly all-purpose adhesive has yet been manufactured and probably never will be. A general-purpose adhesive cannot hope to attain all the individual capabilities and attributes of closely designed ones. Although any of the standard commercial glues will do a satisfactory job if the moisture content of the wood is below 15% and the temperature remains within the human comfort range, there is an increasing trend toward development of special adhesives. Adhesive selection must therefore take into account factors such as species, type of joint, working properties as required by anti-

cipated gluing conditions, performance and strength, and, of course, cost.

One interesting adhesive is water. It is easily spread, wets wood well and solidifies to form a remarkably strong joint. It is delightfully inexpensive. However, it is thermoplastic and its critical maximum working temperature is 32° F. At temperatures at which it will set it has a very short assembly time. But due to its temperature limits water will never capture a very important position among woodworking adhesives.

Glues made from natural materials have been used from earliest times. Although synthetic materials have emerged to the forefront, traditional natural adhesives are still in use.

Hide glue (LePage's Original Glue, Franklin's Liquid Hide Glue) is made from hides, tendons, and/or hoofs of horses, cattle and sheep. It is available in granules which must be soaked in water, but more commonly in ready-to-use form. Hide glue sets by evaporation and absorption of solvent. It has a moderate assembly time and sets in a matter of hours at room temperature. It develops high strength but is low in moisture resistance. Hide glue is used mainly for furniture. Its popularity in recent years has declined drastically with the development of synthetic glues.

Casein glue is primarily a milk derivative although it contains lime and other chemicals in various formulations. It is purchased as a powder that is mixed with water; after mixing, it must be allowed to set for about 15 minutes. Casein glue has the advantage of fairly long assembly time (15 to 20 minutes) but cures rather slowly (8 to 12 hours at room temperature). The glue line is neutral in color but may stain many woods and is somewhat abrasive to cutting tools. The claim of being a good gap-filling adhesive seems somewhat doubtful. Casein has moderately good heat resistance and bonds show significant short-term moisture resistance, but it is not recommended for exterior use. Casein is used extensively for laminating and large carpentry jobs.

Polyvinyl resin emulsions are probably the most versatile and widely used wood adhesives. These are the white glues (Elmer's Glue-All, Franklin's Evertite white glue, Sears' white glue), also called PVA because of their principal constituent, polyvinyl acetate. White glues have a long shelf life and can be used as long as the resin remains emulsified. Setting is by water absorption and quite rapid at room temperature; clamping time of less than one hour may suffice if the joints are not to be stressed immediately. The white glues are non-staining and dry clear. The glue does not dull tools but excess squeeze-out may clog or foul sandpaper under frictional heating because the adhesive is thermoplastic. These glues develop high strength but have low resistance to moisture and heat. An important characteristic is their "cold flow," or creep under sustained loading. This is an asset where dimensional conflict is involved, as in mortise and tenon joints. However, in edge gluing and lamination, "shifting" of adjacent pieces may in time produce visible unevenness at joints. In chair seats, joints may open along end grain due to drastic moisture change.

Numerous modified PVA glues give greater rigidity and improved heat resistance. The so-called **aliphatic resin glues**, commonly called yellow glue (Franklin's Titebond, Elmer's Carpenter's Wood Glue) fall into this group. The low viscosity of the white glues was always troublesome in furni-

cabinet would have tails cut on the sides and pins on the top and bottom.

In any event, determine the size of the pins you will use. With handcut dovetails, the pins are usually about half the size of the tails. This ratio is optional, but if the tails are made too large, the strength of the joint is weakened as the holding power of the glue joint is in the long-grain areas between the pins and tails, not in the end-grain areas behind them. The

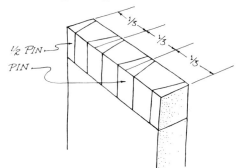

fewer the tails, the less the glue area. But if the tails are made too small, their strength is considerably reduced because there isn't enough wood across their narrowest point. With pins, however, strength is not significantly affected if they are made smaller (in some antique pieces the pins actually come to a point) because there is always enough cross-sectional area for what they have to do.

The first and last pins are called half-pins because they are angled on only one side, not because they are necessarily half the size of the whole pins. This is important when you are using very narrow pins because if you did make the outside pins half the size of the whole pin there would be danger of chipping or sanding through them. But in any case, begin and end a dovetail series with a half-pin rather than a half-tail, because a tail gets its strength only from being glued to a pin, not to the end grain it butts against.

Divide the width of the board that will have the pins into equal divisions, depending on the number of tails you have

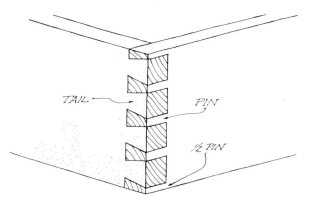

room for, e.g. divide in thirds for three tails, fourths for four tails. These division marks are the center points of your pins. If your pins are going to be 1/2-inch in width at their narrowest, measure in 1/4-inch from each end and 1/4-inch on either side of your division marks. This will give you the placement of your pins.

Check your divisions for accuracy. Then with a bevel gauge set to a 1-to-5 ratio, scribe in the lines with a sharp tool such as an awl or a scriber. Don't use a pencil (except for rough layout) because a pencil line is too thick.

The 1-to-5 ratio can be varied, but anything less will cause fragile corners on tails, and anything above 1 to 6 reduces the

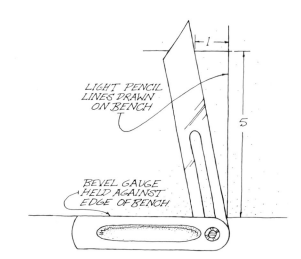

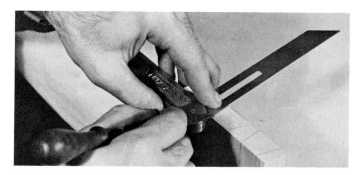

strength of the joint because of a flatter wedge.

At this point you should have the pins drawn out on the end grain of your board. The wider end of the pins should be toward the inside surface of the board. With a square you can carry your lines from the edges down to the marking gauge lines on both sides of the board. To avoid confusion, shade in the areas between pins. A common mistake is to saw on the

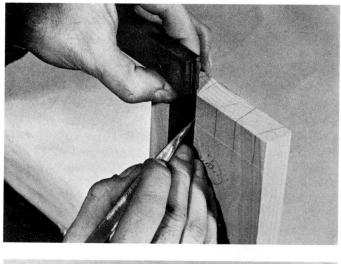

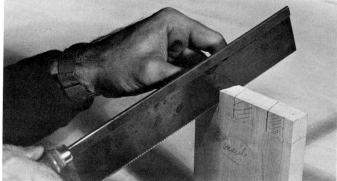

wrong side of the line, or worse yet, to chisel out the wrong areas.

Now, with the piece held securely in a vise, you must make saw cuts down to the marking gauge line. You should use a fine dovetail saw. The thinner the blade, the easier it will be. Remember to split the line on the waste side. You'll find this easier if you imagine the line as having thickness to it, as a pencil line does. It is difficult to saw precisely at first, but you will get better with a little practice.

The piece should now be clamped over a rigid area of the workbench to support it while chiseling. Do not clamp over a vise or allow the piece to extend over the edge of the bench.

Before starting to chisel, it helps to deepen the marking gauge line between the pins with a chisel and then to remove a fine chip out to about 1/8-inch in front of the marking

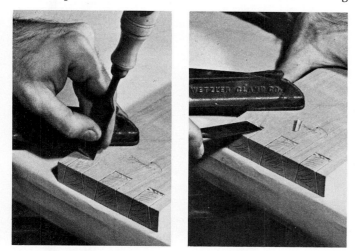

gauge line. This will establish a positive edge to line the chisel against. It will also lessen the chance of the chisel drifting back beyond the marking gauge line during chiseling. Now you are ready to take a heavier cut.

With the chisel held vertically at the marking gauge line, a blow with a mallet will cut across the grain. Then a light cut in from the end grain will remove the chip. A few alternating cuts will get you about halfway through. Now turn the board over and repeat the process from the other side until you have chiseled out the material between the pins.

When you are making the vertical cuts across the grain at the marking gauge line, it helps to tip the chisel forward a few degrees. This is called undercutting and if done when chiseling from both sides it will result in a shallow, concave surface in the end grain between the pins. Remember that

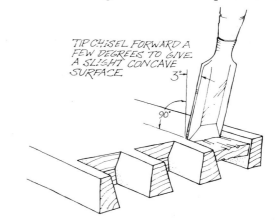

TIP CHISEL FORWARD A FEW DEGREES TO GIVE A SLIGHT CONCAVE SURFACE

this undercut is not visible and does not affect the strength of the joint, but it does result in a tighter looking joint.

Even with undercutting you will still have a little cleanup to do in the corners between the pins. If any of your saw cuts

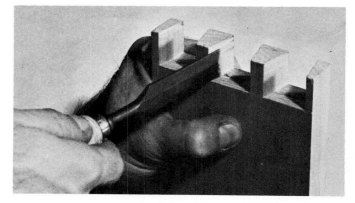

are out of square, you can clean them up a little also, but always use a sharp chisel, never sandpaper or a file, when cleaning up the pins.

You should now be ready to scribe the tails. Position the pins directly over the side to be joined. Make sure that the ends are flush, that the pins are positioned precisely at the previously drawn marking gauge line, that the inside surfaces are facing in, and that the widest end of the pins is toward the inside of the joint. Now scribe around the pins with a scriber or awl. It is important not to move the piece until all the scribing is completed. Clamp the piece in position if possible.

It is easier to scribe from inside the joint rather than outside. The grain will work to your advantage in keeping the

scriber tight against the sides of the pins. From the outside the tool tends to follow the grain away from the side of the pin.

After the pins have been scribed, use a square to scribe the lines across the end grain. Shade in the areas to be removed

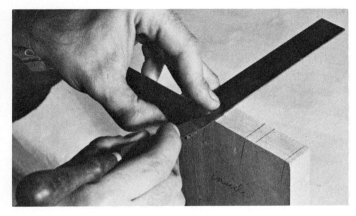

and proceed as you did when cutting out the pins. Be as precise as possible with your saw cuts, remembering to split the line on the waste side. Deepen the marking gauge line with a chisel and remove a 1/8-inch chip. Undercut when chiseling.

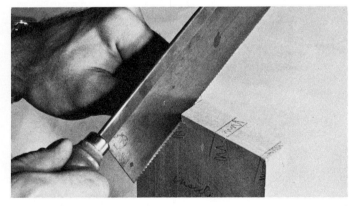

It is probably neater and easier to saw rather than to chisel the ends out. Clean up the corners between tails with a chisel before trying the joint.

Do not force the joint together. If it is your first set, you will probably have more cleaning up to do. With practice you should be able to tap the two pieces together without any cleanup or splits or gaps.

The dovetails should be tight enough to require some tapping when putting them together; however, be careful of splitting. If your dovetails are very tight and require a lot of effort to drive them together, they are probably too tight and may split when the glue is applied (glue swells the joint slightly). Always dry clamp before gluing and use glue blocks —small pieces of a softer wood that are notched so they direct the clamp pressure over the tails. A little sanding to bring the ends down flush with the sides and your through dovetails are complete.

Half-blind Dovetails

Half-blind dovetails are those that show from only one side. They are most commonly used for drawer fronts but they can be used elsewhere quite effectively. The procedure for making them is basically the same as for through dovetails. I will list only the steps that differ.

Half-blind dovetails can be used for joining pieces of the same thickness, but because they are most commonly used for drawers, I will describe cutting them with pieces of different thicknesses—a thicker piece for the drawer front, a thinner piece for the side.

Dress the pieces to be joined to the desired thicknesses and sand and mark the inside surfaces. You will need two marking-gauge settings for half-blind dovetails. First the marking gauge is set to the thickness of the drawer side. With this setting scribe a line along the end of the drawer front on the inside surface only. Now reset the marking gauge to about 2/3 the thickness of the drawer front and scribe a line into the endgrain of the drawer front. The scribed line should be in 1/3 of the way from the outside (or 2/3 from the inside) surface of the drawer front. At this same setting scribe a line around both sides and edges of the drawer side.

The 2/3 proportion can be varied. It determines how long the tails will be. They can be longer, providing they don't interfere with any shaping or face carving on the drawer front. But as tails are shortened, the strength of the joint is reduced.

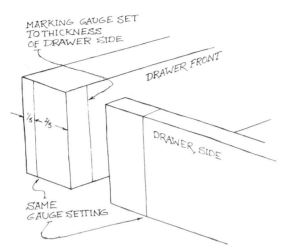

MARKING GAUGE SET
TO THICKNESS
OF DRAWER SIDE

DRAWER FRONT

⅓ ← ⅔

DRAWER SIDE

SAME
GAUGE SETTING

with a square down the inside of the drawer front to the other marking gauge line. Novices usually expect the sawing and chiseling out of the pins to be difficult, but you will find that it is not much different than with through dovetails. Start sawing at the inside edge of the drawer front. Remember to split the line on the waste side, but do not saw past either of the two marking gauge lines.

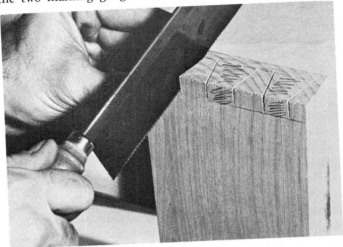

When cutting half-blind dovetails I find it easier to cut the tails first because it is difficult to scribe inside the pins. But others say the pins should be cut first.

On the drawer side lay out the tails. This is done in the

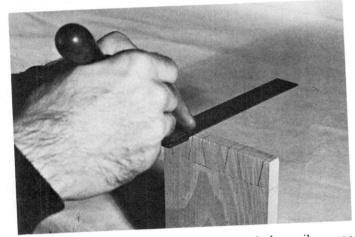

The chiseling is done with the same alternating cuts as for through dovetails. Remember to undercut slightly. The only difference here is that the inside corners will splinter as each chip is removed because the saw cuts do not extend back all the way. It helps to clean out these splintered internal corners after removing each chip. When you reach the marking gauge line do whatever cleanup is necessary and try the joint.

same way as when laying out pins for through dovetails except you will be working on the outside of the drawer side rather than on the end grain of the drawer front.

Saw and chisel out the areas between the tails you have just laid out using the same techniques as in through dovetails. Once the tails are cut out and cleaned up, you must scribe the pins onto the end grain of the drawer front. Clamp the drawer front in a vise flush to the workbench top and lay the

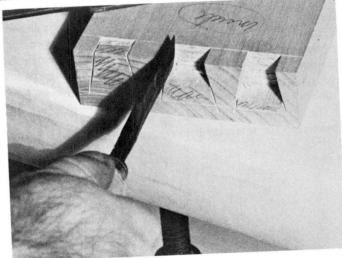

side over it. Be sure inside surfaces are towards the inside of the corner. Line the edges of the boards up, and position the ends of the tails exactly at the marking gauge line. This positioning is critical. If it is not done accurately, it will result in gaps. Clamp or hold the piece securely and scribe the pins from the sides of the tails. The lines should then be extended

For purposes of clarity I have described procedures for cutting each of the types of dovetails on two pieces of wood. This is the best way to practice these joints. However, when actually making a box or a drawer, it is much more efficient and easier to be accurate if you work on all four corners at once. In other words, lay out and saw the pins on both ends of the front and back at once. Scribe the tails on both ends of the sides at the same time. Make all the saw cuts in one operation and then chisel out all the tails at once. But remember to letter each corner so you know which set of tails was scribed from which set of pins.

There are nearly as many methods for cutting dovetails as there are craftsmen. The methods I have described work best for me, and I hope with a little practice they will produce satisfactory results for the reader.

There are several ways to make a mitered mortise and tenon. Often a spline is used, as it is easier to cut. Sometimes

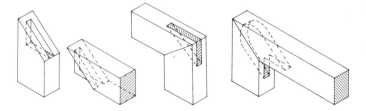

a spline is used purely for visual effect. The spline can also be hidden.

If a tenon should break, a spline can be inserted. The same method is often substituted for a mortise and tenon.

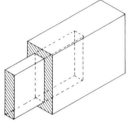

Although it is not as strong, the spline is in most cases sufficient, and is again much easier to make.

There are many other variations of the mortise and tenon joint but virtually all depend on the cheek and shoulder action for their strength. Similarly, the technique used in making these joints is basically the same.

In making mortise and tenon joints, I find it easier and quicker to use hand tools, unless there are so many joints that power tools turn out to be quicker. But this is rarely the case because power tools — whether I'm using a saw, or a router or a drill press with a mortising bit — do take time to set up for the particular job. But even if you plan to use power tools, it's best to learn to do them by hand, so that you understand what you're trying to do with the power tools.

The first step in making the basic two-shoulder joint is to mark both pieces to keep the orientation right. Then I outline

the tenon piece on the mortise piece, but I use a square to put lines just inside (less than 1/16-inch) those marks, because the mortise should be made slightly smaller to allow for subsequent sanding of the tenon.

I pick a drill or bit about 1/3 the thickness of the tenon board. If this size is between bit sizes, I use the next larger one. Although it isn't absolutely necessary, I recommend using a doweling jig to guide your bit while boring the mortise. You'll end up with straight and even sides. Make the

two outside holes first, then the holes in between.

Stop work on the mortise at this point and transfer its dimensions to the tenon board. First measure the depth of the mortise with a rule and make the tenon 1/8-inch shorter

to allow for excess glue. I use a square and a scribe to draw this depth line around all four sides of the tenon board. This marks where the shoulders will go. Don't use a pencil be-

cause its line is too wide and the shoulder must be cut with great accuracy.

Then take a marking gauge and adjust it so its point just touches the nearer side of the holes bored for the mortise. Transfer this measurement to the ends and two sides of the

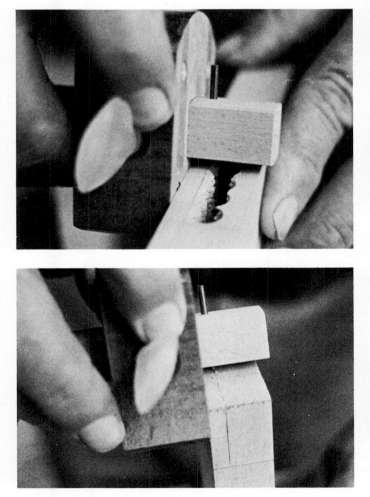

tenon. Then do the same for the other side of the mortise (but continue using the same reference surfaces).

You are now ready to cut the cheeks of the tenon. I use a frame saw for this (as I use for almost all hand sawing because it's the fastest and best saw there is) but if you don't have one, use a dovetail or back saw. The thinner the blade, the easier it will be to make accurate cuts.

The trick to cutting accurate cheeks is to cut the back line and part of the top first; then turn the board around and cut the rest of the top and the front lines. That way you don't have to worry about following two lines at once. When cutting the front line, the saw blade will be automatically

guided at the back by the kerf you made before. You'll also get a little more accuracy in this guiding process if you use a slightly thinner blade for cutting the back lines than you do for cutting the front.

In any event, when sawing the cheeks, "split" the line on the waste side. The tenon cheeks must fit just right. If they're too tight they may split the mortise piece; if too loose, the glue joint may come apart under strain. Furthermore, the surface over a mortise that holds a loose tenon will in time become concave as the wood dries.

After the cheeks are sawed, it's time to saw the shoulders. One trick I've found helpful to improve the accuracy (since the shoulders must be perfectly aligned) is to make in effect a small or mini-shoulder for the saw to lean against. Take one corner of a flat chisel and deepen the shoulder line by

drawing the chisel along it. Then take a second cut at an angle to create half a "vee". You can then use this notch as a guide for your dovetail or frame saw. Finish sawing the shoulders and use a flat chisel to clean up the cheeks, and then round

off the tenon corners slightly for easy insertion. Then sand the edge of the tenon so it will fit into the slightly shorter mortise.

Now finish making your mortise. Take a small chisel and mallet to square off the corners, and a wide chisel (but no mallet) to flatten out the sides. Sand the outside edge of the

mortise piece as you did the tenon sides and you're ready to try the fit. You should be able to push it in by hand with the weight of your body. If you need to hammer it in, it's too tight and you should shave some material off the tenon

100

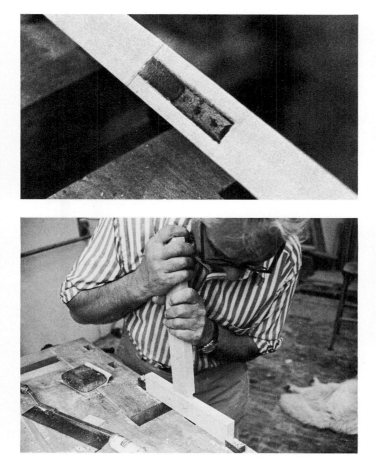

assembled, make a clean saw cut along the shoulder line, making sure not to cut into the mortised piece at all. Do the same for the other shoulder. Don't saw quite completely to the tenon. Instead, finish the cuts with a chisel after the joint is disassembled. If you're making a frame and notice one of

the shoulders is off after you've dry clamped it, make the shoulder correction cuts to all the shoulders on the same side of the frame, so that after correction, the frame stays square (but one blade width shorter). Of course, if a shoulder is really off, you may need to go through the correction process twice.

cheeks because that's the easier piece to correct. If the tenon is too loose, you can glue strips of veneer to the cheeks.

If after fitting, the shoulders are slightly off as illustrated here, there's a trick you can use to align them. With the joint

On complicated pieces where the joints may come in at odd angles, I sometimes don't worry about precise fitting of the shoulders during the initial cutting process, but rely instead on the correction cuts to get the fit I want.

When gluing a mortise and tenon joint, it is very important to put a moderate amount of glue in the mouth of the mortise, and just a little on the beginning of the tenon cheeks and on the shoulders (as insurance).

There should not be so much glue that the glue runs out over the work and the bench and all over the craftsman. Anyway, a tight joint does not allow room for too much glue.

When gluing up a table or chair it is much better to glue up two opposite sections first and later glue them together. If everything is glued up at once, too many clamps are used, and it is more difficult to square the whole piece up at once.

Regardless of the variation of mortise and tenon joint you are making, or whether you are using power tools, the construction process is the same. Make the mortise first and transfer its dimensions to the tenon piece. But don't try to make the mortise and tenon independently.

Carcase Construction

Choosing and making the right joints

by Tage Frid

Furniture construction is broken down into two main categories: frame and carcase. In frame construction, relatively narrow boards are joined—usually with a mortise and tenon joint—as in a chair or table base, or in a frame and panel door. (See *Fine Woodworking*, Summer 1976.) In carcase construction, boards are joined end to end using dovetails, tongue-and-groove joints and the like, as in a drawer or hutch. When designing a carcase, the beginner may find it difficult to know which joint to choose. Some joints are excellent in plywood but weak in solid wood, and vice-versa. Many beginners are so concerned with the "craft" aspect that they design in the most complicated techniques. They use a complex joint where a joint easier to make would work just as well. I always choose the strongest but easiest joint to construct. I cannot see spending time over-constructing a piece. And I expect my furniture to last long after I do.

Most carcase joints can be made by hand, but are usually more easily and precisely made on a circular saw. I would advise people who don't own a circular saw to buy a table saw and not a radial arm saw. The latter is limited in function and not as accurate or flexible. It was designed for cross-cutting rough lumber to lengths, and even then is limited to a certain width. Many of the joints described here would be dangerous and impractical to make on a radial arm saw. I prefer at least a ten-inch table saw, and it does not cost that much more than an eight-inch. Buy one with at least a 1-hp motor, as an underpowered machine is much more dangerous to work with.

Joints at corners

In the article on dovetails, (*Fine Woodworking*, Spring 1976), it is stated that dovetailing is one of the strongest and most attractive methods of joining the ends of boards together. This is true if you are going to make joints by hand. But most carcase joints lend themselves to machine fabrication. The closest machine joint to a dovetail is a finger or box joint. Because of the greater number of pins and the resulting total glue surface, it is stronger than a dovetail, far easier to make, and just as attractive.

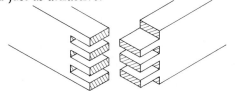

Tage Frid teaches furniture design and construction at the Rhode Island School of Design, and has been a professional woodworker for close to 50 years.

The lock miter is used for either solid wood or plywood. Its advantages are that it is hidden to the outside, and that it requires clamping in only one direction, because of the built-in locking action. The "double-tongued" lock miter is the best and fastest production joint for plywood but it requires a shaper with special knives, (available from Woodworkers Tool Works in Chicago; see page 62). Only one shaper setting is required—the first piece is run through vertically, the second horizontally. The same clamping benefit holds true here. I use this joint only in plywood. In production work, the time saved pays for the relatively high cost of the cutter.

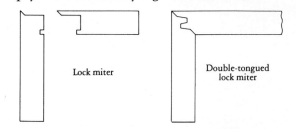

Lock miter   Double-tongued
                              lock miter

The spline miter really lends itself to plywood, but can be used in solid wood on smaller pieces such as boxes. The grain direction of the spline must follow that of the pieces being joined. The spline should be placed 1/5 to 1/6 of the way in from the inside corner so as not to weaken the corner. Because of the 45-degree angle, all pieces must be glued up simultaneously, a real disadvantage in a piece with many parts. Also, a lot of clamps (in all directions) are required to ensure tight glue lines.

A lesser-used spline miter with a parallel spline has several advantages but can be used only in plywood. This spline is just as strong as the diagonal one. The spline slots are minutely offset (about 1/32 in.). Clamps are needed only parallel to the spline, and the offset pulls the pieces tightly together. The ease of clamping this joint is a real advantage. You can glue the inside members and sides first, and when they dry, glue on the top and bottom.

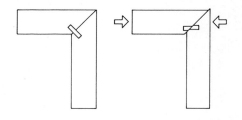

A corner tongue and groove, rounded or square, is good for either type of wood. In plywood the grain of the corner piece must run lengthwise along the edging. However, in solid woods, the grain must run in the same direction as the grain

SEE PAGE 96
SEE PAGE 91

Making a Lock Miter

Set the table saw fence to just inside the board thickness. Set a single blade to a height 1/5 to 1/6 of the thickness. Make the first cut using a miter gauge (1). Set the dado blades to the desired width (about 2/3 the thickness). Mark off the blade height from the other board and cut the dado. A tenoning jig is much safer here than using the fence (2). Scribe the other dado side to the first piece. Set a single blade to the height of the top edge of the dado. Saw to make the second tongue (3). Cut off the tongue on the dadoed piece to the right length (4). Tilt the blade to 45 degrees and miter the mating tongues (5 & 6). Keep checking back and forth between pieces as you make each cut to test for a good fit, or make a scrap set as you go along.

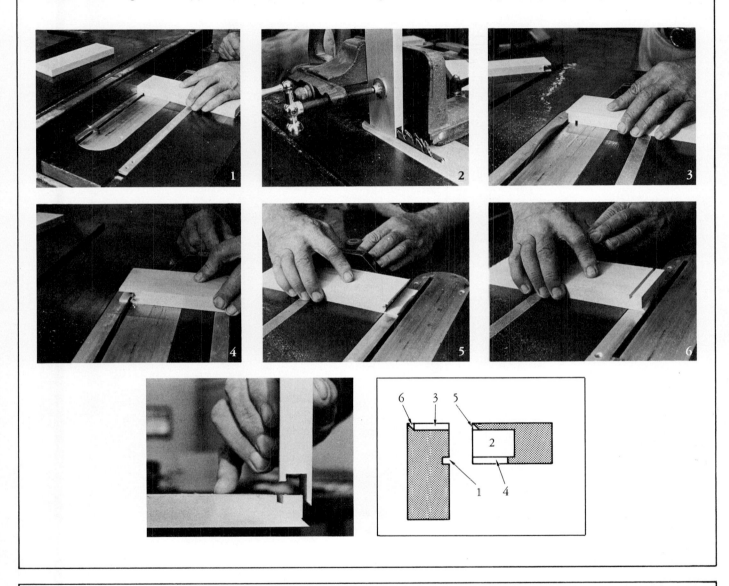

Making a Spline Miter

To make a spline miter set the blade at 45 degrees and cut the pieces using the miter gauge (1). Lower the blades, move the fence to the opposite side of the blade and cut the two spline slots (2). This method keeps the cuts parallel to the edge and prevents the pieces from skewing.

Making Multiple-Spline Joints

Mock Finger Joints

The mock finger joint is made using a simple jig on the table saw. The carcase pieces are first mitered and glued. A jig with a 45-degree vee cut out of it is made and a dado cut is sawed into the jig. A spline is fitted into the cut. The jig is screwed to the miter gauge. A cut is made at the desired arbitrary distance from the spline (1). The pieces are set in up against the spline and the first cut is made. The first cut slips onto the spline and the next slot is made (2). The process is continued down the length (3).

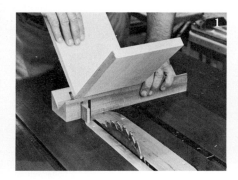 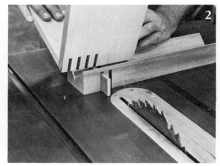 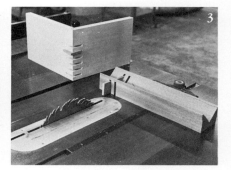

Mock Dovetails

For a mock dovetail the jig is exactly the same as in the mock finger joint. A fence is set up on the router table that is no higher than the bottom of the vee on the jig. A board is attached to the back of the jig to provide a greater surface running against the fence (1). The process is exactly the same as the mock finger joint (2,3). The length of spline is angled on both sides to fit into the dovetail slots (4).

The first piece is lined up with the left side of the jig and the second with the right so that the two align properly. Or a piece of plywood can be made to serve as a guide. If the joint is made with a dovetail jig the splines will have to be rounded on two edges. Or the splines can be made smaller and left square since there is plenty of glue surface. The joint can also be made on a mortiser, using a jig just as in the mock spline joints.

Full-Blind Splines

of the sides so that expansion is constant. The grain should run diagonally from tongue to tongue. Any shaped corner molding can be used. The inside is shaped first, the pieces are glued together, and then the outside is shaped.

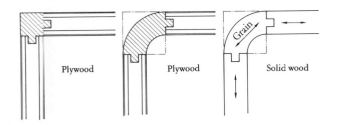

The doweled miter is used where structure is not crucial—in small boxes, knickknack cabinets, spice racks, etc. It is easy to make, and aligns itself correctly for gluing because of the dowels. A dowel center is useful for transferring the position of one hole to its corresponding hole. This joint works in solid wood or plywood.

I generally do not use a butt joint with dowels, but when I do, I find it advantageous to angle the dowels. This adds needed strength to the joint.

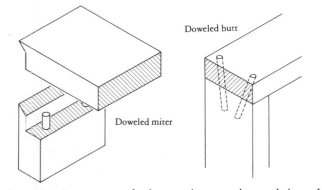

Several joints are made by cutting a miter, gluing the corners together, and then cutting slots to receive splines. Water-based animal glue in an electric glue pot is perfect for gluing the miters since the glue is strong and dries in just a few minutes so you can then finish cutting the joint. These joints have great strength and pleasing decorative qualities. With jigs, they can be made extremely fast. The first is a mock finger joint—it resembles a finger joint without the alternating fingers. For the same effect in a small piece, thin, handsaw kerfs are spaced down the joint. Pieces of veneer are hammered to make them thinner, and glue is squeezed into the saw cut. When the veneer splines go into the slots they swell from the moisture of the glue. (A loose through dovetail can be repaired in the same way, by evening out the gap with a saw cut and diagonally inserting a veneer strip.) A mock dovetail is made similarly, but using a router mounted in a table. If desired, a contrasting wood can be used for splines as a decorative detail.

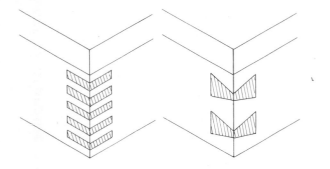

If the splines are to be hidden, the spline slots can be cut using a router with a machine dovetail jig. This joint is considerably stronger than a full-blind dovetail because of the greater glue surface.

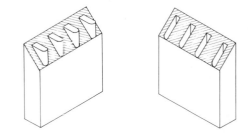

The tongue and rabbet is not the strongest joint but is good enough for the back of a drawer (although not as strong as a dovetail). It is very easy to make. The proportions must be strictly adhered to, as they are determined by factors of strength. The groove should be no deeper than 1/4 to 1/5 of the board's thickness.

The half-blind tongue and rabbet is made like a lock miter but without the miter. It is particularly good for drawer fronts, but in that case be sure to put the drawer stop somewhere other than in the front because of the limited joint strength. This joint can also be made with a router.

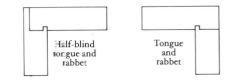

Machine-cut dovetails made with a router and dovetail jig are useful where great quantities must be cut, or where the extra strength of a hand-cut dovetail is not needed. I use them when I have stacks of drawers to do for kitchens. Otherwise, I prefer hand-cut dovetails for their strength and looks. Besides, when you've made them for many years you'll find them easier to do than setting up the router.

The through and half-blind hand dovetails are explained in the dovetail article in the Spring 1976 issue of *Fine Woodworking*. The full-blind dovetail (and similarly the machine-made, full-blind spline joint) is not used to be "crafty," but is used where strength is important, as in a freestanding cabinet without a back, or in a cabinet with glass doors.

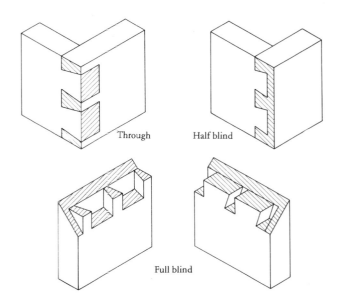

SEE PAGE 91

Joints not at corners

A simple tongue and groove can be used for any type of wood except composition boards. At the ends of boards the tongue is set off center so that the outside shoulder isn't too weak. Fiberboard and particle board are made of waste materials and so there is no grain strength. Since a tongue would break, a spline must be used with these materials. The spline should go into the carcase side about 1/4 of the side's thickness, and twice that amount into the perpendicular piece. Setting the spline further into the side will weaken it, and keeping it shorter in the perpendicular piece will not add enough strength.

I would never use a fully-housed dado joint. There are no shoulders to lock the wood and help resist sideway stresses. Also, if the wood is sanded after the joint is cut, the piece becomes too loose. If there are imperfections in the wood, the piece will not fit tightly.

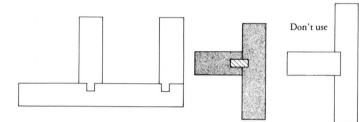

Don't use

Another strong joint is a series of small mortise and tenons. For extra strength, the tenons should run through the sides and be wedged from the outside at assembly.

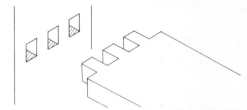

The sliding dovetail is an excellent joint for perpendiculars. The double-shoulder version is machine cut with a router and a dovetail bit. The single-shoulder joint is cut by hand with a dovetail plane and its corresponding saw, and with a router plane. The machine version is excellent for production. If

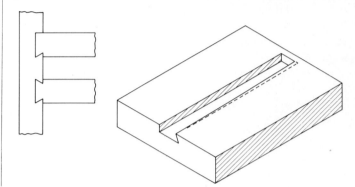

Making a Finger Joint

A simple jig on a miter gauge makes cutting this joint very simple. A correct fit is solely dependent on how accurate the jig is. Raise the blade a hair higher than the thickness of the boards: It is easier to sand a little off the ends of the joint than to plane the whole side. Make a cut in the board with the dado blades. Then make a spline that is exactly the same size as the slot and fits into it snugly (1). Line up the blade to a position precisely one spline thickness over from the first cut. Screw the jig to the miter gauge. With the spline in the slot, cut the first finger with the board edge up against the spline (2). Slip the finger slot onto the spline and continue down the board, moving over one each time (3). Start the second piece lined up to the open sawcut so the first cut makes a slot (4). Continue down the board (5) and the two should fit together perfectly (6). I recommend you do a small test to check the accuracy of your jig before cutting the final pieces.

Making a Full-Blind Dovetail

The pieces are marked and the excess above the pins and tails is removed. The remainder that will form the top miter must be a square. A 45-degree angle is cut at the edge (or at both edges). The pins are marked, cut and chiseled out. The tails are marked from the pins, sawed and chiseled out. With a little luck, they might fit. If for some reason the corner is slightly open, hit it lightly with a hammer when the piece is being glued. This will bend the fibers over and close the imperfection. For a round corner the dovetail is made exactly the same but without the upper miter.

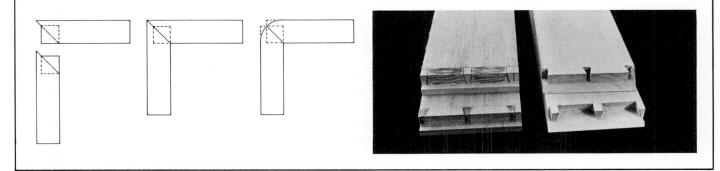

Making Hand-Cut Sliding Dovetails

Hand-cut sliding dovetails require the special dovetail plane and saw (1). The position for the groove is marked with a framing square and scribed. The angle of the taper is drawn in. For lumber 3/4 in. or thicker I use about a 1/8-in. taper. If the groove is to be stopped in the front I mark off where the joint ends. All lines are scribed and scored deeper with a chisel. This is important since the cutting is across the grain. A slight vee is pared off of each line the whole way down (2). If the joint is to be hidden the end is chiseled out. This stops the groove and provides an opening to start the saw in. The straight side is sawed at 90 degrees and the tapered side is sawed at an angle using the saw shoulder as the guide (3). The router plane cuts out the mass of material and the groove is finished (4). The depth of the dovetail is marked onto the edge of the other board with the arrow-shaped blade in the dovetail plane which is available from Woodcraft Supply (5). I make the dovetail 1/32 in. shorter than the depth of the groove. The planing is continued until the piece appears to be the right size (6). It should slide in easily at first and become very tight in the last fifth of the groove. One or two more passes with the plane with testing in between should result in the desired fit. If the joint is hidden, the front of the dovetail is pared off.

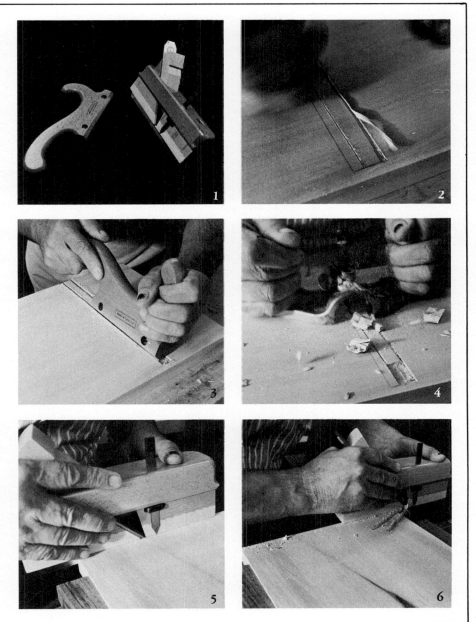

only a few sliding dovetails are required, the hand method is preferred. It is extremely simple and much faster than one would expect. In the hand version the track is tapered so that the dovetail slides in easily at first and locks at the end as it is hammered into place. Consequently, as the dovetail is forced in tight, a small shoulder is pressed into the straight side and increases at the narrow end. In the machine version, the pieces should mate exactly and thus will require a lot of force to assemble. This is especially true if glue is used on a long dovetail, because the glue will swell the grain, making the piece increasingly difficult to slide in.

With both types of sliding dovetails, glue is not necessary, although a spot can be put at the front to fix it in position, or the whole length can be glued. If two different materials are used (e.g., plywood shelves into solid sides), only the front should be glued so that as movement occurs, the front will remain flush.

In a chest of drawers or similar carcase higher or wider than two feet, some sort of strengthening brace will be required. I use a sliding dovetail in the center brace, and if additional bracing is needed, a tongue and groove out to the sides. The sliding dovetail holds the center in tight.

If you wish to keep joints from showing through in front, you can stop the joints before the front or else cover them. In solid wood I sometimes cut a half-inch strip off the cabinet, run the joints through, and reglue the strip. In plywood I run the joints through and add a facing for the same result.

Backs for carcases

The back of a carcase is an important strength-determining factor. Various methods for inserting backs will require differing assembly sequences, which must correspond to that of the particular carcase joint used. This is an important relationship that must be decided at the design stage.

The easiest and most common way to insert a back is to make a rabbet around the four sides and screw on a piece of plywood after the carcase is glued. This method gives you a second chance to square a cabinet that has been glued slightly out of square. The plywood can be made square or slightly out-of-square the opposite way and this will counteract the mistake. This type of back is fine if the cabinet is designed to go against a wall. Most antique furniture was designed to be placed against a wall, and so the backs were usually crudely made and left rough. Today furniture is used much more flexibly, e.g., as room dividers, so it is advisable to design a piece with the back as nice as the rest of the cabinet. The cost and effort of sanding and finishing the back are minimal in light of the time spent designing and executing the piece. Of course, if the piece is designed to be fastened to the wall, the back must still be finished, but not to the same perfection.

A good method for a freestanding piece is to make a groove for a piece of plywood or solid wood which is inserted at the same time the cabinet is glued up. If solid wood is used, be sure the back is free-floating to allow for movement. You may pin or glue the back just at the center points, which will allow the wood to expand equally out to both sides. Leave a little space in the groove on each side to allow for expansion.

If the sides of the cabinet are frame and panels, a set-in flat back would look out of place. To keep your design consistent you can make a frame and panel back that is inserted using either of the assembly sequences described for a plywood back.

Dovetail square

I do a considerable amount of hand-dovetailing and find an adjustable bevel or protractor a bit awkward. Since pin and tail angles remain constant (I use 12°), I have made a square at that angle that is very easy to use. Mine is made from well-cured cherry with 3/16-in. birch pins. The body is a laminate of two 1/4-in. thick cheek pieces, 6 in. long, and two 1/8-in. center pieces, 3 in. long, cut at 12° on the inner ends. The blade is 1/8 in. thick and 6 in. long.

I assembled my tool dry in clamps to drill the pin holes,

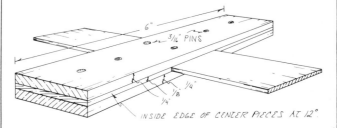

then I removed the blade and pinned the body together dry. After trimming the ends smooth, I lapped all the working edges, including the blade, with 220-grit paper placed on a surface plate.

Reassemble with glue and clamp, and you have a handy tool that never has to be set or checked, and can easily be flopped to pick up the other angle.

—*Don Kenyon, Naples, N.Y.*

Sliding dovetail saw

To make a sliding dovetail saw you will need a piece of hardwood (maple, beech or fruitwood) 1 x 5½ x 13 in. and two flat-head 3/16 x 1-in. bolts with tee-nuts. The blade can be

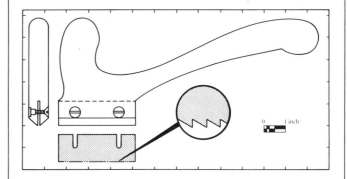

an old band saw or bow saw blade. It should have 10 points to the inch, although 8 will do. I use a ripsaw blade, which I find cuts better and faster than a crosscut. The slots allow the blade to be set to the desired depth.

—*Tage Frid, Foster, R.I.*

Cleaning saw blades

Oven cleaner works very well for removing pitch from bits and saw blades without harming the steel. A clean cutting surface stays sharp longer, gives better results, taxes the motor less and makes for safer use of the tool.

—*Chuck Oliver, Fremont, N.H., and*
George Eckhart, Kenosha, Wis.

Antiqued Pine Furniture

Distressing won't hide sloppy work

by B. D. Bittinger

Antiqued pine furniture has become increasingly popular in recent years. This style of furniture is characterized by thick (1-in. to 1-1/2-inch) table and case tops, and correspondingly sturdy carcase construction. It is constructed from knotty white pine. The antiqued and distressed finish is medium dark brown, with lighter brown highlights.

The line of commercial antiqued pine furniture marketed under the Ethan Allen trademark is a good example of this furniture style. I view the style as a romanticized version of the pine furniture built by skilled joiners in rural America during the last half of the 18th century—not rustic or common, but well-made country pine furniture.

Antiqued pine furniture designs for use in present-day homes are necessarily adaptations, not authentic reproductions. After all, rural colonial families did not have king-size beds with "sleep sets" or stereo and TV cabinets. Freestanding desks were rare and all-drawer chests with large, plate-glass mirrors were unknown. They had as much use for coffee tables and bookcases as we have for dough boxes and flax wheels. Antiqued pine furniture designs are based more on feeling than on fact.

Eastern white pine was used by early cabinetmakers and knotty eastern white pine can still be found. Western white pine serves as well and is available at most lumberyards. There

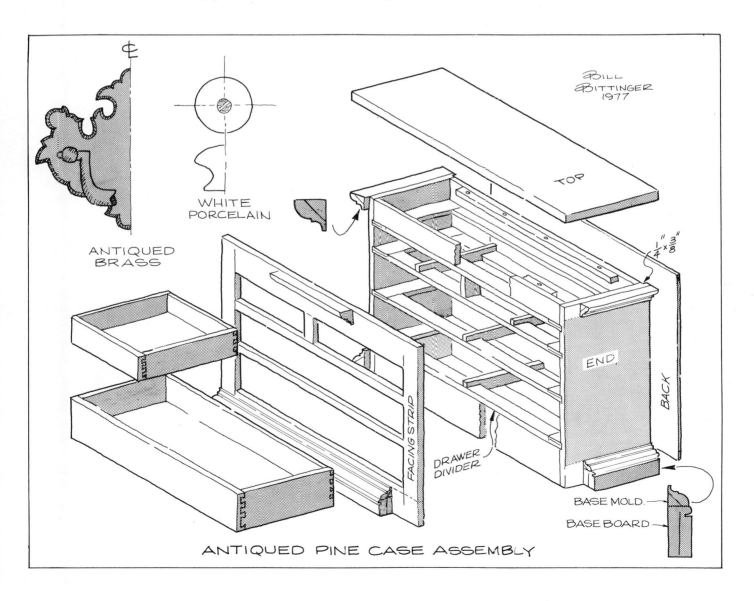

ANTIQUED PINE CASE ASSEMBLY

are several varieties of western pine, ranging in color from al-most white to tan to pink. Kiln-dried knotty white pine is generally available as #3 common 1x12 shelving in lengths of up to 16 ft. Sugar pine is my choice when I can get it. It is usually tan in color with rust grain lines. Some boards also have a distinctive brown fleck marking. The knots are generally small and red-brown in color.

Most furniture parts are less than 4 ft. long and 5 in. wide. In selecting material, I look at a 1x12 shelving board in terms of the number of good pieces it may contain, not its overall appearance. Some white pine boards are full of sap, heavy and sticky, and are useless for making furniture. Thick (4/4, 6/4, 8/4) knotty white pine is not available at most lumber-yards so I usually order from a dealer such as Educational Lumber Co. in Asheville, N.C.

White pine is weak compared to most cabinet woods and this must be considered when designing joints. Tenons in pine, for example, should be as large as possible and somewhat longer than they would be in hardwood. Chair turnings should be hardwood, but heavy pine seats and arms may be used in combination with the hardwood. Pine turnings for table legs should be heavy with simple, bold patterns. I prefer to glue up turning blocks from 3/4-in. stock. Small, firm knots in a turning block will usually cut and finish well.

Tools must be extremely sharp for cutting pine because it is so soft that the fibers tend to tear. I use a plywood-tooth saw blade on the radial arm saw and always crosscut with the good side up. Even with a sharp, small-tooth blade the fibers may break out on the bottom and leave a rough surface. Carving chisels must also be extra sharp.

Let me emphasize that workmanship must be of the highest quality. Antiquing and distressing will not cover or hide sloppy or careless work. Quite the opposite, antiquing will emphasize poor joints, hammer marks, clamp marks, and other evidence of careless workmanship.

Carcase construction

A carcase for a large chest of drawers includes most of the particular problems of working with white pine. The large drawing shows the basic construction of such a case. What follows are the working methods and finishing techniques I have developed for achieving the style I like.

Carcase end pieces (using 3/4-in. stock) may be solid edge-glued pine or frame-and-panel assemblies. Doweling or shaper-edge joining is not necessary with Titebond glue. It is important, however, to align the boards in the clamps, thus minimizing planing and sanding the finished panel. Wide shelving (12 in. or more) should be ripped into at least two strips and the grain alternated before gluing, to reduce cup-ping. Excess glue squeezed out of the joints should be removed at once with a wet cloth. Glue will seal the wood and cause light spots when the stain is applied.

If solid ends are used, special consideration must be given in assembly to avoid restraining the boards across their width, else the case will be damaged by shrinkage or expansion.

Raised-panel case ends are visually pleasing and solve the problems of expansion and contraction. Although a frame

Bill Bittinger, 48, has been a woodworker for 20 years. Trained as an engineer, he is production superintendent at a tire cord factory. He lives in Shelbyville, Tenn.

made from 3/4-in. stock with a 1/2-in. thick panel is light in weight and relatively weak, it is satisfactory for this applica-tion because it will be amply reinforced by the back drawer dividers and facings. The frame is assembled with mortise and tenon joints and the panel is retained in grooves in the stiles and muntins. The front edge stile should be 3/4 in. narrower than the back stile so that after the facing is applied the stiles will be the same width.

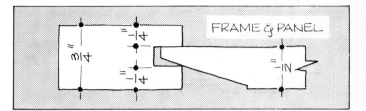

After the end panels (frame-and-panel or solid) are cut to size, a series of 3/4-in. wide by 1/4-in. deep dadoes is laid out and cut to house the drawer dividers. Remember to cut a rabbet 3/8 in. wide by 1/4 in. deep on the back edges of the carcase sides to accommodate the back panel of the case.

Drawer divider units are made from 3/4-in. pine joined with mortise and tenon or half-lap joints. The width of the divider strips will vary according to the overall dimensions of the case. The strips at the ends of the divider frames, which run from front to back, should be about 1-1/2 in. wider than the vertical facing strips of the front frame, so that they can support and act as a bearing surface for the drawer sides.

The carcase is assembled with glue—on the front edge only of solid end pieces—and plug-covered, flat-head wood screws through the end panels. Plugs may be surface-cut round plugs, end-grain round plugs or square patch plugs. Finishing nails, set below the surface, may also be used for case assembly. After setting the nail I use a modified nail set with a square tip (about 1/8 in. by 1/8 in.) to make a square set hole. The small round or square holes will blend with the overall distressed appearance. The facings and back panel will be glued and fastened to the edges of the end panels and to the drawer dividers, to provide adequate strength whether the case is assembled with nails or screws.

The front facing frames may be assembled as a unit with dowels, mortise and tenon joints or half-lap dovetails and then fastened to the carcase; or each strip may be individually attached with butt joints. I prefer the latter. In either case, the facing is fastened with glue and plug-covered screws or finishing nails. If nails are used, they should be located at random on the facing boards to avoid a regular pattern. Plugged screws, however, should be placed in a symmetrical pattern. Whether or not the facings were preassembled with mortise and tenon joints, 1/4-in. dowels may be set into the surface to simulate draw-bore locking pins.

I usually make the base boards about 1-1/2 in. thick to balance the thick top overhang. They may be scroll cut or left full width. The base is assembled with mitered corners and is glued and fastened to the carcase. On some pieces, such as dower chests, the base boards may look better if they are joined with through dovetails. The base mold is a modified stock molding.

The bottom dust panel and back (lauan plywood) should not be attached until the drawer slides are installed and each drawer is accurately fitted to its opening.

Case tops vary in thickness from 7/8 in. to 1-1/2 in.,

depending on the scale of the piece and the width of the carcase facing strips. Tops are made from solid edge-glued pine. I use dowels on edge-glued thick pine to help level the pieces in the clamps. If bread-board strips are not used, the end grain of the top should be carefully sanded or it will soak up extra stain. Case tops are attached with screws from underside in oversize holes in the top mounting strips.

Bread-board strips across each end of the top add to the appearance and strength of projects such as coffee tables and heavy trestle tables. Before joining the strips, I run either a 1/8-in. by 1/8-in. rabbet across the ends of the top or a quirk mold on the joining edge of the strip. Narrow strips may be attached with screws through oversize holes, to allow for expansion. The counterbored screw holes are covered with round or square plugs. The edging strip should be glued only at the center on a tabletop, or at the front edge on a case top. To attach unsupported strips to tabletops that are subjected to heavy loads, I use 2-in. wide stopped splines made of 1/2-in. plywood and two or more concealed tie bolts cut from 1/4-in. threaded rod. The spline is glued only at the center, to equalize misalignment caused by shrinkage or expansion of the top.

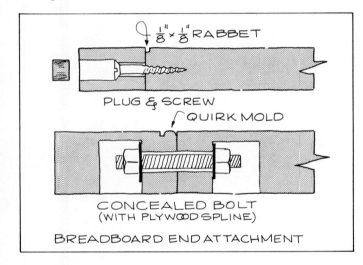

BREADBOARD END ATTACHMENT

Drawers

I don't think pine drawers should be lipped because a thin lip is fragile and a heavy lip is clumsy. I install drawers and doors with 1/8 in. of the edge exposed. When they are rounded by sanding, the chest has a soft—not flat—appearance.

Cut the 3/4-in. drawer fronts for a snug press fit in the openings, and index-mark each front to its corresponding

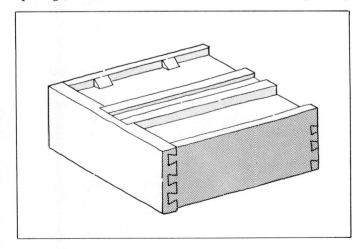

opening. Knots should be at least 1 in. from each end.

Cut the sides about 1/8 in. narrower than the front and about 2 in. shorter than the case depth. Drawer sides should be about 5/8 in. thick. Cut 1/4-in. by 3/8-in. bottom retaining grooves in the sides and front, and cut a mortise on the bottom edge of the back side of the front for the drawer slide part.

Dovetail joints should be cut by hand. It is difficult to obtain sharp clear lines in soft pine with an ordinary marking gauge. I use a sharp 3H pencil with a shop-made marking gauge to lay out the dovetails. Dimension A is usually about

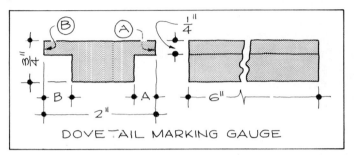

DOVETAIL MARKING GAUGE

two-thirds the thickness of the drawer front and dimension B is 1/32 in. greater than the thickness of the side pieces. Side A is used as a marking gauge on the end of the front and on the matching side piece, to provide cutting lines for the length of the dovetails. Side B is used to mark the dovetail depth line (side thickness plus 1/32 in.) on the inside end of the front piece.

I use another shop-made marking jig to lay out the half-blind dovetail on each drawer front end. The marker is used to draw the pins and the vertical-cut guide lines on the inside of the front.

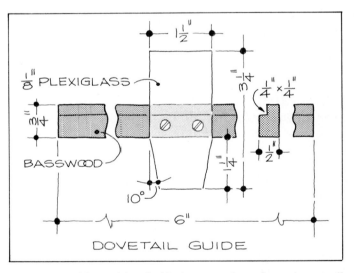

DOVETAIL GUIDE

I start marking with a half-pin on each end, so that a tail will cover the bottom retaining groove in the side, and then fill in between by eye. Each end of the drawer front has the same number of pins and sockets but they are not all identical in size or spacing. Pins in pine should be only slightly smaller than the dovetail sockets. After sawing on the waste side of each pin line, I clamp the front to the bench to remove the waste with a very sharp chisel to within 1/16 in. of the guide lines. I trim the pins and the sockets to exact size with the front held vertically in a vise. Then I lay the side piece on the table saw and stand the front piece on top of it, using the saw fence to hold the front piece vertical. With the ends of the two pieces exactly aligned, I can use a sharp pencil to trace the pin outlines onto the side piece. I cut the tails to size on the band saw. There should be enough interference in the joint to require moderate pressure to assemble. I do not dry-fit dovetail joints because this compresses the pine and causes a weaker joint. The dovetails are assembled with glue.

The back piece is joined to the drawer sides with through dovetails. The bottom (lauan or pine plywood) is nailed to the lower edge of the back part with coated box nails. The drawer slide is attached with brads and glue. Beveled glue blocks keep the bottom from rattling.

When the glue in the assembled drawer joints has set, I sand the protruding ends of the front with a belt sander. This sanding, if carefully done, will leave about 1/32-in. clearance at both sides when the drawer is installed.

Install slides in the case and adjust them to center the drawer fronts in their openings. Sand to round off the top edge of the drawer front, to provide about 1/32-in clearance. A gap of up to 1/16 in. around the drawer is acceptable. Attach the 1/4-in. plywood back panel with glue and small coated box nails to the drawer frame edges and all around the case edges for maximum strength.

Doors

Raised panel doors are included in some case designs such as a hutch base. Doors may be made from 1-in. or 3/4-in. pine stock. But conventional frame construction for a raised panel door of 3/4-in. pine is structurally weak, and the door does not feel comfortably heavy. To avoid weakness and add weight, I set the panel in a rabbet instead of a groove and add a back plate of plywood. First, I assemble the frames (rails, stiles and muntins) with dowels and glue. Then I rout a rabbet 3/8 in. deep by 1/2 in. wide on the inside back edges of the frame, squaring up the rabbet corners with a chisel. Then I cut the panels from 3/4-in. solid pine, allowing 1/8 in. for clearance on all four sides. I "raise" the panels by cutting a bevel all around the front face, so that when the panel is laid into the frame it will protrude by the merest 1/64 in. at the back. Finally I glue a piece of 3/16-in., 1/4-in. or 5/16-in. pine or lauan plywood to the back of the frame only, thereby pressing the panel into the rabbet and completely covering the door.

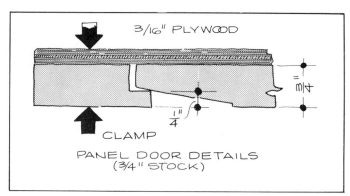

PANEL DOOR DETAILS
(3/4" STOCK)

Moldings

One of the advantages of working with pine lumber is the wide range of commercial moldings. Before mitering and applying commercial flat molding, I glue a pine backing strip to the molding and then resaw to provide a larger glue surface. This is particularly important when attaching large cornice molding around the top of a cabinet. Resawing to 45° also helps in cutting miters on large moldings.

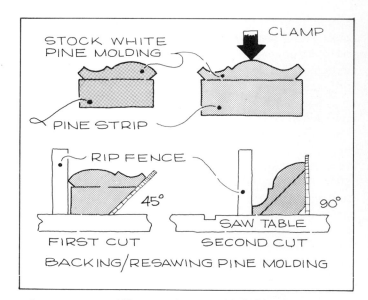

BACKING/RESAWING PINE MOLDING

Large crown molding may be assembled from several parts. The three-part composite molding shown below is made up from: 1) shop-made dentil backup piece, 2) modified commercial flat-crown molding, and 3) a nose-molded pine strip. The dentil backup piece is machined to leave a 1/4-in. to 3/16-in. raised strip. The dentil is laid out and cut after the backup strip is beveled to fit the cabinet. The "teeth" should be laid out from the center to ensure symmetry, taking care to locate one full tooth on each side of the bevel joint. The pieces of crown molding and the pine strips are mitered and installed in turn over the backup strip.

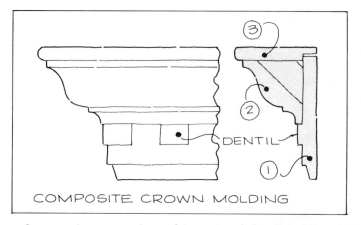

COMPOSITE CROWN MOLDING

Some projects are enhanced by a closed dentil molding (a row of square depressions) along the top horizontal facing strip. This decoration is particularly effective in bedroom sets where it can be incorporated in chests, mirror frames, bedside tables, headboards and footboards.

To make the closed dental facing strip, cut the facing about 1/2 in. wider and longer than finished size. Rip out a strip from the facing board where the molding is to be located. Start the dado layout in the center of the strip to ensure symmetry, and plan the cuts so that a raised tooth, at least full width, will remain on the end of the strip at the facing joint. Cut and sand the dados, joint the glue edges and edge-glue the strip back in place.

Distressing

The piece should not be distressed until after complete assembly and coarse sanding. Experimentation is the only way to determine the amount of distressing that will suit your taste. The procedure includes surface marking and removal of

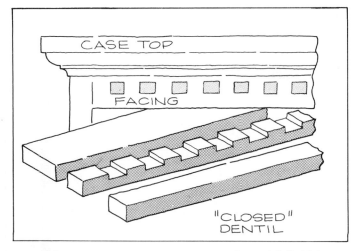

material to create a worn appearance, and special finishing to make the marks look authentic.

I do not like excessive surface marking. I usually make a few dents with the corner of a hammer claw and a few randomly spaced holes with an awl. The claw indentations are triangular and the awl holes appear as small black dots when the finishing glaze is applied. Distress marks are always randomly spaced and are more numerous around the bottom and on the top of a piece than on vertical surfaces. A tall bookcase, for example, would have very few indented distress marks above the height of 4 ft.

Wear distressing should correspond to the imagined, as well as the actual, use of the piece. Stretchers and legs that are rubbed with shoe soles should be much more severely worn than areas touched by other parts of the body. Wear distressing may be done with planes, coarse sandpaper or even rasps and files. In any case, the worn surfaces should be carefully sanded so that no tool marks remain.

After the piece is distressed, I sand with a high-speed orbital sander using 100-grit, 120-grit and 150-grit garnet paper. I complete the sanding by hand with 180-grit garnet paper wrapped around a felt pad. If scratches or other unplanned surface defects show up at this stage, they should be removed by going back to a coarser grit paper. Distressing does not camouflage sloppy and clumsy work or incomplete finish sanding.

Finishing

I use Minwax Early American oil stain to antique pine furniture. Apply the first stain coat to all surfaces, inside and outside, following the manufacturer's directions. After 24 hours, apply a second coat to the outside surfaces. This leaves drawer and case interiors lighter in color than the exposed surfaces. At this point in the finishing schedule your beautiful piece of furniture will look very disappointing—dull and splotchy—but do not despair.

I spray McCloskey Eggshell or semigloss Heirloom Finish for the seal coat and the final varnish coat. Glaze solvents do not soften it and it has good rubbing (sanding) qualities. It can also be brushed on.

After the seal coat is dry (depending on the climate, this may take up to a week) sand all surfaces with wet/dry #320 paper. When the varnish is properly dry, sanding will form a white powder on the surface.

There are a number of antiquing glazes on the market and James M. O'Neill, in his book *Early American Furniture,* gives a formula for mixing an antiquing glaze. I use Tone 'n

Tall chest: Designs are based on feeling more than on fact.

Tique deeptone antiquing glaze, made by C.H. Tripp Co. But I suggest you make up sample blocks to determine your preference. Rub or brush the glaze on the outside surfaces of the project and take care to fill all the distress marks with glaze. Wipe off when the glaze begins to appear dull. The glaze changes the color of the finish even though most of it is wiped off. Leave a film but not streaks. Wipe in the corners and at surface intersections with a wadded cloth so that some of the glaze remains. If too much glaze is wiped off, you can recoat and start over. At this point the finish on your project will look very good and it will improve with the final steps.

After the glaze has dried for 24 hours apply the second coat of varnish. Allow several days for drying and rub again with used #320 emery cloth and 2-0 steel wool. The final step is to coat the entire piece with a good grade of paste wax. The wax should fill any nail set holes. Rub and polish.

If you want an antiqued painted finish, substitute the paint of your choice for the stain and first coat of varnish and proceed as described above. I like the clean, bright appearance of painted interiors on pieces such as hutch bases and dry sinks. Light blue paint goes well with the antiqued finish.

I usually use antiqued brass drop bail or white porcelain pulls and mortised antiqued brass hinges. Black-finished H or L hinges and hardware are also suitable for some pieces.

These comments on design, construction and finishing also apply to small decorative pine projects such as spice cabinets, letter boxes, spoon racks, stools and picture frames.

METHODS OF WORK

Poor boy's scriber

Perhaps my poor boy's scriber might suggest a useful project. The point is a nipped-off 6d nail in a hole drilled under-

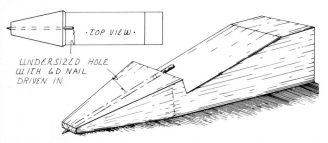

·TOP VIEW·

UNDERSIZED HOLE
WITH 6D NAIL
DRIVEN IN

size for a drive fit. This gadget eliminates error that a round-pointed tool might make because of the angle at which it is held.

—*Earl Solomon, Orchard Park, N.Y.*

Repairing mallets

Wooden carving mallets tend to check unless well cared for. I solve this annoying problem by whipping a line around the face of a badly checked mallet. I use heavyweight string

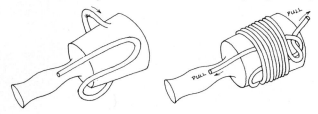

PULL

PULL

and apply two coats of well-thinned white glue afterward. The glue soaks into the string and prevents it from fraying and unraveling.

—*Riff Masteroff, Arlington, Va.*

Wooden box hinge

This box hinge is easy to make and provides a built-in lid stop. First fit the hinge pieces to the lid. A short sliding dovetail is probably the best joint. Set the lid on the box and scribe the outline of the hinge pieces on the back. Cut the

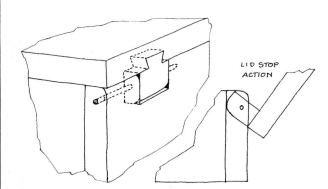

LID STOP
ACTION

slots in the back. After measuring pin location drill pinholes in from the side of the box with the lid in place. Redrill the holes through the hinge pieces for easier operation. Install the pins. An ordinary nail works well. The hinge and the back edge of the box should be slightly rounded off.

—*Jim Richey, Houston, Tex.*

Dealing with Plywood

by Karl Seemuller

Plywood is a much overlooked and often abused material for building furniture, largely because of the horrible production furniture pumped into the market by short-sighted designers. But plywood has a lot to offer and is relatively easy to work with. The key to using it successfully lies in understanding its strengths and weaknesses, and in designing work specifically for the material. It does not help to think of plywood as a substitute for solid wood or as its poor cousin. Such an approach can result only in a finished piece that is a substitute for the real thing. If you are going to use plywood make the full commitment and design for it.

Why bother to use plywood when you have the technical skill to use solid woods? Cost is a major consideration. The cost in time and material of a plywood piece is a fraction of that of a solid wood piece. I am speaking in terms of a small shop that produces furniture many people can afford. If you design one-of-a-kind pieces for yourself or for museums, plywood is probably not the material for you.

Plywood offers quite a few advantages to the designer. It is available with just about any veneer. It comes in nice flat finished sheets ready to be cut into components. It is designed to resist seasonal changes in dimension. And plywood joinery tends to be very simple, though exacting. The cost is about the same per square foot as the board foot cost for solid wood in the rough. But solid wood needs to be rough dressed, edged, glued up, surfaced and sanded to bring it to an equivalent stage.

On the other hand, the very flatness of plywood dictates planes or simple curves. Solid wood offers much more versatility. Adding solid wood edgings to plywood softens some of its harsh quality. Solid wood also provides better colors and grain variation in the finish. The finish surface of plywood is veneer only about 1/32 inch thick, so there is not enough depth for the colors to develop fully. And the wetting or steaming process tends to bleed or leach colors out of finished veneer. However, a careful selection of veneered plywood can often bypass this problem.

Hardwood plywood is available with either a veneer core or a lumber core. In the veneer core, the core has a plywood construction. In lumber core, the core is solid wood, usually mahogany, poplar or basswood. The staves are glued side by side, and covered on both sides by layers of crossbanding and a face veneer. Veneer core is suitable for most applications; it is stable, uniform, and cheaper than lumber core. Lumber

Karl Seemuller has taught at Philadelphia College of Art. When he isn't busy using plywood he works with sculptural form in solid woods.

core is used where additional strength is required. There is also hardwood plywood with a core of particle board, with all of the latter's advantages and disadvantages.

Several machines are used for working plywood. In addition to a table saw, either a shaper or a router is necessary. Carbide blades and bits are a must as the glue in plywood quickly dulls steel. Either a set of tongue-and-groove shaper cutters or a slotting bit for the router is helpful. If you do more than an occasional piece, a shaper and a good set of tongue-and-groove cutters are indispensable. An invaluable asset of these cutters is that they joint the edge of the plywood at the same time that the tongue is cut, thereby ensuring a perfect fit.

It is in the realm of joinery that plywood is most abused. You can cut and join plywood in almost any way you desire and it will go together. Unfortunately, this is precisely what many people do. The result is a product that deteriorates quickly. In solid wood, no one considers cutting dovetails out of short grain, but plywood is often equally misused.

A major problem is how to cover the ugly raw edges that pop up everywhere. The most common solution is simply to glue a strip of veneer over it. Ouch! You are just asking for trouble. We are working with wood, not plastic laminate. One basic design consideration is to avoid any sharp veneered edges or corners. The veneer must be protected from sharp blows or knocks that could easily chip or crack it. Veneer is not fragile, but it does need some help if it is going to give proper service. This problem is solved by using a piece of solid wood edging. It can simply be glued in place, but it is better to attach it with a sturdy joint. I prefer the simple tongue and groove.

This creates another problem. We now have an obvious strip applied to the edge. I take the easy way out. I cannot hide the edging, so I make it an important part of the design. Now, the fact that it is hiding the core and protecting the veneer becomes secondary to its visual importance.

The next problem is joining the plywood at the corners. While the standard solutions are variations of a mitered corner, either spline or locked (never plain), a better solution is to use solid wood in the corners, joined to the plywood with tongue and groove joints, and left square or rounded off. Or you can use a spline miter and inset a small square "wear" strip along the outer edge to give the protection needed. Interior partitions of plywood are best joined by a tongue and groove, so that inevitable variations in the thickness of the plywood don't affect the fit.

Precise joinery is crucial to successful plywood construction. An error might result in cutting through the thin veneer. If you should cut through, do not get into a sweat figuring how to fix it; you cannot. Avoid the error. Work carefully and precisely so there is no need to fudge the joints. Proper use of the router and shaper will prevent these errors. Always keep the important surface of the work against the shaper table or router base to ensure a uniform dimension from the veneer to the tongue. Always use hold-downs on the shaper to keep the work in firm contact with the table. When cutting solid wood edging, keep it slightly fuller than the plywood. In this way you can sand the solid wood to meet the veneer rather than the reverse. When using a one-shouldered tongue and groove in a partition, sand the member before cutting the tongue. This will prevent a sloppy fit later.

Plywood can easily be bent into simple curves. If the curve

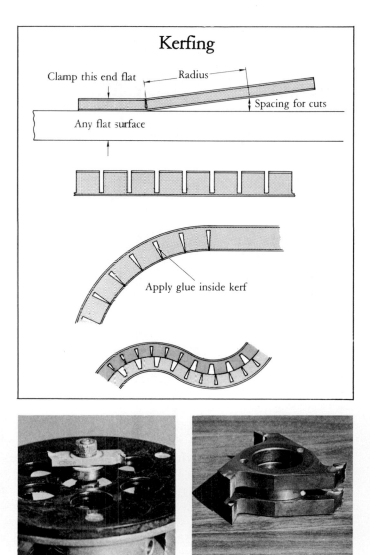

Tongue-and-groove joints can be made with a carbide-tipped slotting cutter in a router, left. At right, shaper cutters shown in the tongue-cutting configuration. Groove cutter is not shown.

is shallow it can be made by laminating several 1/4 or 1/8-in. pieces together over a form. As you might expect the springback will be quite large, but the resulting piece will be very strong and stable.

Another method is to run a series of kerf cuts in the plywood. In this way a 3/4-in. piece of plywood can be made into a curve with less than a 5-in. radius. For this operation I prefer a lumber core. Use a carbide blade, preferably one with a thin kerf—the thinner the better. The procedure is simple and economical. Large jigs or forms are often unnecessary. The kerf cuts must be spaced properly so that once the curve is made, the cuts all close up tight, restoring strength to the plywood.

If the inner surface is important visually, two thin kerfed pieces can be used instead of a single thick one. This is particularly helpful with an "S" curve. For example, instead of a single 3/4-in. kerfed piece, use two 1/2-in. or 3/8-in. pieces. Kerf them in the same manner as before, and bend them into shape with the kerfs facing each other. The result is a very strong form, finished both inside and out.

Plywood is limited and cannot offer the same potential as solid wood. But remember, it is not a substitute but a distinct material. Design for it specifically and you will have come more than half the way to a successful piece.

Desert Cabinetry

Coping with six percent moisture

by Thomas A. Simons IV

The climate of the desert Southwest can have a devastating effect on furniture. People moving there from the East often watch their antiques, which have survived hundreds of years in a relatively humid climate, break up before their eyes. Cabinetmakers suffer similar discouragement. It is rare to find even experienced cabinetmakers who have not had pieces ruined by cracks or broken joints. As atmospheric conditions change, wood expands or contracts until an equilibrium moisture content is reached. Furniture from the East Coast has an equilibrium moisture content of twelve to fifteen percent. When this furniture is brought to the Southwest, its equilibrium moisture content may decrease to six percent with significant shrinkage resulting. Normal midwestern hardwoods are kiln-dried to approximately twelve percent. When that lumber is shipped to the Southwest, the moisture content will decrease and cause shrinkage. Furthermore, seasonal humidity and temperature changes affect the moisture content of the wood and cause movement, which may result in shrinkage, expansion, distortion (such as cupping, warping, bowing or springing), and even splitting.

Wood moves different amounts in different directions. Lengthwise movement is negligible. However, radial movement is significant, and circumferential (or tangential) movement is approximately fifty percent greater than radial movement. Therefore, joints between end grain and edge grain, and between plainsawed lumber (with tangential movement across its face) and quartersawed lumber (with radial movement across its face) will be subject to significant stress upon changes in wood moisture content. (The same is also true in the lamination of different types of wood with different movement characteristics.) This stress generates tremendous forces which can break joints and split wood.

Many cabinetmaking techniques used to minimize wood movement can be seen in New Mexican Spanish Colonial furniture (hereafter, Spanish Colonial furniture). Modern Spanish Colonial furniture is the embodiment of a desert cabinetmaking tradition stretching back for centuries. The Arabs from Syria and Egypt and the Berbers from Northwestern Africa (collectively called the Moors) introduced designs and techniques from their homeland during their long occupation of Spain. By the beginning of the 17th century when colonists supplanted Conquistadores in New Mexico, the Spanish-Moorish furniture design confluence had produced the popular mudéjar style. Although most colonists took little or no furniture with them, they did imitate the traditional and mudéjar designs popular in Spain when they left. Their designs and execution were cruder than Spanish renditions and in native pine rather than the traditional Spanish hardwoods (mostly walnut). Nonetheless, they incorporated many

An early Spanish Colonial through tenon (below, left), with irregularly shaped wedges to ensure uniform pressure. Effects of wood shrinkage can be seen in protruding dovetail billet on table (below) and protruding tenon on leg of modern Spanish Colonial chair (right).

of the cabinetmaking techniques used by the Spanish and Moors before them.

The relative isolation of New Mexico and the fact that the original designs produced simple furniture that held up well under the rigors of frontier life enabled Spanish Colonial furniture design to endure for hundreds of years. Even today, in small villages all over northern New Mexico, local craftsmen use the same furniture designs and techniques as their forefathers. In the larger towns and cities this same basic design and construction, often supplemented with Spanish and Mexican design and modern techniques, is used in commercial production.

One of the most conspicuous construction techniques in Spanish Colonial furniture is the doweled mortise and tenon joint. Of course, the mortise and tenon were not used merely to accommodate wood movement. Until the development of doweled joints, the mortise and tenon joint was the only one to use in many types of fine joinery. Nor would it be accurate to say that the doweling of the tenon is solely a desert cabinetmaking technique. It was used in fine furniture in many countries and was considered the best insurance against joint breakage from any cause. For whatever reason the doweled mortise and tenon joint was used in other countries, it does appear probable that its almost universal use in Spanish Colonial furniture and its continuation after virtual abandonment elsewhere is at least partly due to its ability to hold tight even when the glue joint is broken by shrinkage. The joining of edge grain to end grain is normally the point of greatest weakness and susceptibility to wood movement damage in furniture construction.

A characteristic feature of the Spanish Colonial doweled mortise and

This well executed headboard illustrates the extensive use of spool turnings typical of Spanish Colonial woodworking.

tenon is the almost exclusive use of only one dowel. European and American cabinetmakers often used two dowels at either side of the tenon to increase the strength of the joint. The absence of this extra dowel in most Spanish Colonial furniture is possibly due to the fact that shrinkage across the face of the tenon will cause stress to build up between the two dowels and split the tenoned piece. The use of only one dowel prevents such stress from developing.

Another characteristic of this joint, although seldom seen today, is the wedged tenon. Traditionally the wedges were driven in at the edge of the tenon. This compression of the pine tenon minimized loosening of the joint through shrinkage. To wedge the tenon with the crude tools they had, the New Mexicans broke with the almost universal Spanish tradition of using blind tenons and began cutting most mortises through. Modern makers of Spanish Colonial furniture have continued to use the through tenon for stylistic reasons even though the main reason for its use, ease of tenon wedging, has been largely abandoned.

Offset tenon doweling is sometimes used in the Spanish Colonial doweled mortise and tenon joint. The dowel hole is bored through the mortised piece (with a waste piece inserted in the mortise to prevent breaking out of the mortise sides). The tenon is inserted, and the mortise dowel hole marked on it. The tenon is then removed, and the dowel hole bored, offset slightly toward the shoulder of the tenon. A tapered dowel is then cut 1/8-inch shorter than the dowel hole. When the dowel is inserted, glue is used only on the final 1/4-inch to prevent the dowel from protruding when the piece shrinks.

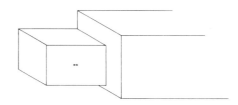

When driven home, the tapered dowel wedges the tenon shoulders tightly against the mortised piece, resulting in a joint that will stay extremely tight even if the tenon shrinks away from the mortise sides.

Another movement-accommodating feature in Spanish Colonial furniture is the dovetailed billet. It was a unique Spanish method for attaching trestles to table tops. It was not widely used in colonial New Mexico, probably because the early New Mexicans could not execute it satisfactorily with their crude tools, but has become a standard technique in modern Spanish Colonial furniture. It is made by first cutting female dovetail dadoes the width of the table top at the places on the bottom where the trestles attach. A tight-fitting male dovetail billet is driven into each dado, cut off flush with the sides and often molded. The trestle is usually then attached to the billet by hinges, screws or bolts. Thus the table top is free to float on the billet while the legs are still firmly attached. This system not only prevents splitting but also controls the cupping tendency of plain-sawed table tops. When the table top shrinks, the billet will invariably protrude. An improvement on the technique is to drive in a short billet,

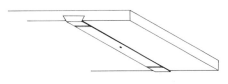

leaving approximately 1-1/2 inch of dado at each end. Then end plugs approximately 1-3/8 inches long are glued into each end, leaving shrinkage joints of 1/8 inch. To prevent all movement from accumulating on one side, a dowel is inserted through the middle of the billet and into the table top.

The next three movement-accommodating techniques can be traced directly to the Moorish influence in Spain. The first is multiple paneling. Also used on furniture, this technique is most common in large door construction. The rationale for multiple paneling is as follows: a wide panel will shrink considerably across its face, thus loosening the panel in the frame and exposing the unfinished panel tongue and even the panel edge. Multiple panels across the same width will each shrink less and cause less tongue exposure and loosening per panel. Moreover, the smaller confinement of the wood gives it less room to distort on the panel face. An additional feature of this frame and panel construction (and an essential

feature on any frame and panel) is that the panels are never glued into the frame groove.

Another Moorish technique is the sheathed door. It is made by sheathing a rigid door frame on one side with

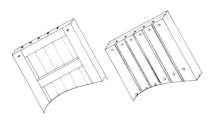

vertical boards. The boards are joined without glue by a shiplap or tongue and groove joint. Each board is then attached to the frame at the top and bottom by a nail, screw or bolt. Thus, each board is held independently and can move freely without affecting the shape or appearance of the door.

The technique of replacing solid panels with a series of turned or shaved spindles is also derived from Moorish woodworking. Shrinkage in the spindles is inconsequential compared to that in a panel, and ordinarily does not

affect the appearance of the piece. This device can be seen in cupboards or trasteros, as well as in certain headboard designs.

The early New Mexicans sometimes substituted a doweled finger joint for the traditional through dovetail in their chests or arcos. Characteristically they used wide fingers and doweled through only one side. A superior joint was produced, however, in 15th-century Spain where the fingers in each side were doweled. The resulting joint held

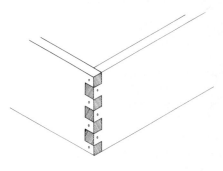

even with broken glue lines, as long as the bottom or top remained in place.

The double dovetail or butterfly key across edge joints has come into fairly widespread use in modern Spanish Colonial furniture. Although many times only thin inlaid ornamentation,

A multiple-panel door in pine. The panels were beveled with a gouge. The use of spindles (below, right) in the central section of this trastero door accommodates wood movement and also allows the contents of the cupboard to be viewed.

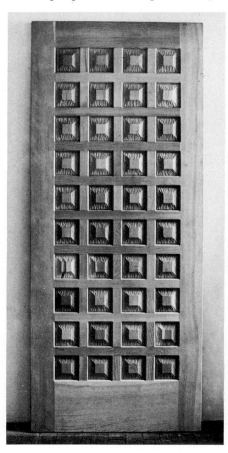

the key can significantly inhibit edge joint breakage due to shrinkage distortion when amply made and carefully inlaid.

Careful edge joint preparation by the Spanish Colonial furniture maker reduces the possibility of joint breakage caused by shrinkage distortion. (Edge joint gluing is a relatively recent phenomenon in New Mexico and Spain. Early cabinetmakers had single pieces of almost any needed width or thickness, or used an unglued tongue and groove joint.) Often a gap in an edge joint must be planed true before gluing even though it can be pulled up with clamps. Further shrinkage may increase the spring and break the joint. Sawed edges are jointed before gluing unless extremely smooth and straight. If possible, prepared edges are glued relatively quickly before further wood movement distorts the edge line. The glue joint is allowed to dry thoroughly before surface planing or sanding. This is to prevent a depression from forming at the glue line when the wood, which swells with the moisture of the glue, shrinks back to its original position. If several plainsawed boards are glued up, the annual ring arc in the end grain is reversed alternately, so that cupping of the individual boards does not cup the entire piece.

Wood selection is another important aspect of the Spanish Colonial furniture maker's wood movement awareness. An extremely popular wood is the very stable Honduras mahogany. Relatively stable black walnut and white pine are also used extensively. The most movement-conscious cabinetmakers try to use relatively straight-grained material. They also try to use quartersawed lumber in preference to the more beautiful but less stable plainsawed material. (Unfortunately, quartersawed lumber is now practically unavailable.) Also, when laminating, the Spanish Colonial cabinetmaker tries to choose material of similar movement characteristics, matching wood types and avoiding a combination of plainsawed and quartersawed stock.

When possible the Spanish Colonial furniture maker chooses lumber that has had time to air-dry to the ambient equilibrium moisture content over lumber recently shipped from the kiln. (The rise of solar-heated kilns may soon allow lumber yards in the Southwest to dry furniture wood down to acceptable

Low humidity has caused the wood to shrink to such an extent that the edge of the panel is exposed. At right, butterfly keys on a mitered joint. The middle key was inaccurately laid and required the use of filler.

moisture levels, thus allowing production shops to use properly dried material.)

Some Spanish Colonial furniture makers use relatively "wet" kiln-dried wood to their advantage by making female pieces out of it before it dries and making male pieces out of drier wood. After gluing, the female piece shrinks to hold the joint more tightly.

Many Spanish Colonial cabinetmakers now use synthetic glues, most notably aliphatic resin. However, some continue to use liquid hide glue extensively. The low moisture resistance of the glue is less of a problem in the desert, and its tough elasticity allows it to stand a fair amount of joint movement before breaking.

Movement accommodation considerations have played little part in the choice of finishes. In colonial New Mexico little or no finish was used on furniture. Today relatively low moisture-resistant oil finishes are the most popular. One of the reasons for this could be that the finish on furniture does little to retard seasonal or longer moisture content changes, and shorter changes affect the wood moisture content insignificantly. One rule of furniture finishing almost universally followed by the Spanish Colonial cabinetmaker is to finish both sides of any board liable to cup, and to use a finish with similar moisture-resistant

qualities on both sides. A final traditional rule of the Spanish Colonial cabinetmaker is to avoid endbanding of solid stock if at all possible. Not only does it lead to an unsightly overhang of the end band, but it will break the banded plank if secured tightly at more than one point.

The Spanish Colonial cabinetmaker is in many ways the present embodiment of a long and fascinating tradition of furniture making. However, the movement-accommodating techniques that have developed as part of that tradition should not be of interest solely to the desert cabinetmaker. Wood moves with the temperature and humidity of the air around it. In a New York City apartment which is heated in the winter and open in the summer, wood moisture content may change more than in the desert. Few cabinetmakers know whether the lumber they use is at its equilibrium moisture content, or whether the furniture they build will be moved to a markedly different climate. For these reasons every cabinetmaker, no matter what style of furniture he or she produces, must make design and execution decisions with the possibility of wood movement in mind. The history of Spanish Colonial furniture construction can offer valuable techniques useful in minimizing the effects of that movement.

Spiral Steps

The trick is to make them strong and graceful

by Edward G. Livingston

Trying to describe the innermost workings of the concept and construction of a design, be it a building or a door knob, is risky business. Risky, primarily because such analysis quite often falls short of explaining thoroughly just what transpired. Risky too, because even though the artist may be doing the explaining, there is a loss in translation between his creative processes and his verbal ones. With that in mind, we would like to take a calculated risk and show the innards of our library ladder.

First, in explaining "why" the ladder: it was created as an experiment. It was the joy of experimenting with the creative process rather than any urgent necessity that triggered the concept. The ladder was a challenge in the functional sense because it was and is a basic instrument used to defy gravity. It is easy enough to get above the ground all right, but how do you get above the ground with a certain amount of grace and aplomb? That is indeed a challenge! A spiral stair, whether it is a full-story size or a partial stair such as a library ladder, provides by its very spiral nature, the intrigue of potential grace and aplomb in climbing. It does in fact beckon to be climbed, so why not enhance this by eliminating as much possible—the extraneous structural supports, for instance—and allow the essence to stand out?

Another large obstacle was solving the actual technical problems relating to fabricating the unit. In other words, "Okay, you have cooked up an idea. Now, how in the world do you build it?"

This part of the conceptual process is extremely important because sometimes it is impossible to translate an idea properly.

A man once said, "Well building hath three conditions — commodity, firmness, and delight." The man, Sir Henry Wotton, was talking about the basics of architectural design, but I like to think that those basics are more universal. I feel that: "commodity" — the function of the design; "firmness"—the structure; "delight"—the aesthetics; are the guts, feathers and all of any of our creative endeavors. Combining Wotton's basics and the intrinsic challenges of the ladder, plus the creative impulse in me, into a physical whole is the sum of the experiment.

The physical aspects of putting together a unit like the ladder are patience, glue, and wood—in that order. The first part of the structure is basically a laminated column with alternate armature laminations left void—thus creating a mortise type of receptacle to receive the tenon type end of the individual riser assemblies. The spiral of the stair is provided by the second set of column wedge laminations, which flank either side of the armature laminations and differ in that their cross section is in the shape of a wedge or pie. The armature laminations are interrupted by the risers. The wedge laminations are continuous for their individual full length. The riser laminations provide a nest for the riser itself, and the wedge laminations lock the riser in the nest.

The second part of the structure is the foot. Its importance and complexity are deceiving. It was also the most difficult of the design features to resolve simply because the total unit required a large stable underpinning which was hard to build without making it look too large and too heavy.

The design was resolved by providing floor support continuously along the same axis as any anticipated applied weight from above. The foot follows exactly the same curve as the treads above. The flow of the curve allows the foot a little respite from weight and size and at the same time provides continuity with the flow of design above. The complexity of the foot exists because of its curve. In order for the foot to have any strength in bending, it has to be cross-laminated so by the time the foot reaches from toe to the heel at the column, there is a stack of six laminations each juxtaposed grain-wise so as to reinforce each other.

The last part of the structure are the tread riser assemblies—simple laminated cantilevers. The risers at the column end are in effect tenons that actually project completely through the column. The only atypical tread riser assembly is the first one at the floor and this because it actually embraces the foot as the foot approaches the base of the column.

Assembly of the total unit can be tricky because the twisting motion the wedges provide makes it difficult to obtain straight line pressure points in applying clamps. Also the wedges themselves have a tendency to pop out of their intended plane as pressure is applied. There is also a problem of keeping track of a needed reference point. Everything about the unit is either twisting or curving, and unless care is exercised the fabricator will be wondering about up from down.

Normally we first glue up the armature pieces, risers included, with a wedge piece added on one side as reinforcing. When these have cured, we then juxtapose the armature-wedge assemblies and glue. This allows for more control of the otherwise slippery wedges. We keep all of the column edges rough at this point to allow for the maximum availability for clamping area. Also in order to keep everything true, i.e., the column vertical and the risers horizontal, we use as a reference point the vertical line made by the take-off point common to all the riser assemblies.

After the column is completed in the rough, the foot

assembly is inserted in the slot provided by the lowest riser armature. This armature is then beefed up by two full dimension laminations on both sides to provide adequate glue line support for the incoming foot assembly. This juncture is an important one because it is the point where all the accumulated vertical stresses in the column assembly are transferred to the foot.

With the foot on, the column straight up and down, and the riser armatures poking out in place, the tread side wings can be added. It is best that the side wings be preassembled and sanded because it is a difficult maneuver to get sanding equipment in the tight space between treads after the pieces are assembled.

The one redundant feature of the ladder is the finale or handhold at the top of the column, which is a series of built up laminations of a different wood applied over the column end—a blob of a different wood made integral with the column end.

After the unit is together the column is sculpted with a seven-inch automotive disk sander with 16-grit abrasive, thus providing the continuous flow of the twisted column. From then on it is finish sanding, an oil finish, and a wipe of the brow!

Finally, the time involved in fabricating the unit is approximately 40 hours, with over half of that time devoted to the necessary sanding. The glue used is alphatic resin and there is no hardware or metal involved in the structure. The wood is Japanese oak throughout except for the handhold.

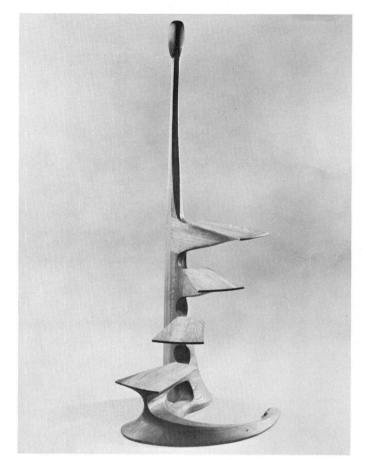

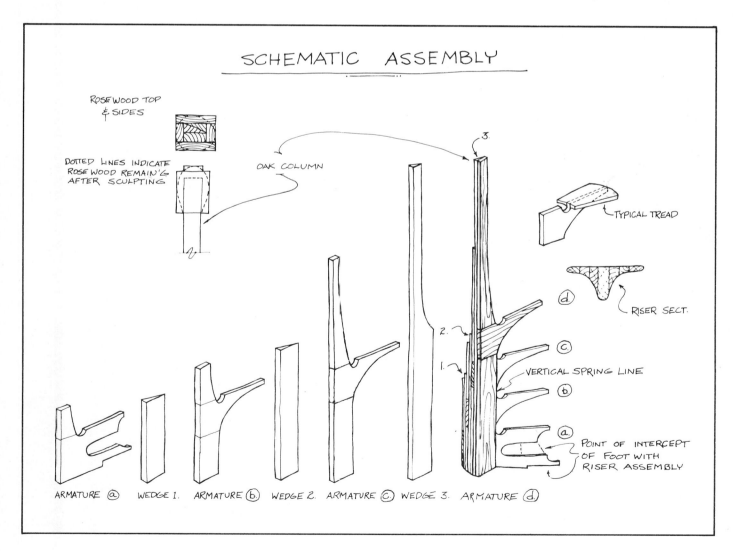

SCHEMATIC ASSEMBLY

ROSEWOOD TOP & SIDES

DOTTED LINES INDICATE ROSEWOOD REMAIN'G AFTER SCULPTING

OAK COLUMN

3.

TYPICAL TREAD

(d.)

RISER SECT.

2.

(c.)

VERTICAL SPRING LINE

1.

(b.)

(a.)

POINT OF INTERCEPT OF FOOT WITH RISER ASSEMBLY

ARMATURE (a) WEDGE 1. ARMATURE (b) WEDGE 2. ARMATURE (c) WEDGE 3. ARMATURE (d)

Two Sticks

Ancient method simplifies layout of big jobs

by Hank Gilpin

The stick method of measuring and drawing is by no means new. I'm certain it predates all other methods used in designing furniture, since the availability of large pieces of paper is a relatively recent luxury. Prior to the introduction of S-curves in the late 17th century and the multiple-angle joinery of the Chippendale period, most furniture was joined very simply and readily adaptable to stick layout. The introduction of complex joinery and curved forms in furniture has not diminished this method's usefulness because even today most wooden objects are based on rectangles and squares. Contemporary English cabinetmakers use this method for nearly all construction except chairs, which are difficult to lay out on a stick. However, the simple Carver chairs of colonial America and the delicate chairs turned by the Shakers are obvious results of the stick method. In reproduction work the stick is very handy. If you are asked to duplicate a Sheraton bow-front chest, all you have to do is hold a stick to the front and scribe all the elements of the chest onto the sticks. Then you need only a full-scale drawing of the front curve.

I was introduced to the stick method by Tage Frid during the construction of a library circulation desk that measured 15 ft. by 18 ft. Frid grabbed the scale floor plan we'd drawn up, took a few measurements and covered two sticks with mysterious pencil lines. He made a cutting list, somehow related to those marks on the stick, attacked a 24-sheet pile of plywood, cutting, grooving and tonguing and in less time than it would have taken to execute a full-scale drawing (I'd still be hunting for an 18-ft. table) all the parts for the desk were cut to size,

Hank Gilpin makes furniture in Lincoln, R.I., and teaches woodworking at Rhode Island School of Design.

tongued and grooved, and ready to be glued together.

None of this really sank in until I had my own shop and was faced with my first big job. But, once I had adapted to the sticks as a substitute for full-scale drawings and devised my own method of marking, I wondered how I ever worked without them. Every element of a job can be drawn on just two sticks: doors, drawers, carcases and frames, drawer sides, bottoms, pulls, hinges, edge-banding and shelves.

In this article I'll use a kitchen to illustrate the stick method of layout, but everything I'm going to discuss can be applied to any large job that is to be constructed in your shop and installed elsewhere. I'm focusing on a kitchen because it is a job you are likely to obtain; everybody needs one. Undoubtedly this will be a larger job than you've ever done, possibly including fifty feet of cabinets. No problem. If proper attention is paid to measuring, layout and some standardization, things will progress with staggering swiftness.

The first step is careful measurement of the room with sticks, two pieces of wood 3/4 in. square (it's a handy size), each at least 18 in. longer than half the largest dimension of the room. In an 8-ft. by 12-ft. room with an 8-ft. ceiling, two sticks each 7-1/2 ft. long will suffice for all necessary measuring, with a face of the pair of sticks used per wall. For large or complicated rooms I use two sets of sticks, one for the horizontals and one for the verticals.

Assuming walls B and D are to receive cabinets we'll proceed to measure, or "stick off," the room. Facing B, hold the sticks horizontally at chest height and push them apart until they meet walls A and C. Mark the two sticks appropriately and check for variations at floor and ceiling level, noting any differences on the sticks. This noting of variations in length

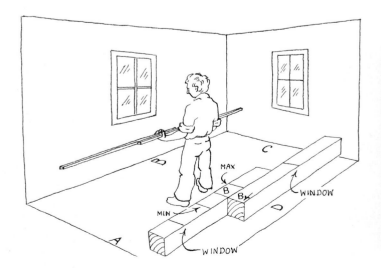

Gilpin sticks off room, noting window position. Stick marks (left) establish scribing allowances for fitting cabinets.

will prepare you to make the necessary allowances for scribing the cabinets upon installation.

If there is a constant, such as the window in wall B, the sticks must be marked to indicate its extreme dimensions, including moldings. Use a straightedge to carry the window lines to the floor and ceiling and again check for variations in the length of wall B. Any other permanent elements in the room should also be marked on the sticks. This might include radiators, electrical outlets, pipes, doors, ducts, etc. This process, if carefully done, gives you an exact, full-scale horizontal cross section of wall B.

To obtain a vertical cross section follow the same basic procedure, but use one of the unmarked faces on the sticks or two new sticks and push them from floor to ceiling, once again marking windows and such. Check and mark variations in height by moving the sticks all along the wall. If the floor has a truly dramatic pitch, not unusual in older buildings, I like to set a level line on the wall 36 inches above the highest point in the floor's rock and roll. With this line acting as an imaginary counter top, and thus a necessary constant, I set my sticks accordingly. This is important for fitting the cabinets around appliances such as stoves and dishwashers, which require a specific counter height.

The process of sticking off should be repeated on all the walls and in any other areas, such as the middle of a large room, that are to receive cabinets. After measuring the whole room and returning to the shop I transfer all the information to clean sticks cut to length, and often to a new stick for each marked face of the old ones. Since a 16-foot stick isn't easy to come by, I use short lengths overlapped and nailed together.

Now you must design the kitchen around the available dimensions. It is at this point that you discuss entrances and approaches: cabinet styles, paint, light, heat, type of wood, sinks, tiles, floors, everything, but most importantly, appliances. A real nuisance these refrigerators, stoves, ovens and dishwashers, but these are the fixed elements in the evolving picture. So they are where you start. It is imperative that you have all the dimensions of each and every appliance your customer desires and that once a decision has been reached you state firmly but diplomatically that no changes can be allowed without increase in cost. When considering all the other aspects of the room, remember that the final appearance of your work, which will dominate the room and thus be most open for criticism, depends to a great extent on forethought and coordination of details. This usually means working with

a number of subcontractors who may not be as concerned with esthetics as you are.

Once all of this preliminary discussion is completed you have to sit down and design the job. Referring to the sticks for overall dimensions, make a rough floor plan that includes all the appliances and various cabinet, drawer and counter combinations. Be careful to consider function with the esthetics.

It is helpful to make this floor plan to some scale, and 3/4 in. to the foot is easy to read and not overly cumbersome. Many cabinetmakers draw scale elevations to accompany the floor plan, but I find most customers just cannot project two-dimensional elevations into a vivid picture of the finished project. I've scrapped the elevations and instead present perspective sketches incorporating as much detail as possible. These sketches, along with the floor plan and a wood sample, give the customer a fairly good picture of what to expect. After you've done a few jobs it is always possible to take prospective customers to see a finished product, the best way of solving the problem of explaining ideas.

I know all this talk of appliances and plumbers seems contrary to the discussion of woodworking but I've learned that the preliminary planning, though time-consuming and a bore, is absolutely essential to a quick, trouble-free job.

Here is one of the basic structural approaches I use when building a kitchen. This is only *one* way of doing the job, and not *the* way.

I use 3/4-in. veneer-core plywood for all carcases, usually birch for interiors and hardwood-veneered plywood for all visible exterior surfaces. It's wise to check the thickness of the plywood stock you buy as it often comes through a bit under 3/4 in. and this discrepancy might cause joinery problems. The carcases are joined by tongue-and groove in two basic forms, each with a 1/4-in. tongue. One uses the standard centered tongue and the second uses an offset tongue. The offset joint is simply a way to add a small amount of strength to what is obviously a less than convincing corner joint. By setting the tongue to within 1/16 in. of the inside you gain enough strength in the vertical member to prevent the short grain from popping while gluing. Always leave a shoulder, no matter how small, as it adds a bit of strength and helps keep things square.

These joints can be cut in a number of ways, but I find it quickest and easiest to run the groove on the table saw with dado blades and the tongue on a shaper with two pattern bits coupled by a spacer made of long-grain wood that has been

This kitchen includes stove island, counters and wall cabinets. Complete layout was done on two sticks.

fitted to the groove. A new wood spacer should be made whenever you sharpen your blades because the kerf gets smaller each time. I generally find it a good practice to cut the groove first and fit the tongue to it. I also cut the groove about 1/64 in. deeper than the tongue, to allow for glue build-up and any slight inconsistencies in the cutting.

I make the carcases without backs, and the tops need not be solid pieces of plywood—a strip 4 in. or 6 in. wide at the front and back is enough to fasten the counter top to. I make my own counter tops of solid wood, usually 1-1/4 in. or 1-1/2 in. thick, with corners and edges carefully detailed. Sometimes I 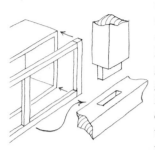 use floor tiles on the surface. After the carcases are glued up I face each with a solid wood frame that has been mortised and tenoned together. Remembering that any given edge of veneer-core plywood is at least 40% long grain, it becomes obvious that nothing more than glue and clamps is necessary to fasten the frame to the carcase. This frame adds the strength that was so menacingly deficient in the tongue-and-groove carcase.

In any case, the weakness of the carcases will become inconsequential once they are screwed to the wall or floor at installation, even if the solid frame is omitted. To do this, I usually glue the edge of a 3/4-in. thick by 1-1/4-in. wide strip to the underside of the top of the carcase, at the back. I mark the location of this strip on the wall and drive nails until I hit a stud, then hold the cabinet in place and drill through for a No. 12 screw. I had a football player chin himself from an upper wall cabinet that was supported by screws into two studs; it held.

Remember that the frame is the element of the cabinet left oversize to allow for scribing as the carcase cannot be cut to match irregularities in the walls. Minor irregularities at floor level can be adjusted by scribing the lower cabinet kickboard supports before fitting the kickboard itself. Occasionally an independent base must be fitted to a room that is really out of kilter, but this does not occur very often.

Our main concern now is transferring this information to the sticks, concentrating on the carcases, the frames, and the spaces necessary for fitting appliances. (Doors and drawers should also be laid out, but style preferences complicate matters and we'll ignore them at this point.) The depth of cabinets is predetermined in most cases, 24 inches or so for floor cabinets and 12 inches plus for upper cabinets. These are only average sizes, not absolutes, and thus, not directly related to the stick layout. As in any full-scale working drawing, the main functions provided are location of all joinery and full-scale measurements for the cutting list.

I'll discuss only the sink cabinet, since it is typical and straightforward, but remember that everything applies to the entire job. After locating the space necessary for the dishwasher, leaving no more than 1/8 in. on each side for fitting, you begin by marking the extreme dimensions of the plywood carcase on the width stick, the one carrying the horizontal cross section of the long wall. The cabinet is to be 36 in. wide so draw two lines, A and A-1, 36 in. apart. Then measure in 3/4 in., or whatever is the actual thickness of the plywood, from each and draw the next two lines. These represent vertical plywood sections. Now mark the height stick. If the height of the cabinet is 34-1/2 in. (without the counter top), draw a line on the stick 34-1/2 in. from the floor mark. Then simply measure down the thickness of the plywood and draw the next line. This represents the carcase top. Assuming a 4-in. kickspace, your next mark should be 4 in. up from the floor level. Again, measure in the thickness of the plywood and draw a line to indicate the carcase bottom. If you have plywood drawer dividers or permanent shelves, they too are marked out at this point. These lines on both sticks represent the carcase elements and locate the joints. I should add that I find it very helpful to color-code the various markings. I use black pencil for plywood elements, red for frames and green for doors and drawers.

Once the carcase elements are laid out you turn to the

Centered and offset tongues join carcase elements, and sliding dovetails fit the sides of this drawer to an overhanging front.

Cabinet at left has large allowance for scribing; it will be surfaced with ceramic tile. Splashboard, right, is carefully detailed.

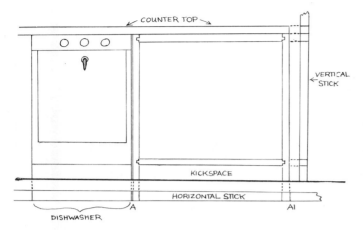

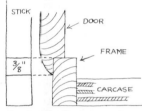

Sink cabinet, left, is marked out on horizontal and vertical sticks. Above, photo at left shows sticks atop finishing cabinet, with marks for plywood carcase and front framing; right, vertical stick locates drawer dividers and finished drawer fronts. Sticks and frames below include a 1/2-in. allowance for scribing to irregular wall.

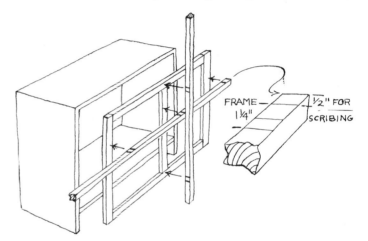

frames that face the carcase. If your design calls for 1-1/4-in. frames throughout, simply measure in 1-1/4 in. from the extreme dimensions on the carcase and, using the red pencil, mark the sticks appropriately. If you are allowing for scribing, this is the time to mark it on the sticks. If the wall to which you are fitting is 1/2 in. off square over the 3 feet needed for the cabinet, mark the frame 1/2 in. beyond the line indicating the outside of the carcase on the length stick and then measure 1-1/4 in. inward from the same line, thus ensuring finished symmetry.

All vertical and horizontal stiles, integral parts of the frames necessary for the division of the doors and drawers, should also be drawn on the sticks. If you have decided to use lipped doors and drawers (3/8-in. square lip) they can be indicated on the sticks by simply measuring 3/8 in. out from the inside frame marks on both the length and height sticks. With face-mounted doors and drawers you must first determine the spacing that is desired between each and then mark each accordingly, remembering that these marks indicate finished sizes and might include edge-banding.

Now, with all the carcases, frames, doors and drawers marked on the sticks, your next step is to compile cutting lists. One will include all the plywood elements (carcases, shelves, and probably door and drawer fronts). The other will include all the frames. I always follow the same procedure to compile the cutting lists. On the plywood list I include a cabinet designation, what each piece is, the number of said pieces, type of wood and size. I indicate the pieces to be tongued and those to receive edge-banding.

You know the depth of the cabinets, so all the carcase pieces will be 23-7/8 in. deep (or 11-7/8 in. in the case of upper wall cabinets) and because all the floor cabinets stand 34-1/2 in., the vertical elements will be listed as such. In general, horizontal pieces have tongues, and verticals have grooves. The first pieces you must measure are the carcase top and bottom. Measure between the plywood marks on the length stick and add 1/4 in. for each tongue, noting same when you add the dimensions to the list. Example: If you have 37-1/2 in. between the plywood marks with two tongues, add 1/2 in., giving you a piece 38 in. long. This may seem academic but it is not often that the pieces will measure exactly 38 inches. You will more often have to fit the cabinet into a space 37-11/16 in. wide and careful measuring becomes imperative, lest you assume too much. Door sizes are simply measured and noted, although you must remember to

subtract the thickness of the edge-banding if it is an element of the design because the marks on the sticks indicate finished dimensions. I make cabinet doors of solid ply, but they could be frame-and-panel for a more traditional appearance.

The frame list is compiled in the same way. All vertical end pieces will be 30-1/2 in. because all the kickspaces are 4 inches, all the cabinets are 34-1/2 in. high, and the frame does not extend to the floor. All other elements are determined by measuring between the frame sections drawn on the sticks, be they vertical or horizontal components, and adding the length of the tenons. In this case all the tenons are 3/4 in. long and shouldered on four sides (strictly personal choice—two shoulders satisfy many builders). Here again I note those pieces which will receive tenons. It is imperative to measure carefully because a 1/4-in. variation might not show up until you try and fit the frame to the carcase. Also, try to use the same ruler throughout the entire job as it is not unusual to find a 1/8-in. difference between two seemingly identical 6-ft. rules.

Once the cutting lists are complete and you have gathered the necessary stock you actually get to do some woodworking. One point I feel is helpful and hopefully obvious: When cutting plywood and lumber to size always start with the larger pieces and work to the smallest. This means you'll be cutting parts for different cabinets at the same time, which can get confusing, especially if you consider that an average-size kitchen might have 100 or more plywood parts and nearly as many frame parts. So this is not the time for casual conversation and extended coffee breaks. A few hours of uninterrupted concentration will prevent large headaches later.

Guitar Joinery

The balance between structure and tone

by William R. Cumpiano

The author with apprentice R. Goldberg.

The major problem confronting the guitar maker is how to counteract the structural changes that will occur in his instrument over time. These changes will alter tonal quality and affect the instrument's playability. The builder relies on joinery to counteract these changes.

A strung-up guitar is a structure undergoing constant sizable stress and requiring utmost economy of materials to render it a highly compliant, frequency-dependent vibrating object—that is, with different sections of the guitar vibrating at different but specific frequencies. A successful guitar design must correctly balance an effective structure with an optimum mass to produce an instrument that will project good strong tone for many years without destroying itself in the process. The designer will usually favor good tone and lightness at the expense of rigidity. He will build into the guitar features that anticipate distortion while allowing for repair through its hoped for 100-year life span.

Interestingly, a guitar's tone is expected to mature and decay within a relatively short time, short compared to the maturation span of several hundred years of violins and other bowed instruments. This is because the architecture is different in each case. When a guitar is played, six long strings are pulled up at the center of a wide expanse of very thin spruce of essentially even cross section. In the violin, four short strings are pushing down on a perfectly vaulted cross section of fairly thick and narrow dimension. The guitar body fatigues first, losing power and volume dramatically when its contemporary violin is just passing adolescence.

Guitar assembly methods vary according to how the builder chooses to join neck to sound box. Factors affecting this choice are: the number of instruments to be built simultaneously, the extent of the builder's facilities, his talents, time and profit margin, and his training and accumulated prejudices. Unfortunately, the sense of responsibility of the builder to his creation and his buyer is predominantly absent today, and most mass-produced instruments are designed with only profit in mind.

The selection of the neck/body joint is critical. The primary requirement is rigidity. Also, it must fit at a precise angle. The angle of neck to body determines the height of the strings off the neck and consequently the instrument's playability. Of equal significance is how easily the joint can be disassembled for later readjustment of the angle.

If we accelerate the effect of string tension on an

instrument we see the following: As soon as the strings are strung the entire instrument flexes longitudinally away from them, like a wooden bow under a taut cord. Soon the area under the string attachment point at the sound box bellies out as if the instrument were being inflated. Consequently, the previously straight neck is forced into a curve. The fingerboard pushes down toward the sound hole in an effort to resolve the stress. The back of the instrument strains, and the stress causes tension against every inch of its seams. The sides try to flatten out and away from the face, as if the whole system were collapsing into its sound hole.

All of this movement is slowed by the stiffening braces inside the guitar box. A stiffening spline or an adjustable pre-tensioning device running through the center of the neck counteracts its tendency to curve.

The untrained eye will notice only that the strings are gradually moving away from the fingerboard, and that the instrument is becoming progressively more difficult to play. From time to time the guitar must be repaired. Depending on the extent of the distortion, the repair might entail readjusting the pre-tensioning device, filing down the string-to-body attachment, or resetting the neck. The latter involves removing the neck and reattaching it at a new angle to compensate for its distortion and the distortion of the sound box.

Neck/body joints fall into two main categories: those requiring an integral heel and neck block (such as the Spanish method), and those with separate blocks (such as the tapered dovetail and the pinned mortise and tenon). A host of other joints, uncommon in modern guitar making, rely on intricate

The three neck/body joints are, left to right, the Spanish method, the tapered dovetail and the pinned mortise and tenon. The last is shown with its pinning tool.

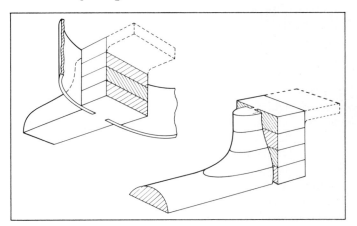

William Cumpiano was a furniture designer/draftsman who turned luthier seven years ago. He builds, repairs and teaches at his studio in North Adams, Mass.

and contrived systems—threads, screws, cams, hooks, wedges and inserts—to hold the neck to the body. Some are bizarre and fascinating; most have been relegated to the dustbin of history.

Some instruments such as the early lutes, citterns and gitterns of medieval times were carved from a single billet of wood, but the oldest surviving assembly technique is the Spanish method. It has outlived all the others because it is simple and adaptable to hand building. It is used by novice and master alike, by hand builder as well as machinist, because it requires less accuracy than the others and does the job as well. Its major shortcoming is that it cannot be undone for resetting, and so it is only used responsibly on instruments with low-tension strings, or short strings and thus short necks. A skilled person can sometimes reset Spanish-method necks, or compensate for body/neck distortion by relying on some arcane tricks of his trade.

In the Spanish method, the instrument's sides are let into slots cut into the neck. The portion of the neck inside the instrument is kept massive and rectangular for ample gluing surface to lock sides, top and back together, and the portion left outside is whittled into the graceful triangulation called the heel.

If you are an experienced hand builder or a well-tutored novice contemplating building a single instrument, you may use the Spanish method/free assembly. You will build the guitar from its face upwards, piece by piece like a Tinkertoy. Start with the guitar face upside down, with its internal bracing members looking up at you. Attach the slotted neck, also upside down. The sides, previously bent, are let into the slots, glued to the face one by one, and carefully lined up with the template outline scribed on the face. The far ends of the sides are both attached to a tail block, similar to the neck block. The back closes the sound box, completing the main structure of the instrument—sound box and neck are locked together rigidly and permanently.

If you need to build several identical instruments, or if your skills are not up to the demanding task of aligning the sides with a template mark on the face, you might choose the variation of the Spanish method that requires an elaborate exterior mold. The mold is a clamping/centering device. You begin by gluing together the sides, slotted neck and tail block. The mold keeps these pieces in place while the glue sets. The product is a neck attached to a guitar-shaped hoop. Then affix the face, and lastly the back. The result is a closed sound box and cantilevered neck, just as in the free assembly. What remains to be done is to attach the fingerboard to the

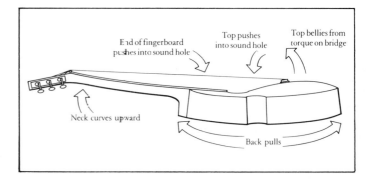

An exaggeration of structural distortions that will occur in time.

neck, and trim and finish the instrument.

The tapered dovetail neck/body joint is the most common production joint. It is also used by many hand builders, but it requires skill with a backsaw and chisel to make the necessary angled cuts. In a factory setup, jigs and hold-downs allow the mating pieces to be cut with an overhead router and a dovetail bit.

The tapered dovetail joint consists of a separate neck block inside the body, exposing a dovetail cavity, its least width pointing down to the back of the instrument. A matching male counterpart behind the heel of the neck slips into the body and down, forming the precise body/neck angle that yields accurate string height. If you've done any woodworking you can see why this joint is more popular with machinists than with hand builders. Yet some hand builders feel it is the supreme neck/body joint.

The pinned mortise and tenon has a vertical mortise exposed on the outside of the sound box. The mortise mates perfectly with a vertical tenon on the neck behind the heel. Whether machined or hand-built, it is simpler to construct than the tapered dovetail with its double-angled cavity. However, the right angles must be perfect if the instrument is to fit together properly.

Two tapered hardwood dowels just long enough to pass through the neck block pin the neck tenon to it. Pre-drilled holes in the neck block and neck tenon are taper-reamed to match the pin, so that as the pin is pushed through, it tightens. The holes in the tenon are minutely offset to those in the block, so that as the pin is forced through, it draws the neck tightly against the body. After the neck and body are completely finished and polished, the pinning is done with the aid of a homemade steel pincer called a pinning tool. It is manipulated through the sound hole, its pincers grabbing the

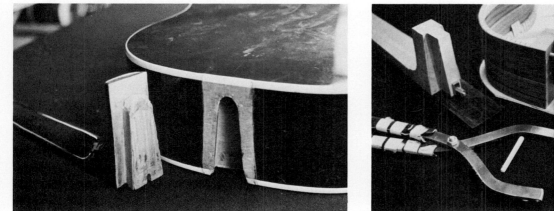

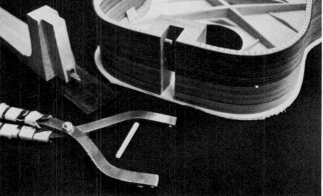

The guitar's braces help control structural distortion while "disciplining" flex and thereby determining tonal quality. The large, flat brace at the left counteracts the top's tendency to split from differing expansions of top and fingerboard. The thicker brace next to it supports the end of the fingerboard. The three short braces around the sound hole restore rigidity where the hole was cut out. The X-brace is the main support for the top, the fan braces above and below support the outer edges. The patch to the right of the X increases the mass for the bridge attachment. The two diagonal braces control the top's flexibility and therefore its frequency response. The small cross-grained diamonds reinforce the book-matched seam of the top. In the drawing, at the left the headstock veneer reinforces the joint; at the right the fingerboard acts as a reinforcement, commonly found on banjos.

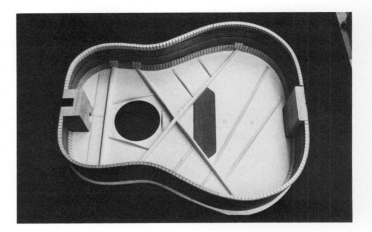

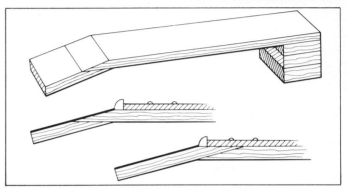

neck block and pin, forcing one into the other when its lever arms are squeezed. A small light bulb inside the body illuminates the process. To remove the neck, the action of the pinning tool is reversed with the help of a small metal dowel inserted into the small end of the pin hole. Pressure on the tool pops the pin out. Removing the neck becomes a fifteen-minute affair, instead of the hours-long job of undoing a tapered dovetail.

With the tapered dovetail and the pinned mortise and tenon, the neck and body are constructed, trimmed, and often even finished separately. The production advantages are obvious. Parts can be conveniently stacked, and the often laborious pre-finish and post-finish sanding at the heel/body juncture in the Spanish method is no longer necessary. The result is a clean, finished joint at the end of the line.

I have often participated in lively discussion with hand builders who eschew these two-piece systems. They feel that something intangible is lost when they work long hours on an object that only at the very last moment becomes a guitar. They feel, understandably, that they can retain a subtle connection with their creation through the entire process only if it is guitar-like from a very early stage in its construction. However, the more pragmatic realize the superiority of the dovetail and pinned mortise and tenon, when it comes to building a salable product that can be guaranteed over the long run.

The pinned mortise and tenon is highly efficient and practical. Its use is not widespread and when it is found, it is on instruments coming from small shops that specialize in individually handcrafted instruments. I have found some controversy about its use. Some people are just prejudiced in favor of the other methods; others legitimately feel that in time the pins may shrink and loosen, or that its rigidity and impact resistance is inferior. And although it is easier to disassemble for resetting, very few repair people are familiar with it, let alone possess the special pinning tool necessary to dismantle and reassemble it. However, I prefer this last joint. It is neat and foolproof, and I have yet to see it come undone when it wasn't supposed to. On the other hand, I have repaired dozens of tapered-dovetail instruments whose necks had slipped due to glue failure or inaccurate fitting. I feel free to guarantee the pinned mortise and tenon on my instruments, since if worst comes to worst, repairs can be made with a minimum of fuss and time.

The rest of the joints in the instrument are simple glue joints with two exceptions: a lap joint on the X-brace found under the top, and the headstock-neck joint. The purpose of the top braces is not exclusively structural. The top braces

control the amount of flex and movement in the top and determine each instrument's vibration characteristics. The guitar box is not only a sound amplifier, but more importantly a sound modulator. Nowhere on the instrument is the balance of mass and structure more finely determined than at the top braces. The size, shape, weight and placement of these braces determine the flex and vibration of the top, thus modulating the sound and giving a guitar its characteristic tone. The angle of the lap-jointed X-brace determines the size of the resonating "working area" (the circular lower portion of the guitar top, which has the bridge as its approximate center) and thus influences the tone; it must be accurately laid out and cut for the instrument to produce the desired sound. All these braces counteract the effects of string tension.

Another important joint is where the headstock meets the neck. On mass-produced instruments, this is usually not a joint at all, but a one-piece neck blank bandsawn from a single billet of hardwood, often Honduras mahogany. A one-piece blank can be made quickly, but it is wasteful of stock and relatively weak, with its short grain in the angled headstock. A better possibility is the composite neck blank. A scarf joint at the bend reinforces the headstock because the long grain follows the shape, and the built-up heel eliminates the need for thick stock.

The sheer economy of all these methods has always intrigued me. They have been refined and perfected over a period of 500 years, and may never be superceded. A musical instrument, like an airplane or a racing bicycle, owes its success to the dictum "less is more" (but not too much less!). Its components must be pared away, thinned out, made so economical that all that remains is its essence: the absolute minimum that will allow it to function properly. Anything more gets in its way. In this process you also end up with something that happens to be a thing of beauty.

FINISHING, TURNING AND MARQUETRY

French Polishing

The disappearing art of getting a fine shellac finish

To many woodworkers the art of satin-gloss French polishing—the building up of a thin, fine shellac finish with a cloth pad—is a deservedly dying one. Not only does it take much skill and experience to produce that transparent, satin-gloss that it's famous for, but also much elbow grease.

As a result, in this day of seemingly instant, effortless activity, French polishing is given short shrift, rarely or briefly mentioned in books on wood finishing.

To Anthony Arlotta, a former cabinetmaker and now a professional finisher and refinisher for many years in New York City, this is a sad state of affairs. He can understand why French polishing for commercially made woodwork has become economically impractical except for the finest antiques. But for the amateur craftsman, who has already spent dozens or even hundreds of hours making a piece of furniture or a marquetry panel, the extra several hours that French polishing takes, compared to the instant finishes, is well worth it. It gives a smooth, thin finish full of luster but without the thick high gloss associated with lacquer.

For refinishing work, it can be used over old shellac, but not over old varnish or lacquer because of the poor bond.

The advantages of French polishing over varnish and lacquer are not only its beauty, but also its relative practicality. That is, if the finish does get scratched or damaged, it's a relatively easy process to rebuild and blend in the new shellac buildup. In fact, Arlotta demonstrates this dramatically by putting some 150 or 180 grit sandpaper to a finished piece, and then, in a few minutes of rubbing, getting rid of the intentional scratches.

There are disadvantages, however. Shellac is water resistant but not waterproof as some varnishes are. And, of course, it is not alcohol resistant, since that is the solvent for shellac. But given these drawbacks, there's no reason why French polishing can't be used for any fine furniture that is properly cared for, especially where the beauty of the grain and figure of the wood is to be highlighted.

For French polishing, Arlotta uses age old techniques, such as mixing his own shellac. (He considers ready-made French polishes inferior, but he does use them—on the undersides of furniture where it doesn't show.) He takes orange shellac flakes or crushed orange shellac buttons, fills a jar about three-quarters full with the dry shellac, and then fills the jar with methyl or wood alcohol, or columbine spirits, as it is sometimes called.

It takes about a week for the flakes or chips to dissolve. Every day he gives the mixture a stir or two; after a week the flakes have dissolved into an orange syrupy mixture. He strains it through cheesecloth if necessary, especially if the buttons were used.

Arlotta doesn't use bleached or white shellac because he's never sure of the impurities in it, and if it's the least bit old, it doesn't dry. Arlotta says the orange shellac has an indefinite shelf life if a skim coat of alcohol is poured over the top and the jar is tightly sealed. The color is not a problem because the shellac is put on in such a thin coat.

If the wood is to be stained before finishing, only *water-based* aniline dyes should be used. Otherwise the rubbing process of French polishing could lift up stains that have other base formulations.

In fact, to create a warmth and mellowness in the wood, Arlotta likes to stain all of his pieces (regardless of the wood), with a weak solution of yellow stain. If kept pale, the stain does not really turn the wood yellow, but does give it a warmth and depth that is hard to match.

(As always in the finishing process, it's best to do extensive experimenting beforehand, for instance trying various dilutions of the yellow stain on a spare piece of wood. And, of course, it's prudent to go through the whole French polishing sequence on scrap before trying it on a treasured piece.)

Water stain raises the grain, so wash with water, dry, and sand before you stain. After staining you should give it another light sanding with very fine sandpaper.

The first step in French polishing is to put on a very thin or light wash coat of shellac (two parts alcohol, one part shellac

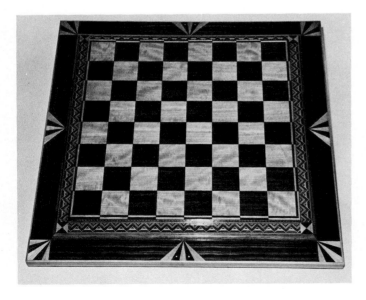

French polish gives chessboard by A. Miele a fine finish.

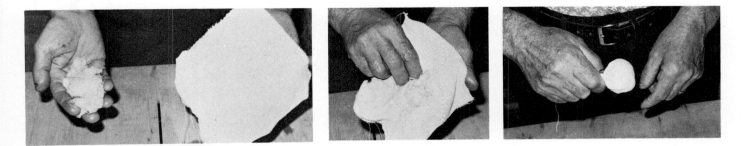

Making up a pad and working in the white pumice sprinkled on the surface, which will fill pores.

stock). This is done with a pad made up of a small ball of cotton wool or cotton waste wrapped into a larger square of cotton or natural fiber cloth and twisted into a ball. The shellac should not be put on heavily as its main purpose is to serve as a binder for the subsequent filling step.

After the shellac dries, usually in a half hour or less, Arlotta goes immediately to the filling process, using 4F pumice stone as filler.

A new pad is made up, this time with more rugged linen or tight gabardine as the pad material (because pumice is a strong abrasive). He sprinkles some pumice lightly on the surface of the wood, the pad is dampened with alcohol, and the pumice is rubbed hard into the pores. As with all French polishing steps, the initial rubbing should be in tight moving circles, then looser figure eights, and finally long straight strokes with the grain. Don't let the pad stop its motion, but keep it moving constantly. Otherwise, you'll get cloth marks where the shellac hardens.

What the combination of the alcohol and the rubbing does is to soften the shellac undercoat and imbed the pumice in it.

When the pumice has disappeared, sprinkle some more on, and add more alcohol to the pad. Keep on with this until the pores are completely filled, the surface seems absolutely flat, and the circular stroke marks have disappeared.

Then put it aside for a week. The shellac will dry completely and shrink slightly, exposing some of the pores again. Do another pumice filling sequence and again put it aside, this time for fewer days. When the surface stays completely flat, the wood is ready for the final polishing sequence.

(It's at this point, too, that any blemishes or defects in the wood would be fixed using wood powders.)

But assuming a blemish-free surface, a new cotton or wool pad is made up. Some shellac stock is poured onto the inside ball (the outer cloth then acts as a filter). The pad is squeezed to spread the shellac throughout, and flattened, and then just enough alcohol is put on it to make it lose some of its tacky feeling. A drop or two of lemon oil is touched here and there onto the wood surface (to act as a lubricant), and the padding process is begun.

Use the same small overlapping circles to put on the shellac. Glide the pad on and glide it off, but never stop its motion. Put enough pressure on the pad to rub the shellac in, but not so much that it takes off or "burns" the coat underneath. Recharge the pad with shellac and alcohol as needed. Add more lemon oil occasionally, and keep up the rubbing process, going from the circular strokes to the figure eights to the long straight strokes.

Repeat the process as often as you want, until you've built up the desired finish. You'll know that you've rubbed enough when the stroke marks disappear. The longer into the padding process, the lighter the pressure on the pad should be.

At the end, you'll want to apply alcohol alone to the surface to take up the lemon oil and give the final polish. Arlotta uses a new pad that is barely damp with alcohol and uses straight strokes with very light pressure. Stop when you've got the surface to where you want it.

That's the essence of French polishing. After the filling step you can build up the shellac finish as many times as you want—once or twice for a really spare finish, to several or many times for a heavier build up. There is no drying time between steps and you can pause or stop anywhere in the process (as long as you glide the pad off).

And if the finish itself does get damaged, you can sand the affected area with fine paper and rebuild it to match the overall piece, provided you have no deep dents or gouges.

Unlike lacquer and heavy varnishes, there's no solid film to crack or chip off. There's only a very thin coat of shellac that has been padded or polished on.

After the final polish, you should wait a few weeks before you put any protective coats of wax (like butcher's wax)—if you want to wax it. But it's really not necessary.

Good polishing! But remember, keep that pad moving!

[Note: If you are unable to find locally the materials mentioned, try H. Behlen and Bros., Inc., Box 698, Amsterdam, N.Y. 12010. They carry all the materials (both wholesale and retail). Minimum order is $25.00.]

Finish samples

Every woodworker and wood finisher has experienced the frustration of trying to describe the peculiar merits of a particular finish to his customers or to his fellow craftsmen. Words fail because the essence of a fine finish is sensory—one appreciates it through the fingertips and the eyes. My answer is a collection of finish samples, which I have been developing and refining for the past three years. Constant questions from my refinishing students and patrons forced me to develop it as a tangible answer; my system should work equally well for the amateur craftsman or the professional.

Start with 40 or more pieces of wood about ½ by 4½ by 9 inches, a convenient size for handling and storage, yet large enough to display the finish. Mahogany is a suitable wood because it is so often encountered in old furniture that needs refinishing. My collection includes both plain-sawn and quarter-sawn wood, and I keep a piece of raw wood as a control. It's a good idea to bleach a couple of pieces too; they will come in handy later on.

All the pieces should be carefully sanded at the same time, following your usual techniques, to ensure uniformity. I use

garnet paper and start with 100 grit until all the milling marks are gone, then I sand with 150 grit before filling. I apply paste wood filler to one face, edge and end of the sample to illustrate the contrasts that will appear in the finished piece, and then sand to 280 grit. When all the wood is prepared, it is ready to receive the finishes you most often work with. The samples can be set aside and worked up one at a time, or you can do intensive work to build up a nucleus of the more common finishes and add more, or play with variables, later on.

The possible variables include finishes on raw woods, finishes over various sealers, stains and fillers, and finishes over other finishes. Additives in finish materials, such as driers and stains, produce interesting results. Several blocks of wood, all finished with the same material and then rubbed out with abrasive flours to show the development of a polished surface, say more than words ever could. Finally, finish samples can be subjected to stresses such as alcohol, chemicals, water and burns to test your efforts.

It takes many hours to produce a fine set of finished specimens, but the extended exercise is worth the effort. It leads to conformity in each finished product and makes the finisher familiar with a wide range of materials and their application. The result is a unique educational tool that can be shared with others and always expanded. It will last forever, and it saves a lot of talking.

—David Adamusko, Alexandria, Va.

Oil/Varnish Mix

Making oil more durable

by Jere Osgood

There is a basic decision to be made when choosing a finish for a piece of furniture. Would you prefer a matte oil finish or a glossy varnish or lacquer?

For many years now, a matte oil finish has been very popular because it penetrates the wood and becomes part of the surface, and because it is easy to put on. But it is not really durable, especially for often-used table tops. On the other hand, a good water and alcohol-resistant finish would mean a varnish or lacquer which is more of a surface finish, frequently glossy, and much more difficult to put on. The various varnishes or lacquers also require a fussy environment—warm, ventilated and dust-free—for application.

If you do prefer an oil finish, you have several choices—including an oil/varnish mix that I have found to be particularly effective.

Linseed oil is of course in wide use as a finish. But it has a long application time (a matter of weeks), requires continual upkeep, and is not water-resistant. Its advantage lies in the fact that it is easy to apply, though time-consuming. A ruined spot is easy to repair with a little wet rubbing, using a rag dipped in oil and thinner. It is also pleasant to use, is easy to clean up and can be put on in a dusty, slightly cool shop if absolutely necessary.

Various synthetic penetrating oils, and Watco oils in particular, are a tremendous improvement over linseed. Watco is more water-resistant and can be used on tables if they are treated with care. The other advantage is that you can deliver your work in three days, instead of the three weeks it takes for linseed. But Watco is a little hard to locate in some areas, although many of the mail-order woodworking supply houses now carry it.

Oil and Varnish Mix

The best general finish I have had experience with is the oil and varnish mix. I can't claim to have originated it but I have pushed its use. It seems to have a long history, and variations of it are used by many furniture craftsmen because of its durability where an oil finish is needed. Its advantages over Watco are that I find it slightly more water-resistant, easier to obtain, and it has more of a body to it (but still penetrates like an oil). It doesn't need any special shop environment or equipment. A little dust or another piece being worked on nearby will cause no difficulties, though a clean, dry shop would probably be best. And the ingredients should be available at most local paint-supply stores.

The piece to be finished should have all planing, scraping or sanding completed so that a later wet-rubbing step deals only with raised grain or unevenness in the finish.

Materials needed are a pure, boiled linseed oil with no driers or additives. Parks brand is pure and is generally available, at least in the northeast. Behlen's oil is of course pure but may be harder to obtain. Pure turpentine is required; do not use mineral spirits or other substitutes. Also needed is a good-quality synthetic varnish. Try for a minimum of 50% alkyd resins (the resins are the solids) in the varnish. Use a gloss varnish so it won't contain flattening agents. The two brands I have found to be good are Valspar Gloss (50% alkyd resins) and McClosky's Ultra Spar Marine Varnish (52% alkyd resins). Clean, absorbent, lint-free rags are required—an old diaper is perfect. Also needed are 400-grit silicon carbide wet-or-dry paper for wet rubbing and a small cork or heavy felt rubbing block about three or four inches square. Mixture proportions are one part pure, boiled linseed oil, two parts synthetic varnish, and three parts turpentine. Mix a minimum of one quart the day before if possible, so it can ''make'' overnight.

Application steps

First day: Flood the surface of the piece using a brush or rag. If you see dry spots, apply more. Keep the surface saturated. After two hours, check for tackiness and wipe off with a rag if the mix has started to thicken. Thickening may take two hours or all day, depending on wood specie, humidity and temperature. In any case, the surface should be wiped off before being left overnight. If you let it get too tacky, it will be difficult to wipe off and will leave crusty spots.

Second day: Generally a repeat of the first application but don't apply quite so liberally and watch carefully for thickening, because there is not as much absorption by the wood. The time it takes to become tacky will be much shorter than with the first coat—even as short as an hour or less. When it does, wipe it off with a rag.

Third day: Flood the piece (or a section if it is very large) with mix and do the wet rubbing. Pour some of the mix into a pie plate or other flat dish. If there are some slightly crusty spots from the previous day, it might be better to thin the rubbing mix half-and-half with turpentine. Put a few pieces of 400-grit wet-or-dry paper in the plate to soak. Wrap one of these on the block and rub evenly back and forth, with the grain only, until the whole surface is covered and is smooth everywhere. This will flatten the raised grain, eliminate crusty spots and smooth out to an even thickness the finish that has been put on. Curved surfaces can be rubbed using a folded leather pad behind the paper. After this wet sanding or rubbing is complete, the piece should be vigorously buffed clean and dry. Do this by hand with clean rags, not with an electric buffer, because this finish does remain soft for a period of time. An electric buffer might possibly take too much of the finish off.

The piece is finished now, but with some woods I have found a slight sweating occurs, i.e., ''mix'' comes out of the pores. If this happens, it can be taken care of by a treatment on the fourth day—a light moistening application of mix, and then buffing it dry immediately.

You can use the wet sanding technique as a rescue for a dried or gummy oil finish at any stage. Add a lot of thinner to the mix if it is a big disaster. For wet sanding you can

Hickory wine locker by the author was finished with an oil/varnish mix over a three-day period.

Third-day application of oil/varnish mix involves wet rubbing with sandpaper to flatten raised grain and smooth out finish.

substitute very worn 220-grit garnet paper for the 400-grit wet-or-dry paper, but it disintegrates quickly. 4/0000 steel wool can also be used, though it tends to shed particles that can lodge in pores or corners. Damaged spots in this finish can be repaired easily by scraping the bad spot and/or wet sanding with some of the mix, depending on how bad the spot is. Then reapply more finish.

While this oil and varnish finish can't compete with the durability of a varnish or lacquer, it does meet some of the demands for a more durable oil finish.

Checkered Bowls

Reinterpreting in wood the designs of the American Indian

by Irving Fischman

After turning bowls for several years, I have recently begun to explore the classic designs used since antiquity in pottery and basket making. I am now particularly interested in the pottery and basketry of the Indians of the Americas. Simple shapes—such as truncated cones or bells—are used to counterpoint intricate painted or woven patterns. I have tried to reinterpret this design approach into a different medium, wood.

One bowl in particular has a simple bell or trumpet shape and a checkered pattern of teak and black walnut, woods that are richly contrasting. To make this bowl, familiarity with lathe work and a supply of clamps, both band and deep throated, are essential.

Basically, the bowl is made of three layers of wood. A 15 or 16-inch square of one-inch walnut forms the top layer of the bowl and an 11-inch square of two-inch teak forms the bottom. In between is a checkered ring of teak and walnut one inch thick. Both the top and bottom pieces should be

planed or sanded flat and cut into a disk shape.

To provide a means of attaching the faceplate, I glue a piece of 3/4-inch Baltic birch plywood directly to the bottom of the teak. No sheet of paper is used between them because the mass is so large that the paper might fail during turning. I use birch plywood because it is far stronger than either fir plywood or solid wood.

The checkered ring in the center of the bowl is not an inlay as first observation of the completed bowl might suggest. It is a separate layer composed of solid truncated-wedge-shaped pieces glued together to form a ring. This technique is much easier than inlaying on the curved surface of a turned bowl and the pattern can be seen on both sides of the bowl—in the manner of Indian baskets.

The ring has twenty-four pieces, the smallest number that I felt would have a pleasing visual effect. Larger numbers of pieces are possible, but the accuracy of the angles of the pieces becomes correspondingly more critical.

Bowls in various stages of construction are shown in a flow sequence.

With 24 pieces the base angle of the wedge is 82.5 degrees or 7.5 degrees from the vertical. If the outside edge of each wedge measures 1-7/8 inches, the ring will have a diameter of approximately 14 inches (from the formula circumference equals pi times diameter; the circumference in this case is 24 times 1-7/8 inches).

The wedges are cut from identical pieces of one-inch teak and walnut three inches wide by 27 inches long. In cutting the wedges on the table saw, the blade is kept vertical and the cross cut guide is set at 82.5 degrees. First, the end of the board is trimmed to this angle. Then the board is flipped over and the 1-7/8-inch base length is marked on the edge. This is used to set the distance between the fence and the blade. Because the crosscut guide is on the opposite side of the blade from the fence, using a fence for measuring each subsequent piece would cause the blade to bind. Therefore, we actually measure to a short hardwood block clamped at the front of the fence, which acts as a distance marker. Now we cut 12

identical pieces each of teak and walnut, flipping the board after each pass to get the wedge shape.

If the angle has been set correctly, the 24 pieces should form a perfect ring. This can be checked by clamping the pieces dry with the band clamp. Slight errors can be corrected by sanding.

Alternating the teak and walnut blocks, glue is applied to their edges and a belt clamp tightened around them. (A tourniquet could be used instead.) I simultaneously clamp the whole ring between two disks of 1/2 or 3/4-inch plywood, protected with wax paper, to assure that the ring is flat. I use yellow glue (aliphatic resin) throughout because it hardens and is stronger than white glue. Plastic resin, resorcinol, or casein are other possibilities. After allowing the glue to dry thoroughly, the ring is removed and touched with a sander or plane to make sure it is flat.

It should be noted we are gluing end grain which is not especially strong. However the ring will be glued between two

Approximate cross section of bowl showing placement of the layers. Bowls are turned by eye without templates.

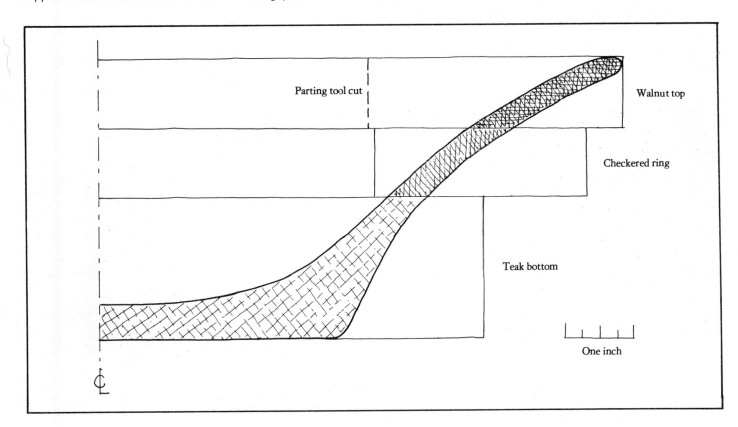

Parting tool cut

Walnut top

Checkered ring

Teak bottom

One inch

135

Truncated segments are cut with the cross-cut guide set at 82.5 degrees for 24-piece ring. Block clamped to rip fence safely eliminates need for measuring each piece.

Tourniquet clamp holds glued segments together while two plywood disks protected by waxed paper are clamped to hold checkered ring flat between them.

Checkered ring is touched with sander to make sure it's flat; then it's glued between the two-inch teak base block and the one-inch walnut board that will form the top rim.

solid layers and we have the advantage of not turning end grain.

The entire turning block can now be assembled. The teak base (with birch plywood block already attached), checkered ring, and walnut top are glued together and clamped using many clamps to assure good contact. Concentric alignment is important and either circles or crossed diameter lines drawn on the blocks will help. The block is allowed to sit one or two days to assure that the glue in the interior is dry.

A faceplate is now attached to the birch plywood on the completed turning block. Because of its large size, the block must be mounted securely on the outboard side of the lathe. I use a heavy duty lathe with four speeds—600 and 1200 rpm for faceplate turning—2400 and 3600 rpm for spindle turning. The handrest is mounted on a moveable tripod.

With the lathe at its lowest speed, a heavy scraper is used to round the walnut top disk, both for balance and to determine the final dimension of the bowl. Then a gouge is employed to rough the outside shape. Starting at the bottom, material is removed from each of the three layers until there are no gaps between the layers and the tool cuts solid material throughout its path. Keep in mind that the three layers will cut differently—the easiest is the teak and the hardest the walnut. Also, teak is notorious for dulling tools and frequent sharpening and honing will be necessary. Final outside shaping is accomplished with a scraper, taking very light cuts. Any small tool can be used to apply the radius on the bottom edge.

At this point I usually sand the outside of the bowl completely since I can apply as much pressure as I like to the still solid block. In other words, I don't tackle the inside until the outside is completely finished.

The inside of the bowl is tackled with the handrest facing the top of the bowl. First I remove with a parting tool a central disk of walnut eight inches in diameter. This disk

Outside of bowl is turned and finished first with lathe set at low, 600 rpms. Top walnut board gives the bowl stability during this stage. The handrest is on a moveable tripod.

matches the hole in the checkered ring and has not been removed until now to assure rigidity during both the gluing and the outside turning process. Because the parting tool is not coming in from the side, be sure to widen the groove that it makes so that it doesn't get caught. When the cut is completed, the central disk is easily removed.

Now I usually remove some material from the center of the bowl, so that the handrest can be moved in to act as guide for roughing out the inside. I prefer the scraper for this operation so there is no chance of the tool catching in the wood.

The bowl takes shape very quickly now. The sides, completed first, are made parallel to the outside and between 1/4 and 3/16-inches thick. Don't make the sides any thinner or stability becomes a problem with these laminated bowls. The sides taper slightly at the rim and gradually increase in thickness at the base. A higher lathe speed should be used to finish the bottom. The bottom is left between 3/8 and 1/2 inches thick to give the bowl a solid feel.

The interior and rim of the bowl are now sanded. Teak sands very nicely, and I use only grits 60 to 120, wetting the surface occasionally to bring up the grain. The entire bowl can now be burnished with a clean rag if desired.

The completed bowl is split from the Baltic birch backing and the bottom is hand planed or sanded flat. Finally, I prefer to give the bowl a rich oil finish, but a glossier finish can be tried.

The finished bowl takes five hours to complete and about $10 in materials. The present design can readily be seen as a jumping off point for many variations. Contrasting veneers could be placed between the layers to form stripes in the finished bowl. Different numbers of pieces and different woods could create other patterns.

However, I feel that the basic design approach—using a simple shape to compliment intricate patterns—is essential to a satisfactory finished product.

Thickness of bottom is measured and kept between 3/8 and 1/2 inches to give bowl a solid feel. Use a higher lathe speed for bottom. Author sells the bowls for about $80.

Inside of the bowl is now turned and completed. Sides are turned first parallel to the outside and no less than 1/4 to 3/16 inches thick in the interest of stability.

Once outside is completed, a parting tool is used to cut the central disk from the walnut top. Widen the groove so the tool doesn't get caught.

When cut is completely through, centrifugal force holds disk in place until lathe is stopped. The disk should be made smaller than the inside of checkered ring.

The Bowl Gouge

Using long-and-strong tools to turn the outside

by Peter Child

Woodturning gouges are of three types: one designed for bowls, one for between-center coving and small rounds, and one for roughing square stock to cylinders and sweeping curves, also between centers.

The blade of a bowl gouge is always "long and strong," meaning heavy duty. A good new one measures 12 in. from cutting edge to tang. It has a deep U-shaped flute with much meatier metal at the bottom, or keel, of the flute than at its two wings. Bevel angle varies with how tall a person the turner is, but it is always less than 45 degrees, although not so small as to make the edge fragile. There is no second bevel as in a bench chisel or plane iron, and there is no point. The edge is shaped square across.

Four sizes of bowl gouges are in current production: 1/4 in., 3/8 in., 1/2 in. and 3/4 in., ranging in weight from 4 to 16 ounces. Each size has a particular function. The 3/4-inch is absolutely the largest that can be used correctly; any bigger gouge is not a bowl gouge, however long and strong it may look. The heavy-duty handles should be about a foot long, and hefty—weight and length are necessary for control. This is why bowls should be turned outboard and should not be attempted between centers, where the lathe bed restricts movement of the gouge.

Coving gouges, for between-center work, are of medium strength and have a longer bevel and a lighter handle than bowl gouges. They also have pointed, "lady fingernail" noses

---

Peter Child, author of The Craftsman Woodturner, *operates a full-time turnery and for the past dozen years has taught turning at his studio in England.*

and a much shallower flute. Common sizes range from 1/4 in. up to 3/4 in. The roughing-down gouge serves for larger work.

Roughing-down gouges are of medium strength, deeply throated, semicircular rather than U-shaped in cross section, beveled at 45 degrees, and of even thickness. Their lack of keel makes them unsuitable for bowl work, whatever the size. They range from 3/4 in. up to 1-1/2 in.

Depending on the mood of the factory grinder, the bevel of a new tool can be any angle or length at all, and so the purchaser will have to reshape it. Any point must be removed so the edge is straight across. The bevel should be hollow ground right up to the cutting edge, without a second bevel. A skilled operator can thus provide himself, straight from the grindstone, with an edge that has a fine sawtooth cutting burr. Such an edge would horrify a cabinetmaker or carver, but it is most practical for a turner as it can be resharpened in seconds on the grindstone. An absolutely flat bevel does the same job as one hollow ground, but takes longer to obtain and maintain with a flat stone. Although the final result will be much sharper than the sawtooth edge, it may not last long enough to merit the time and care taken to obtain it. Also, with a stone it is very easy to round the bevel, exactly opposite to hollow ground. The slightest belly is intolerable since it causes the tools to lose most of their usefulness.

When cutting, the whole length of the bevel is in full contact with the wood. Take a piece of wood and hold it in the bench vise. Use the gouge to make a groove in the wood, as though starting a carving. In controlling the cut there

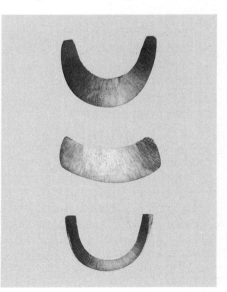

The different sizes of bowl gouges corresponding to cabinetmaker's planes are shown below. From the right, the 3/4-in. gouge is equivalent to a scrub plane, the 1/2-in. and 3/8-in. are jack and smooth planes, the 1/4-in. is a block plane for cleaning up end grain. A turner with a new set should start by grinding all the bevels to the angle of the 1/2-in. tool, second from right. To try your hand without investing in a whole set, choose the 3/8-in. or 1/2-in. gouge. At right, starting from the top, head-on views of the three kinds of turning gouges, all at 3/4 in. Bowl gouge is ground square across; spindle or coving gouge is ground to a pointed nose; roughing-down gouge at bottom is ground square across.

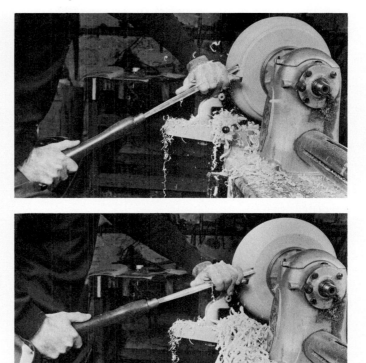

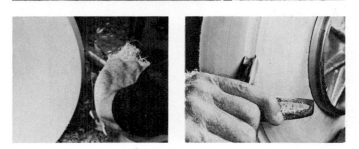

Child slices curls of wood from the rotating disc. Proper gouge work depends upon correct stance, hand position and coordination of eye, hand and leg. With the bevel always rubbing (bottom middle photo) the trick is to roll the tool over in the direction of the cut, while lifting the handle straight up. The cut begins at 12 o'clock high (left) and slices a downward arc to three o'clock (top and middle right). He watches the progress of the cut at the silhouette at the top of the whirling disc. His right hand rolls and slides the

handle up the thigh; his right leg supports and powers the thrust of the tool, his left palm presses firmly on the rest, the thumb pushing the blade and the fingers curled around and controlling it. The shaving is narrow at the start and broad at the end, but its thickness does not change. At bottom right, the gouge digs in. The wing away from the direction of cut, here the left wing, has been allowed to touch the wood. It scores a deepening ring in the bowl, ending in a sharp tear, startling the operator out of his careless stupor.

should be no space between the bevel and the wood. Now try to make a similar groove with the bevel not in contact, holding the handle more or less upright. It will be almost impossible. A gouge can remove wood without the bevel rubbing and without conscious effort, but only because the power of an electric motor is scraping it off. Only with the full bevel rubbing is it possible to take clean cuts.

There are two main methods of turning a bowl. One is to screw the wood to the faceplate and turn the outside and base first, perhaps with a flange or lip, and then remove the wood, reverse it, and somehow reposition it on the faceplate to turn the inside. The other way, my method, is to flatten and sand the bottom of the blank first, then fix the base to the faceplate and turn the outside and inside in one operation. There is a little more cutting against the grain, but the troublesome end grain is the same in either case. And I am saved the tricky problem of getting the bowl back onto the lathe in exactly the right place, since I never take it off.

Let us move to the lathe to cut the outside of a bowl with

the long-and-strong gouge. The blank is sawed to a disc, screwed to a faceplate and mounted outboard. The tool rest is parallel to the axis of rotation, set about center. The height of the rest is adjusted according to the height of the operator, so that the gouge cuts at the center of the disc or slightly above center. (We assume the operator is right-handed and cutting from left to right, from the face of the disc toward the faceplate.)

Every cut has to be fully under control from beginning to end. The operator has to stand centrally behind the gouge, with its handle upright. He cannot see the bevel. With the blade on the rest, the heel of the bevel rubs the revolving wood. The cutting edge is not yet touching the wood.

Keeping the blade on the rest, he gradually lifts the handle straight up until a thin shaving appears at the center of the U-shaped channel. This indicates that the whole bevel is rubbing, without the turner having to move to one side to look. At this stage, the blade will be in contact with the front, not the top of the tool rest.

The left hand holds the blade close to its cutting edge and on the rest, palm over the blade, first and second fingers curled around it, and thumb, if not curled around, then pushing against the side of the blade. This hand does not move for the duration of any one cut—the fingers may move slightly at the end of the cut, but the palm remains where it is. The right hand holds the long handle very close to the bottom in a tennis or hammer grip.

The shearing cut of the gouge starts at the top (12 o'clock high), coming down in an arc to finish at 3 o'clock. The first cut is started about 1/2 in. from the right-hand edge of the disc and removes wood from left to right toward the faceplate.

The shaving is removed first by the center of the blade, then, progressively, by its right-hand edge or wing, so that only half the cutting edge is occupied. To do this the turner rolls the blade over to the right and at the same time lifts the handle straight up. This coordination has to be learned and the way to do it is to start a thin shaving with the center of the gouge and keep the shaving at the same depth for the duration of the cut. If the blade is rolled too much the shaving will finish thicker than it started. If the handle is not lifted, the cut will be straight across and not in a downward shearing arc, which is the best cutting action. Do not attempt to remove too much wood with one cut—a cut that traverses a half inch at a time is ample for practice, and this should be done again and again, keeping the shavings the same thickness throughout.

Sometimes the gouge digs in, a startling and unpleasant jump that leaves an unsightly gash in the wood. All sorts of circumstances can lead up to this shock—bevel not rubbing, gouge out of control due to incorrect holding or wrong position, blade not sharp, or overcutting. What actually happens is that the unwitting operator allows the blade to roll in the wrong direction, from right to left, and the left wing of the blade comes into contact with the wood. This is what digs in.

To avoid this, I emphasize rolling and lifting the gouge and using its center and right wing only. This motion keeps the left half of the blade away from the wood and out of harm's way. This "wrong half" is the only cause of a dig-in.

Time and again I am puzzled at seeing an operator standing in one position, albeit a correct one, and endeavoring to traverse more and more wood with each cut. To keep the blade cutting he has to roll it over more, move his hand along the rest (incorrect), and lift the handle uncomfortably high. This is overcutting, an awkward motion which can easily lead to a disastrous dig-in. I now firmly believe this mistake is a result of training, probably in other crafts. Consider a cabinetmaker hand planing at his bench. He stands still. Likewise a woodcarver and a potter with his clay. But to keep constant control of a gouge, a turner seldom stands still for long.

After a disc has assumed a distinct rounding, say from half of full thickness to almost the faceplate diameter, try the following. Take an even cut from full disc thickness toward the right. The gouge will tend to come off the cut after about 1/2 in. of travel. Do not force it to cut further, but move your feet a little to the right and take up the cut from where you left off. You should find absolute control in cutting, and a comfortable action. Remember that each cut is still from 12 noon to 3 o'clock. The bowl might look a little ridged, but

not much. A practiced turner can do the whole area from middle thickness to faceplate in one or two sweeping cuts, but his feet are continuously moving him sideways to the right. The majority of bowl turning is done by body and legs, not hands alone.

The normal stance of a right-handed operator is left leg in front of right, with the right hand holding and providing thrust to the gouge. To make a smooth and even cut over wood containing end grain, hard and soft areas and perhaps knots can be quite difficult. The blade may skip over a hard area, then plunge too deeply into the soft.

Try this. Stand directly behind the gouge in the correct position, but reverse your legs so that the knee or mid-thigh of the right leg touches the end of the handle. It will feel most peculiar at first. Take a cut, but with the handle not quite in contact with the leg. Next, take a cut with the handle butt touching your leg and either raise your heel to lift the handle, or slide it up your thigh. The handle is always lifted straight up, not sideways, so the leg can support the tool over the full cut. Turners use this leg action to control depth of cut, whatever the terrain, and as a third hand or power source to remove large shavings in minimum time. The 3/4-in. gouge cannot be used to full capacity with the hands alone, unless one has the mighty thews of a blacksmith.

While the left wing of the blade must be kept away from the wood to avoid dig-in, no harm will result if the gouge is rolled so far that the whole right wing is cutting. Try having the bevel rubbing, but not cutting, and rolling the tool to the right over the whole working area. Repeat the exercise, but deliberately look away from the blade—don't watch what you are doing. This should convince you that nothing untoward will happen, and will give confidence to an otherwise apprehensive and tense approach. Now start a cut, looking at the blade, and immediately transfer your gaze to the top of the disc. A suitably placed lamp will help. You will be able to see the effect of the cut without looking at the cutting edge. The coordination of roll and lift, so difficult for beginners, is automatically simplified when the eyes transfer information directly to the hands. If the gouge is rolled over too far, the cut will immediately thicken and you will see it happen at the top of the disc. Your eyes will send a correction directly to your hands. As a bonus, you can govern the shape of the bowl much more easily. By starting each cut just before the finish of the previous one, you can reduce and practically eliminate ridging. The gouge does the work almost alone.

A basic woodturning principle is that all cuts are made from large diameter to small, and never going uphill from small diameter to large. Too deep a practice cut can lead into this, so watch it.

Up to now we have assumed the turner is right-handed, and most technical writing ignores the hapless left-hander, who must mentally reverse all the directions. But when a bowl bellies out in the middle so one has to work both right to left and left to right to keep working toward the smaller diameter, then a right-hander must also learn to switch directions and hands. If he doesn't, the fingers are pulling the blade and it can easily roll back the wrong way and dig in. A gouge blade should always be pushed, never pulled, and the hand that is doing the pushing has the opposite leg supporting the handle. I always tell my right-handed pupils they will be better turners when they learn to do it left-handed and I am nearly always proved right.

Natural stains

All my stains are made from natural materials—nuts, wood and plants. They are very true in color. First you must gather material for the color you desire. The dry husks of black walnut shells give a deep brown tone. Dry beechnut husks make a deep yellow tan, plug tobacco an antique yellow, red swamp cedar chips a reddish-brown. I have used other nuts and woods; I suggest experimenting with whatever is available to you. My mother, part Indian, suggested many natural matrials to use for stains, and so was a great help in my search. The Indians used a homemade lye, but I found an easier answer—non-sudsing ammonia.

Place the materials to be leached in a jar, pour in the ammonia until the material is covered, and let sit. Black walnuts absorb the liquid, so it may be necessary to add more ammonia to keep the husks saturated. How long you soak the material affects the deepness of the color. Tobacco leaches out in a week. Black walnut shells still have color after a month and can sometimes be washed and used for a second batch.

After the tone is right, strain the juice off through a nylon stocking into a clean jar. (Don't use cans, because they will rust.) Leave the jar open for several days until most of the ammonia smell has dissipated. It can be used right away, but is strong-smelling! For a lighter tone, dilute with water; for a darker stain, let the liquid evaporate. Because the stain is water-based, the wood will need light rubbing after application. The stain works well under oil or varnish finishes.

Be sure to use non-sudsing ammonia. Sudsing ammonia will carry the color to the top with the suds.

—*C.H. Dimmick, Sparta, N.J.*

Cutting circles

A good method for cutting perfect circles on a band saw: Take a strip of plywood or chipboard about a foot wide and several feet long. Divide it lengthwise in a line. Lay it on the band-saw table and cut a slot from one edge to the center line. Along the line from the slot, mark off the radii of the circles you wish to cut and drill pilot holes. Countersink these holes on the back of the board and insert a wood screw in any hole. Mark the screw, remove it and grind it so only a point protrudes. Now you can put the screw in the appropriate

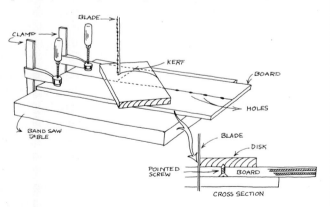

hole, clamp the board to the band saw table, and pivot the blank you wish to cut on the protruding point. You can finish the edge of the circle with a similar setup on a disc or belt sander.

—*Larry Green, Bethel, Conn.*

Bowl Turning

On the inside

by Peter Child

It is preferable to turn the outside of a bowl until it is ready to finish-sand before removing any wood from the inside. This should prevent troublesome vibration. Then, starting on the inside, there are three main problems facing the amateur:
• the outward thrust of the whirling wood on the gouge;
• starting a cut exactly where wanted without the risk of any sideways "kick," which if not expertly controlled can ruin the work, especially at or near the rim of the bowl;
• two inside areas that have perforce to be cut against the grain and thus can tear out.

The long-and-strong bowl gouge at work on the outside of a bowl shears an arcing cut from hour hand 12 noon to 3 p.m. or to 9 a.m. depending on which way we are going. It should follow that the same action would be correct when taking out the waste from inside the bowl.

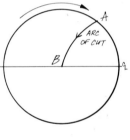

However, doing it this way actually invites a dig-in because whirling wood tends to throw the gouge blade over onto its back. The trailing edge and wing (the right-hand half of the blade) contact the wood and damage is inevitable. Without starting the lathe, place the gouge blade, bevel rubbing, at point A. Rotate the disc toward you slowly by hand and at the same time try to travel (bevel in contact but not cutting) from A to B. The wood surface pushes the blade back over to its right-hand edge, and the effect is more pronounced the nearer the blade gets to point B.

To start the cut correctly, set the rest below the center of the disc. With the gouge handle only slightly down from horizontal, the cutting edge can enter at A, the same height as the center of the bowl B. For small bowls—up to 7-in. diameter—entry near the outside rim is fine, and the cutting arc is slight. In large diameters, entry can be made anywhere along the straight line A to B. The gouge will enter quite easily an inch out from B, and successive cuts can be

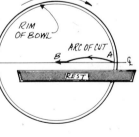

taken until point A is reached. However, the farther away from B, the more skittish the gouge will behave, and the more difficult it will be to start cutting exactly where wanted. In large bowls the arc of the cut ends before B is reached and the cut finishes in line with and across to B. Cutting from above and down to B can cause trouble.

I will now give a simple instruction. Place the gouge blade

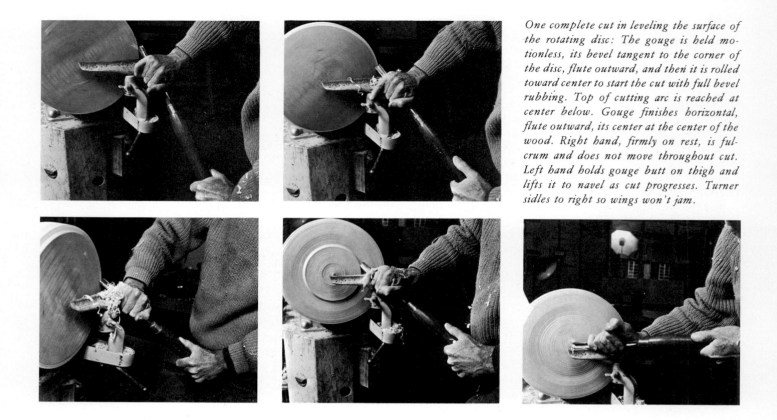

on its side, flute facing towards center, handle only just downward from horizontal. Push the blade in and start the cut. There appears to be no reason why this should not work every time, and the instruction surely could not be made any plainer. Sadly, the majority of my pupils disagree. So I have had to analyze why. First, the front surface of the disc may not be quite flat so it wobbles in rotation, and the unevenness can knock the gouge away from the desired route. So we will level it from outside to center.

A 1/2-in. gouge is held on the rest, handle almost perpendicular, edge at disc center height, distanced a little way outside the rim of revolving wood, and with flute facing outward. The handle is pulled slightly forward towards the body so that the full bevel of the blade will make contact with wood as soon as the cut starts. The blade is rolled over to the left and makes cutting contact with the wood while rolling. This forward roll of the blade is what provides control. Then the handle is lifted sideways to the right to continue a light cut to center. The rolling action can be stopped else the cut become too thick, and just enough forward pressure is used to keep the cutting edge traveling smoothly to center. If the full distance cannot be accomplished in one sweep, start where you leave off, and begin again. This is the quickest and cleanest way of flattening any disc, including tabletops.

Even with the front surface nicely flat some will still not be able to enter the wood on target—the first attempt sends the blade outward into limbo, or at best, along a crazy path in the wood surface. If this happens the turner must smooth it before trying again. Otherwise the blade can find the path again and really go crazy.

There is an easy way out which I do not recommend, but it can be a start and may lead to increased confidence, and then

Peter Child, English master turner, continues the discussion begun in Fine Woodworking, Winter '76 *of using long-and-strong bowl gouges.*

a determination to succeed. Use a 1/4-in. parting tool horizontally at a scraping angle to put a groove or notch into the wood at the site of proposed entry. Only a very shallow groove is required. Then hold the gouge blade, handle just down from horizontal, flute facing toward center, and cut. The groove will hold the blade and there will be no sideways "kick." When this has been proved, discard the parting tool and try a slight vee-cut made with any suitably shaped scraper. Even this should be enough to stop the blade from slipping outward. Now try the proper method. Present the blade as described and push it slowly forward so that it just contacts and rubs the wood. Hold this position for a few seconds, then slowly but firmly push the blade into the wood.

The square-nosed, deep-fluted, long-and-strong bowl-turning gouge is the most difficult tool to master, but when mastery is fully achieved the tool is a joy to use and well worth the effort. After the many years in which the woodturner's hook tools were in use, the comparatively modern cutting gouge has been so thoroughly developed that it can do its job by itself with the minimum of guidance by its user—if the user knows what to do!

It will be obvious by now that only half a gouge blade can be used at any time, which half depending on whether the cut is from right or left. The inside of a bowl can only be cut from right to left, using only the center (where the point would be in a spindle gouge) and the left-hand wing. The best cutting action is a roll from center to engage part or all of the left-hand wing.

To simplify matters we will dispense with the rolling action at first. Start a cut as described. If the blade is just pushed straight forward without any sideways movement of the handle, then all the left-hand wing will enter the wood and jam. In order to use the left-hand edge to full effect, the extreme end of the left-hand wing must be kept just clear of the wood, and to do this the handle has to be moved progressively over to the right. At entry the bevel is not in contact with the

See page 138

Starting a cut: Gouge just contacts wood, with left-hand corner of blade clear to avoid a dig-in. The bevel, center, as yet has no support from the wood, so the tool must be held very firmly and pushed straight in to start its arc toward the center.

wood, but the sideways movement puts it in contact and then the blade cuts more or less cleanly. Cutting thus, in a straight line from A to B and ending up with the center B in the bottom of the flute, is the first step in using the gouge properly.

More than just "hand-power" is needed to use a heavy-duty gouge to its full capacity. The right-hander will naturally have the palm of his left hand on the rest, with any unrestricted fingers curled over the blade. The nearer the hand to the cutting edge, the more control is gained. Therefore, he has only the grip of his fingers to prevent the gouge from ripping outward, especially at the starting cut. The left-hander is much better placed, as he naturally has the palm of his right hand behind the blade.

The correct position is:
● right hand on the rest behind the blade with what fingers that can do so curled around it, and thumb possibly against the barrel of the blade;
● left leg in front of right, right leg back with knee bent, so that pressure can be exerted by the left leg to provide the "push-power" for the cut.

In action, the right hand is a pivot for the blade (the palm does not move during any one cut). The butt of the handle is held on the left leg, and the left hand holds it at the very end in a hammer grip. With both blade and handle held firmly, the only way a cut can be made is with a sideways swing of the hips. The cut is a scoop.

Looking down on the work, A to B is the distance traveled by the handle in a complete cut from rim to center. In a small bowl, this is insignificant but in a 12-in. bowl the handle has to travel quite a way, and you are holding it.

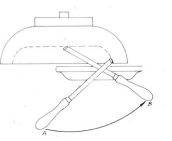

A professional turner is mobile, and walks the distance A to B with the gouge cutting its way continuously from rim to center. The handle never leaves the body, which provides the power. An amateur can start a cut as described, swinging to the right as far as is comfortable without actually falling over, stop the cut, step a little way to the right, continue the cut, and so on, in several stages. Depending upon the height of the lathe and the turner's height and leg-length, the handle can be on the leg, rising to the upper thigh, into the groin, and possibly ending up on the rib cage when the cut is completed at dead center.

Gouge nears completion of cut, top, coming down toward center line before horizontal push to center itself. Close-up shows full left half of blade cutting, but tip of wing is clear.

Turner fails to shuffle to right, and left corner of gouge enters wood, causing a jamming ridge.

143

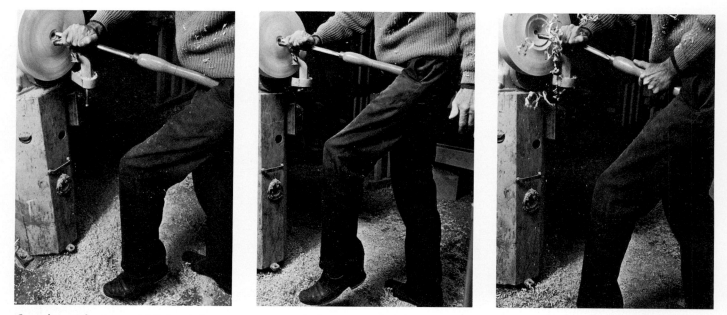

Cut taken without use of left hand demonstrates proper body control. With right hand as stationary pivot, power comes from thigh as left foot lifts entirely off floor. Photo at right shows full-power cut:

Left leg provides lift, while left hand governs forward roll of tool. Palm of right hand does not move, but turner swings to right to keep blade cutting without jamming.

There is a second method of removing the waste from the inside of a bowl, one that many amateurs might prefer. Take a disc, say, 3 in. thick, and before mounting it on the lathe, drill a hole in the center about 1 in. in diameter and 2-1/2 in. deep, thereby removing the core of the center so that waste can be removed progressively from hole to rim. When starting the first few cuts from the side of the hole, the amateur can try an experiment that may prove the importance of body control. The gouge is presented to the right side of the hole, the flute facing left, the handle held against the left leg slightly down from horizontal, with the right leg behind the left, and the right knee bent.

The test is to be able to take the first couple of cuts without any help from the left hand. The left leg pushes the gouge into the wood and the body swings over to the right so that the blade travels to center through the pivot of the right hand. It will be found necessary to raise the heel of the left foot off the ground to lift the handle, and after the first two cuts, the entire left foot has to leave the ground and you resemble the stork. However, in successive cuts, instead of the left foot leaving the ground, the left hand is used only to lift and roll the gouge, and the leg and body power the cut.

The perfect gouge cut is a rolling action of the blade from left to right using only the left-hand wing of the gouge and swinging over to the right so the tip of the left-hand wing is just out of the cut. This shearing action is kind to the two areas of wood where we have to cut against the grain. Any other cut or scrape can wreak havoc in these areas and no amount of sanding will completely remedy the damage.

Try placing the blade into a cut with the middle just in contact and the right-hand wing backed over just short of dig-in contact. Then roll the blade over to the left to engage the center and left-hand wing. This push-roll towards the middle counters the outward thrust and a much better cut is obtained than by merely pushing the gouge towards center without any roll.

Thousands of words have been published for and against using scrapers in turning. Those in favor say that in comparison to gouges, which are difficult tools and can be dangerous,

scrapers are easy to handle and with careful use can achieve the same results. Those against maintain that the best finish is a cut finish and scrapers are just not needed. The truth, as usual, falls between.

When a bowl has been cut and fashioned to such a degree of finish that it does not need any scraping—then, and only then, should a scraper be used. A good cut finish is improved by scraping. A bad finish can easily be made worse. Only the minimum of wood should be removed by scraping. A scraper should be used as a finisher—not as a wood remover.

The scraper tends to bounce back and forth as the bowl revolves and different surfaces—end grain, quick-growth areas, knots—come round and have to be dealt with at speed. Every bounce of the tool can inflict slight damage, especially to the two end-grain areas. The bounce can be overcome by forcing the scraper into closer contact with the wood but the damage caused by this viciousness is much worse.

For maximum control, a scraper has to be of heavy thick metal, with a blunt angle bevel (almost none at all), and equipped with a long handle so that, like the gouge, the hands hold the tool but the body does the work. Unlike the gouge, the scraper bevel must not come into contact with the wood. The edge must be kept sharp, either by honing or straight from the grindstone. Since the edge can be blunted in two or three strokes, depending on the type of wood, I prefer the grindstone method of sharpening as it is quick.

The scraper blade is held firmly down on the rest and the handle tucked into the side of the body. Imagine that the wood surface consists of peaks and valleys. The scraper should remove only the peaks without touching the valleys. This minimizes bounce.

However sharp the tool, it is still a scraping edge, not a cutting one, so the wood fibers are laid over in one direction. All my lathes have reverse switches so I can scrape both ways.

To finish up, I find the best abrasive paper is open-coated garnet, of the "finishing" variety. The "cabinet" grade is much too stiff. I use two grits, 100 followed by 150. Very rarely I might use 220, but nothing finer. With reverse, I can sand the bowl both ways.

Split Turnings

Using green logs to turn a camel

by John Kelsey

Although it is one of the oldest machines used by man, the lathe is fixed in our minds as a device for making bowls and cylinders. But it is also a multi-purpose machine for making parts of infinite variety — a general-purpose tool whose product is a means to an end rather than an end in itself. If one can visualize a cross-section, one can generate that form in three dimensions by turning. And then one can cut the turning anywhere at all to get an entirely new shape.

Here I will describe the turning of a rocking camel large enough for several children or adults to ride. This project requires a good-sized lathe, a bandsaw or a chainsaw, and hand tools. The materials were a station-wagon load of walnut branches scavenged from an abandoned farm where veneer cutters had removed the boles, one four-foot by five-foot sheet of ¾-inch solid birch plywood and some ¾-inch dowels. The beast was turned from the walnut; the plywood and dowels hold it together.

These methods could be used to make herds of camels or a menagerie of cows, horses, ostriches and giraffes. Indeed, any animal seems possible. But the point is to illustrate an approach to the lathe, using it to turn sculptural parts between spindles. The byproduct is a large toy to delight little children that doesn't cost much money.

I think camels are my favorite animal but I chose one here because my daughter had asked for a two-seater rocking horse. I had access to a large file of photographs of camels in various poses at the local newspaper library. A superb source of animal anatomy is the book *How to Draw Animals* by Jack Hamm (Grosset and Dunlap, New York, 1969, paper, $3.95).

From the photos I blocked out the forms that would be

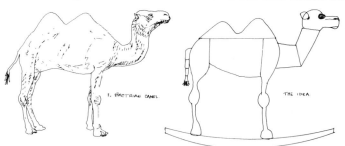

needed. Including the rockers and such details as eyes, ears, tail, the entire camel consists of just ten turned forms; eight or nine could have done it. So much anatomy from so few turnings meant most of them would be cut into two or more parts. This also provides the key to preventing green logs from checking and a way of holding the parts together: fox-wedged dowels pass through a plywood keel or centerboard running from head to tail and dividing the animal in half.

When a log dries it shrinks. Most of the shrinkage is at right angles to the annual rings, or radial, and around the rings, or

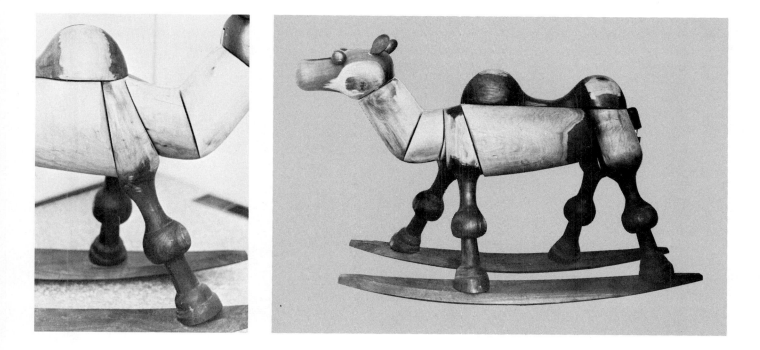

tangential. It checks because the circumference is three times as large as the diameter—as the rings of wood shrink, they try to squeeze the log smaller and can't. The stresses are relieved by wedge-shaped cracks radiating from the irreducible kernel that is the center of the annual rings. Splitting a log in half before it shrinks allows the stress to be distributed — the cut diameter merely cups as the circumference contracts, and the pieces generally remain intact.

When a tree is felled the exposed end grain dries very quickly and the logs check at the ends. But it takes years for drying to proceed far into a log, and slicing off the end exposes wet, intact material. When such a log is brought into a heated shop and turned, however, the protection of the bark is lost and a large proportion of end grain is exposed. It will check seriously overnight. To avoid trouble, a log should be completely worked in a single day. If it must be left overnight, wrap it in plastic with its own moist shavings, or bury it under a heap of shavings to keep it wet.

Before mangling any camel walnut, I turned a sketchy model at ¼ scale to be sure my conception was reasonable. I worked with photographs near the lathe in an attempt to capture the flavor of flesh in the solid wood. It seems neither reasonable nor desirable to try for realism, and few dimensions will be given here—it is cut-and-try to the scale of the maker's own body.

My largest walnut branch, for the camel's belly and rockers, was 14 inches in diameter including bark, and five feet long. It had a dog-leg crook. I wanted rockers between three and four feet long, so I cut off a chunk to use later for humps and grunted the rest up onto sawhorses. Green walnut weighs about 60 pounds per cubic foot. I use a large, logger's crosscut saw to buck the logs; a chainsaw would have done better and could also replace the bandsaw throughout the job.

I removed the bark with a hatchet and gauged the center by eye, taking into account the crook and aiming to get the largest possible cylinder at the midpoint. Fearing that such a great, uneven mass would not clear the ways of the lathe—a Crescent with a 7½-inch swing radius—and also afraid the log would break free and crush me, I began working it toward round with a power plane and an axe. A conventional center spur quickly tears itself a flat-bottomed hole in soft green stuff, so I use a three-pronged gadget with the usual cup or

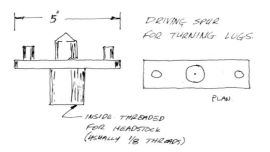

free-spinning tail center. One could also use a faceplate with large screws, but only if the end of the log is cut truly square to the axis of rotation.

I had never turned such a large log before, so I stood well clear when I switched on the machine. The entire lathe bucked and vibrated, but in a steady, rhythmic manner. The log showed no sign of breaking loose. The machine was bolted to the concrete floor, but it was loose on the bolts and this was just as well. If the bolts had been tight, the vibration surely would have cracked its castings. It is futile to try to

Turned log before it's cut to make belly and rockers

damp this kind of vibration unless one has an enormous lathe such as metal spinners use. Instead, I use a handrest mounted on the lathe ways, not a floor stand, so the hand and tool vibrate in phase with the lathe and log. Obviously, if the tool post fouls the log, one must resort to the floor stand. As soon as the log is cylindrical the vibration mostly ceases, unless the heart and sapwood vary greatly in density and are unevenly distributed through the mass.

Green wood is lovely to turn. I use a one-inch gouge and a large skew, at low speed. The walnut cuts cleanly and quickly —great curly shavings. Fresh surfaces are greenish-brown and turn dark after a few hours' exposure to light and air.

This log was turned to a cigar shape, finishing about twelve inches in diameter at the center and three inches at the ends, and 42 inches long plus an allowance for cutting away the holes left by the lathe centers. The silhouette of this cigar determines the rock of the animal — long and smooth or tight and quick. Any flats left from sloppy turning will be felt as bumps in the ride.

A thin, springy slat can be used as an approximate guide to curvature. I usually sand green turnings to 50-grit, pause for coffee to allow the outer layer of wood to dry a little, and sand to 120 or 150.

The diagram shows how this cigar was cut into four pieces:

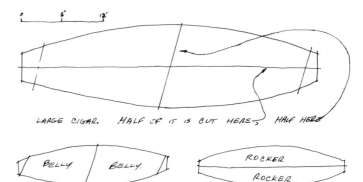

two long quarters for the rockers and two crosswise quarters for the belly. The handrest can be used as a pencil guide to lay out the lengthwise cuts before the log comes off the lathe, bearing in mind where the irregular swirl of the yellow sap and brown heartwood will appear in the end. Then I used four plywood squares with circular holes to make a cradle to guide the torpedo slowly through the bandsaw.

146

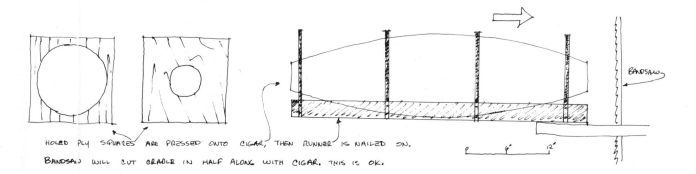

HOLED PLY SQUARES ARE PRESSED ONTO CIGAR, THEN RUNNER IS NAILED ON.
BANDSAW WILL CUT CRADLE IN HALF ALONG WITH CIGAR. THIS IS OK.

The long quarters that form the rockers could be left V-shaped at the top, and the animal's legs mortised to fit. I chose to cut them flat by tilting the bandsaw table to 45 degrees and clamping two small boards to the fence ahead of and behind the blade. This formed a guide trough against

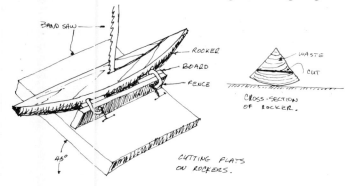

which the curve could run, passing the blade at uniform thickness. (One could make curved staves from turnings for large barrel shapes this way.)

The short quarters that form the belly were bandsawed crosswise, about 15 degrees from square. This angle determines the stride of the camel. The tail ends of these pieces were sawed at a similar angle, so the two sawed faces were approximately parallel, and a flat was planed on top where the humps would go. Most of these faces won't show

Camel is assembled as split turnings are attached to "back bone" of solid birch plywood using dowels and fox wedges.

on the finished beast and needn't be planed smooth. Or else the surfaces can be run over a jointer.

Before making the legs, I bandsawed the plywood to the rough shape of the camel, making sure it was oversize in every dimension, and traced the outline of the belly onto it. Then I drilled three holes for dowels and used the plywood as a template to drill matching holes two inches deep into each half of the belly. The easiest way is to clamp the walnut to the ply and drill through. Later the bottom of each hole would be widened in the direction of the grain for the fox wedges that

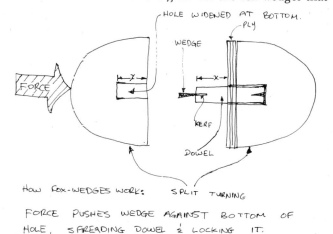

HOW FOX-WEDGES WORK: SPLIT TURNING

FORCE PUSHES WEDGE AGAINST BOTTOM OF HOLE, SPREADING DOWEL & LOCKING IT.

lock the construction together. But for now I used two of the holes to loosely pin the camel's body to the board.

A walnut branch seven inches in diameter and four feet long made a pair of camel legs, joined together at the shoulder. After roughing to a cylinder, I marked a section about a foot long at the center and worked down to a knee and foot at each end, as in the drawing. Then the legs were

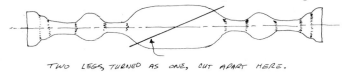

TWO LEGS, TURNED AS ONE, CUT APART HERE.

cut apart on the diagonal. This flat face butts against the centerboard. To make a clean joint with the belly, and also to loosen up the camel's canter, the front shoulders were cut again on the diagonal to make a second flat face at right

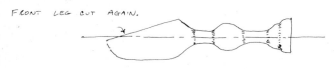

FRONT LEG CUT AGAIN.

angles to the first. The belly is narrow enough at the back to require no second cut on the rear shoulder.

The legs were pinned to each other through the centerboard, just like the body. But because they walk, one dowel from each must go into the opposite belly piece and this strengthens the construction. Although they weren't split in half, the legs haven't checked. I believe this is partly because they aren't very thick and partly because the center of the rings isn't the center of the turnings. Branches grow that way, with more wood on the bottom of a curve than on the top. Thus the center of the annual rings passes through the bulbous foot, knee and shoulder, but is cut away elsewhere. Constructions like this could also be turned with large tenons to fit holes ("circular mortises") like kitchen chairs.

I blocked the camel upright on two sawhorses until the rockers, held level in pieces of the cradle that had guided the large cigar through the bandsaw, could be slipped under the feet. Then, using a small block in the same way that one levels table legs, I marked a base line on each foot and cut them.

A single tapered cylinder made the neck, split in half lengthwise and pieced together to match on each side and form a bend. Dowels hold it together, as usual.

With this much made and loosely assembled, I traced around the walnut and bandsawed the plywood to size — leaving two inches sticking up from the neck to tenon the head on. A little chopping with an in-cannel gouge widened the holes for the wedged dowels. Large clamps forced the beast together. Then I turned the camel over, clamped the rockers into position, drilled through into the feet, countersunk for the heads, and drove six-inch lag screws home.

Saw, Surform and rasp cleaned up the discrepancies between the two sides. When the humps and tail were added, the plywood only showed along the back of the neck. It could have been hidden here too by cutting it undersize and filling the gap with a strip of solid wood.

There must be a million ways to cartoon an animal's head in solid wood. Found, green wood is cheap enough and soft enough to try several variations — on the lathe, you can almost model it like clay. I finally turned a ball with snout, cut a slice off the chin and pinned it back on again to form lips, added a few veiner cuts, and chiseled a deep V-groove for the nose which was one-quarter of a scrap turning. I used a dumbbell-shape for eyes, turned with the center of the rings on center for that spaced-out look, and pinned it into a gouged channel atop the nose. The ears were a small barrel turning with a tenon on each end, cut on the diagonal to make two and driven into holes. I planed the bottom of the

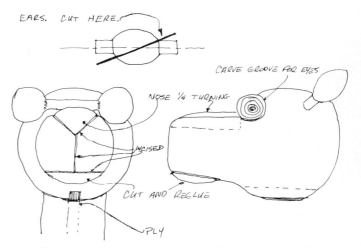

head flat to meet the neck, cut a slot for the ply and fastened it on with two vertical, wedged dowels.

The humps were the most difficult turning to work out. The problem was keeping enough height while paring the width so they would fit atop the body, and retaining a saddle between them. I made a large ball with a thick stem, split it into quarters and removed wedge-shaped pieces as in the

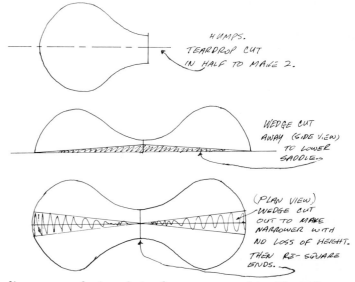

diagrams, and pinned the four parts together. The tail was easy — a cylinder cut in segments and drilled for a length of rope, knotted behind a dowel driven into the plywood. Then sandpaper and several quarts of Watco, and a happy child.

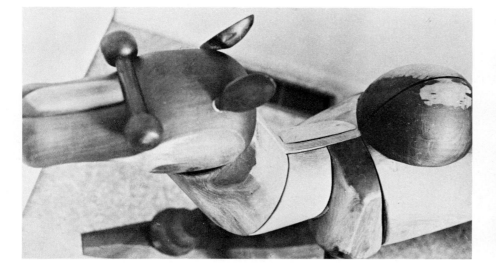

Author Kelsey astride his beast

148

Green Bowls

Turn unseasoned wood, dry it, then turn again

by Alan Stirt

A big problem in bowl turning is obtaining thick, wide, dry wood. You might be able to get 4-1/2 or 5-inch thick mahogany or 4-inch teak from an importer. In the Northeast you might find some 3 or 4-inch maple, birch or cherry at local mills. These planks usually contain numerous checks and splits. If they are sound, they will be more expensive than thinner material. If you want to turn a number of bowls, such sources will be quite frustrating in terms of cost and available species.

However, green (unseasoned) wood can readily be found and is often free. Even exotic woods are much cheaper when bought in the log. Working directly from the log gives you an opportunity to fit sizes and grain patterns to your own requirements, rather than accepting material that has been milled to a predetermined size. Green planks also offer advantages over dry wood. You can get larger sizes (the sawyer won't mind cutting extra-thick planks if he knows that *he* won't have to dry them), and the material will be in better condition.

In rural areas, logging waste — often containing the most figured wood — sawmill slabs and storm-damaged trees are usually free or sold cheaply. Firewood piles yield nice chunks of local hardwoods. Small local mills usually are glad to cut logs to whatever dimensions you want. Here in northern Vermont, mills charge $40 to $50 per 1,000 board feet for milling logs that you bring them. If you buy a log from the mill and have it cut, the cost is 20 to 30 cents per board foot. If the log is in good condition, such material is virtually check-free. Even in cities, green wood can be had from local tree-removal services and highway departments.

After you've found a supply of green wood, you have to dry it. One way is in planks or bowl-size blocks, but this is unlikely to produce perfect material. The easiest method is to turn the wood when it's green. Once the wood is in a bowl shape it dries much faster and with fewer defects than a solid chunk. You might start with a slab of lumber 4 or 6 inches thick, but if you turn the walls of the bowl down to an inch, it dries more like 4/4 stock. The analogy isn't exact because the grain orientation of the bowl isn't the same as that of milled lumber, but proper drying procedures minimize the differences. As the bowl dries it will warp and shrink, but once it is dry the walls are thick enough to be turned true again.

As an example of green turning, I'll show how to get a dry bowl from a green log of lignum vitae about 9 inches in diameter. It had been drying for about two years, but it was still quite wet. Similar procedures can be used for most hardwood species, both native and exotic.

First, cut about an inch off the end of the log to find check-free wood. If the log has been in the sun, it may be necessary to cut a series of thin slices to reach sound material. In some hardwoods small center checks run the whole length of the log, but these will be removed when trimming the block for the lathe. Next cut off a cross section as long as the diameter of the log, and rip this piece along the grain through the center of the log. If there are any center checks, make this second cut parallel to them and the saw kerf will often obliterate them. It is important to make sure the center of the tree —the pith—does not end up in your bowl as it will almost certainly split. Note any other checks and defects and plan your cuts to eliminate them from the final shape. Next, flatten the outside of each slab. This will be the bottom of the bowl. The flat surface will make the block safe to cut on the band saw. On the lignum vitae I roughly flattened the bottom with a 1-1/2-inch carving gouge, but these cuts can be made with a chain saw or a band saw. To cut down vibration and make turnings easier, I taper the sides of the block. I used the gouge but the easiest way is to saw a tapered circle. My band saw just doesn't have the capacity to make this cut.

The more you refine the shape with hand or power tools, the easier the initial turning will be. How far you go depends upon the size and species of your block of wood, the size and weight of your lathe, and your confidence and skill in using your tools. It's best to start with a balanced shape and discover how much unevenness you and your lathe can take. Even a small, out-of-balance piece can cause a lot of vibration.

First I turn the back of the bowl, with the face that was at the center of the log attached to the faceplate. Use long screws to grip the wet wood since the bowl will be absorbing a

Bowls turned from green wood by the author. Largest, 15 inches across, is of quilted, broad-leaf maple. Others (clockwise) are from zebrawood, white ash and cherry burl.

number of hard knocks in getting it true. Even if you don't usually wear a face shield when turning, it's important to wear one now. In the early stages chips will fly in all directions and some of them will be rather large.

Before turning on the lathe make sure the wood will not hit the ways or the tool rest. I start at a low speed and use a gouge, taking light cuts at first.

Don't try to decide the exact shape until all the rough spots are gone. Once the bowl is true, stop the lathe and carefully examine the wood. Note any defects which have to be removed, and interesting grain patterns to develop. The shape and the grain can be made to work together to create something more than just a bowl. On the lignum vitae bowl, I cut quite a bit off the bottom to ensure an interesting balance and pattern of heartwood and sapwood.

In shaping a bowl, I find the gouge to be the most efficient and enjoyable tool. The wood cuts cleanly and thick, curly shavings usually fly from it. Lignum vitae is an exception, preferring to come off as chips. Some woods, particularly butternut, are so soft and stringy when wet that they are hard to cut with anything but a gouge. A scraper just pushes the fibers around. To cut the straight foot, I use a 1/4-inch gouge with a slightly pointed nose.

When the contour of the bowl is done, flatten the bottom and make a pencil line to help reposition the faceplate.

Before remounting the bowl, I drill down to 1 inch from the bottom using a 1/2 or 1-inch bit. This gauges the depth and makes the gouge work easier. The faceplate can now be mounted on the bottom, using shorter screws because the wood will be running true. If you align two of the screws with the grain direction, the holes will probably remain in line during drying. Jot the screw size on the bowl for remounting later.

First I clean up the front, taking light cuts with the gouge. This can be a great help in reducing vibration, particularly if a chain saw was used to cut the log and the front is uneven. Now the bowl can be hollowed out. Because the wood is wet the tools stay cool and large amounts of wood can be removed before resharpening. I usually start at the center and work out toward the rim.

It's important to keep the thickness uniform throughout, so the bowl will dry evenly with less risk of checking. The thickness is very important in determining drying time, and a bowl turned down to 1/4 inch would dry very quickly with little chance of checking. However, it would distort more than a thicker bowl and when dry would be nearly impossible to turn truly round. For most native woods leave the walls and bottom about an inch thick. I gauge the thickness with calipers as the bowl nears completion, and examine it carefully for checks and knots. Checks present when the bowl is wet will get larger as it dries, and knots will often start checks that spread through the wood.

If you're satisfied with the condition of the wood, start the lathe and coat the bowl with a heavy layer of paste wax. I use Johnson's paste wax because it's cheap and I purchase it by the 12-pound case. Wax the bottom after removing the faceplate.

It's a good idea to rough-turn in an uninterrupted sequence. If you have to stop before the bowl is hollow, wax the wood to keep it from drying. I have had unwaxed pieces start checking in minutes in a heated shop.

Generally, the slower the drying the less risk of severe warping and checking; however, if the drying is too slow the wood may succumb to fungus and decay. And the slower the bowls dry, the more storage space the turner needs.

One controlling factor is the coating on the bowl. If left unsealed, the end grain will dry much faster than the rest. This can result in checking. Wax evens the drying rate and slows the whole process. So far I have used only paste wax. I'm sure any sealer that would adhere to wet wood would work to some extent. If I find that one layer of wax is not preventing checking I'll add more. The more layers of wax, the slower the drying and, up to a point, the less the chance of checking.

Each species of wood dries differently. In general, the higher the density of the wood, the longer it will take. But even within a single species the density can vary greatly. Sapwood will generally dry faster than heartwood and can cause extra distortion in bowls where both are present. Among domestic hardwoods, cherry and apple check easily while elm, walnut and butternut are excellent; in general, fruitwoods are more susceptible to checking than nutwoods. Ash may check within minutes.

This particular variety of lignum vitae proved to be very stable. Although I had to be very careful about checking, hardly any distortions occurred (by using many layers of wax and slow drying conditions I lost only one bowl out of 15 completed ones). These bowls I turned from 1/2-inch to 3/4-inch thick. I dry most native wood bowls, turned 1-inch thick, for about three months. I dried the lignum vitae bowls from six to twelve months, according to size and thickness.

You have great control over the drying environment, and the environment is crucial. Temperature, humidity and air circulation are the important factors. In the winter I never start bowls drying in a heated room. Usually I'll dry them in a spare room which stays around 45 or 50 degrees with moderate air circulation. After some weeks — the exact time depending upon the experience with wood of this species and grain formation — I move the bowls to a heated room.

A room which has good drying conditions during a period of high humidity can become an oven when the humidity drops sharply and stays down. Often the conditions can be changed just by opening a door, for increased circulation and faster drying, or closing it, to retard drying. If you want to be more scientific, you can outfit a room with temperature and humidity controls.

Once I found some 12 by 6-inch cherry bowls had checked during their first few days in my "normal" drying conditions. I dug out the checks with a gouge and rewaxed the bowls. Then I put them in my cellar which has high humidity. The bowls gradually dried without checking. However, they developed an unattractive blue-green stain from a fungus which thrives on high humidity. I completed the drying in a heated room and then finish-turned the bowls. The stain went deep into the end grain and was visible after finishing. I later dried the cherry in conditions that represented a compromise between my spare room and the cellar.

It pays to experiment with the facilities you have available; such experimentation should be a never-ending process. I have arrested checking by placing bowls in paper bags for a few weeks to choke off air circulation. Once you have an idea of the principles involved there are endless ways to deal with problems.

To determine when the bowls are at equilibrium with the

relative humidity and temperature of the surrounding air, weigh them periodically. When they stop losing weight they are dry. Under average conditions, most native woods rough-turned to a thickness of 1 inch will dry in about three months.

I should mention an alternative to the drying procedures I use. The green bowl can be soaked in a heated solution of PEG (polyethylene glycol 1000) before drying. The chemical replaces the water in the cells and prevents them from shrinking. I experimented with PEG a few years ago and was not satisfied with the results. The slight differences in appearance and finishing qualities mentioned by PEG's proponents were real differences to me. Also, I was having success with natural drying and saw no need to continue with PEG. It can be useful, however, because with it you can turn bowls that include the pith of the tree. I know one professional turner who's satisfied with the results and I'm sure there are more. For further information, contact the Forest Products Laboratory and Crane Creek Company, both in Madison, Wisconsin.

When your bowl is dry it can be finish-turned. First, plane the bottom flat. Before mounting, drill a hole to mark the finished depth. This will prevent turning through to the screws, which penetrate about 3/16 inch. I usually am able to use the same screw holes as in the rough turning, and I use the same length screw. Mount the bowl on the lathe and check to see that it clears the rest and the bed.

I true the outside first, with the lathe at low speed. I usually use a gouge but I found light cuts with a small round-nose scraper ideal for the lignum vitae, which is very hard when dry. A larger tool might have taken too big a bite and forced the bowl off the screws. I finished off the outside shape with a skew scraper.

At this point I usually sand the outside of the bowl. I turn most bowls relatively thin and when I am done hollowing, the walls vibrate. It's much easier to sand before hollowing, with little vibration. I start with 50 or 80 grit and work my way up to 220. I always wear a mask because the fine dust can be quite harmful.

Now I clean up the rim of the bowl with a gouge. Next I get the inside rim true and work my way down to the bottom, using a gouge and scraper. I advise against using the scraper on the sides of deep bowls because it can really make a mess of end grain. When I'm satisfied with the contours and thickness — measuring with calipers — I sand the inside of the bowl using the same grit sequence as on the outside. The bowl can now be hand-sanded, if desired, to remove circular scratches. Finish as you like.

The above procedures are only guidelines and can be adapted for almost any wood you'd care to turn. Exact methods of turning and drying should be worked out individually in one's own particular situation. I've had some failures and will have more in the future, but I've had a high rate of success. It is very satisfying to make a bowl when you control the whole process from log to finished form.

Before turning the back of a bowl cut from a green log (top photo), try to make it as round as possible. With the back turned, the faceplate is then attached to the foot, and the bowl is rough-turned. Then the whole bowl is liberally coated with paste wax (bottom photo) to control drying. When dry, the bowl is remounted and finish-turned.

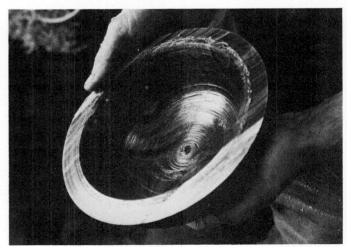

151

Patch-Pad Cutting

A basic method for cutting marquetry

by John N. Beck

The patch-pad method is one of several ways to cut and assemble wood veneers to form geometrical, floral or pictorial designs. The veneers are stacked between cardboard or plywood, and taped or tacked closed to form a "pad," which is then cut up with a jigsaw. This method has certain advantages. All the pieces are cut at once; and a single sawcut cuts the line between two adjacent pieces. (In some other methods each line is sawed twice.) Also, by using the cut pieces in different combinations, several pictures can be assembled from the same pad. In addition, by stacking sets of veneers, one can cut several identical pictures simultaneously. For the craftsman interested in selling his products the time saved by this method is considerable. For the occasional marquetarian there is no other method by which multiple cutting can be done.

The main problem of making wood inlay pictures is fitting the pieces. The patch-pad method accomplishes this to within the thickness of the saw blade used. No trimming of oversize pieces is necessary. Layers in the pad are made by taping choice veneers selected for specific picture pieces into cheaper veneer seconds called "wasters," to keep the layers even in thickness. The pad is sawed in a horizontal position with a vertical blade. Consequently, all edges are square and join precisely when butted together.

Cutting is the same with a hand or power jigsaw. I use a Rockwell Delta 24-in. throat, 1/3-horsepower jigsaw. If the picture is larger than the depth of the throat, the pad can be sawed into several smaller pads. An electric foot switch which

---

John N. Beck started marquetry shortly after coming to this country from Austria 38 years ago. He sells many pieces which are displayed in his Littleton, N. H. bakery.

turns the machine on and off leaves my hands free. Blade size is not determined by pad thickness, but by the size of the pieces to be cut. I usually choose a 4-0 jewelers' saw blade because the pieces in my pictures are generally small; for larger pieces a 2-0 is sufficient. I buy my blades from H. L. Wild, 510 E. 11 St., New York, NY 10009, saw list $.25. The blades are of high quality and break less than others.

The first requirement is a paper tracing of the desired picture. Two copies are needed: one is used as a master tracing upon which the names of the desired woods are indicated; the other is used for the assembly of the cutout pieces. A piece of acetate is cut to the exact size of the paper tracing, laid over the tracing, and the lines copied exactly with India ink to form a third picture template. This is called a "finder," helpful in choosing and orienting the grain patterns. All tracings should have 1/2-inch margins.

Two pieces of corrugated cardboard are cut to the exact size of the tracing. These form the top and bottom of the pad. On one cardboard the design is duplicated by tracing it over carbon or graphite paper with a ballpoint pen. This serves as the top of the pad.

In the picture shown here, I used a poor grade of maple for wasters. Any waste veneer will do providing it is the same thickness. The first piece in the pad is a poplar veneer chosen for its grain design which makes a perfect sky. I laid the finder (with the design tracing on it) over the poplar to select the most fitting grain pattern, and marked the finder edges (including the margins) on the desired poplar, which I cut to the exact pad size. I then layed it on the corrugated cardboard that forms the bottom of the pad.

For the white in the waves and the seagulls, I used holly veneer. I didn't have any holly the full size of the picture, so I

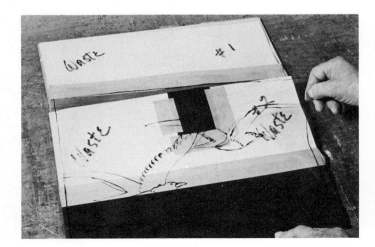

152

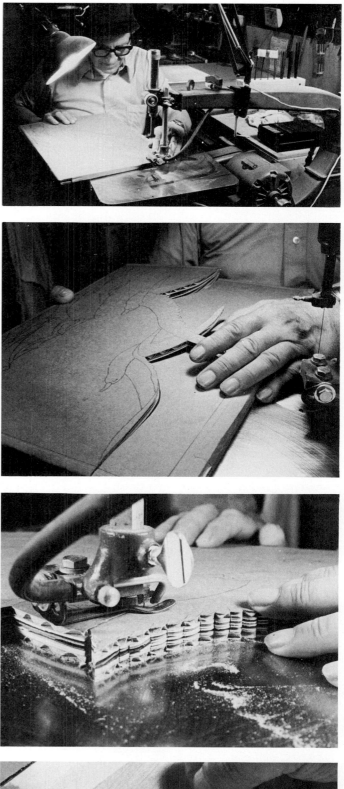

In photograph opposite below, the pad is being made up of good veneers and "wasters," using an acetate finder to help orient the grain. Next to it is the back-lit assembly table, with a sheet of masking tape ready to take the cut pieces. In the sequence of photos on this page starting at right, the author cuts the pad on his jigsaw, places the pieces on the masking tape, and uses sand heated on a hot plate to put shading on the veneer. The finished picture is shown opposite, with reverse side up, ready for gluing and mounting.

cut two pieces one overlapping the waves and the other covering the birds. Since the birds reached from one end of the sky to the other, wasters would have been impractical, so I used another piece of holly, again overlapping the bottom piece. This formed the second sheet in the pad. The third veneer was a sheet of oak dyed with ferrous sulfate to a dark bluish-gray. This formed the wings. Since the seagulls occupied only about two-thirds of the picture, the veneer was cut to that size and a waster taped to it. The fourth sheet contained black-dyed veneer for parts of the waves and the water, and to it I attached a waster of maple veneer, into which I patched another piece of black veneer for the wing tip of one bird. The last sheet contained a green-dyed ash veneer, also for the waves, with a waster for the balance of the picture. All of the joined pieces in the pad were taped together with gummed craft tape to form one sheet. The pad was then ready to be taped at the edges and sawed. (The orange beaks of the birds were so small that I cut them separately and then fitted them into their proper places. The same was true of the eyes. I drilled two holes through the pad, and after the birds were assembled, inserted small pieces of black-dyed veneer.

To assemble the cutout pieces a sheet of masking tape is made, the same size as the picture plus a margin. To do this, lay the design on a clean wooden surface, with the bottom of the design at the edge of the table. Fit a 2-foot carpenter's square around the design on the top and left side. Mark the size of the picture on the right with a pencil and remove the design. Place a piece of 2-inch masking tape, sticky side down, from the inside corner of the top of the square to the pencil mark on the right. This tape is as long as the picture, including a margin for a reinforced edge. Remove the framing square and lay down strips of masking tape below the

first one. Cut them off on the right in line with the pencil mark. Continue down to the table edge. You will have a complete sheet of tape the size of the picture. It is important to reinforce both sides with a narrow strip of masking tape to facilitate removing the sheet from the table. Starting with the upper left-hand corner, the whole sheet can be peeled up slowly. The masking tape should not overlap more than 1/8 in. between strips, to ensure visibility of the design when placed on the assembly bench, which is a square pine frame, topped with a piece of plate glass of the same size. Underneath the plate glass is a fluorescent light.

Place the second tracing of the picture onto the glass and fasten it with tape at the corners. Place the sheet of masking tape over it; it should conform exactly to the size of the tracing. It is fastened sticky side up with tape in each corner. When you turn on the light the lines of the design will show through the masking tape, which is now ready to accommodate the cutout veneer pieces.

As you cut the pieces out of the pad, lay them down on the illuminated masking tape until the complete picture is formed. Since the pieces are removable, they can be corrected if improperly placed. Throughout the assembly process you have a clear view of the picture.

Next, remove the corner tapes and lift the picture off the design. Tape 1-1/2-in. gummed craft tape over the whole picture with a minimum of overlap. Turn over the picture and pull off the masking tape strip by strip until you see the completed picture in reverse.

Prepare a glue-size of half water and half white glue and brush the exposed side of the picture with the solution just enough to dampen it. Cover the brushed side with a piece of waxed or silicone paper and lay the whole picture between several sheets of newpaper to absorb the excess moisture. If you don't have a veneer press, lay the picture between newspapers and then between two boards, and weigh them down with something heavy. At room temperature the picture will dry in about two days. Inspect the picture for open sawcuts. The glue-size should have filled most of them, but if not, any open spaces should now be filled with wood filler. I use Duratite with a little black acrylic added. I mix it with water to a paste, and apply it to the open sawcuts. Press again to ensure a flat surface; it will take only a few hours to set and dry. Then sand with a fine garnet paper to make it absolutely smooth and even. The picture is now ready to mount on a panel, frame and finish.

If you intend to sign the picture, do it after the first or second coat. Rub the spot with 000 steel wool and it will then take your signature with India ink. Or if you have a pyroelectric pen you may use that before the finish is applied.

Some of the dyed veneers I use may be made from a solution of one or two ounces of ferrous sulfate (which may be obtained in most drugstores) in a gallon of water. Maple immersed into this solution will turn various shades of gray. Philippine mahogany will turn a near black and some types of oak a deep blue. One might experiment with other types of wood. Make sure that the veneers have been immersed long enough for the solution to penetrate completely through the wood. One can check that by taking a small strip off the edge of the veneer. Wet veneers coming out of the dyeing vat must be packed between sheets of newspaper to absorb the moisture. When they are only slightly damp they should be pressed between pieces of dry paper.

154

METHODS OF WORK

Trimming veneers

Matching veneer pieces on a long edge requires a truly straight cutting procedure. Bookmatching is particularly fussy, for any departure from a straight line is doubled when the pieces are positioned. The traditional solution is to clamp the veneers between cauls and hand-plane the exposed edges. It doesn't work well—the cauls do not distribute pressure properly to the veneers (usually puckered), and planing a three-foot length to a few thousandths of an inch is rarely a happy adventure.

By using a form of pattern routing, employing a piece of ground tool steel as the pattern, the precision cutting of veneer edges becomes routine. The ground stock is available at any tool and die supply house. Although it is expensive, (about $25 for the size shown) do not stint on size; accuracy is based on the stiffness of the steel cross section. To avoid distortion, do not heat-treat the bar or machine it in any way. Simply embed and bond to the upper jig section. I used

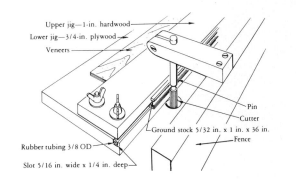

Upper jig—1-in. hardwood
Lower jig—3/4-in. plywood
Veneers
Pin
Cutter
Ground stock 5/32 in. x 1 in. x 36 in.
Rubber tubing 3/8 OD
Fence
Slot 5/16 in. wide x 1/4 in. deep

polyester resin, instead of epoxy, to make the ultimate retrieval of the steel simpler. Polyester resin develops about one-third the strength of epoxy on metal.

To clamp the wavy veneers, I use a rubber tube that is simply pushed into a snug groove in the lower board. I suspect that foam weather-stripping would work as well.

The upper jig member should be made of a hardwood (mine is cherry) but the wider lower member can be made of plywood. If after clamping a full load of four veneers there is some visible bow in either piece of the jig, do not be alarmed. The only necessity is support along every inch of the veneer edge. Unsupported veneer will chip off.

To use the jig, first set your router into a shaper table. Use a straight carbide cutter. Attach a metal pin, equal in diameter to that of the cutter, to the fence so that the pin is centered on the cutter and about ½ in. above it. Great precision is not required; eyeballing the pin location is adequate. With the pin guiding the steel bar, the cutter will generate a nearly perfect edge on the veneers in one pass. Even such hard and brittle materials as Brazilian rosewood are easily cut.

—*Leon Bennett, Riverdale, N.Y.*

When screws snap

When a screw snaps off in hard wood and there is no way to get it out, I take a 2-in. length of steel gas line. Make some saw teeth on one end and put it in a drill. When the screw is out, fill the hole with some 5/16-in. dowel.

—*Edwin A. Chard, Jr., Rochester, Ill.*

Marquetry Cutting

by Peter L. Rose

Woodworkers who have never tackled marquetry before have a variety of cutting tools and methods to choose from. Depending on one's patience and skill, some will work better than others. The aim, of course, is to have tight-fitting joints requiring no wood filler except for intentional esthetic reasons.

Basically, there are two ways of cutting veneers for marquetry—with a knife, and with a saw. The knife is good for pictures with many straight cuts and geometric designs and for cutting borders and miters. But it's difficult to cut sharp turns on the harder veneers, although there are some superior marquetarians who use a knife exclusively. Also it's difficult, if not impossible, to cut neatly through two thicknesses of veneer at a time with a knife.

The saw overcomes the disadvantages of the knife by allowing tight turns and the cutting of more than one thickness at a time. But it, too, can be difficult to handle, has limitations of size, and can run into much more expense if power equipment is chosen.

Knives to choose from

The knife most used in marquetry is the X-acto knife with a #11 blade, a blade that has an extremely sharp point. It is a comfortable knife to hold and the blade is sturdy, but frequent sharpening is required. The X-acto knife's main disadvantage is that because of the thickness of the blade, it makes a V-shaped cut, spreading the veneer apart at the top. Many marquetarians overcome this by cutting their pictures from the back using a reverse pattern. When seen from the front, the cuts will have a much tighter fit.

Another good choice is the scalpel or surgical knife, again with a #11 blade. This is a flat, slim knife that uses blades about the same thickness and sharpness as razor blades. Because the blades are thinner and sharper, the scalpel cuts the veneer more easily than the X-acto knife. However, the blades are fragile and break easily. They are usually replaced rather than sharpened.

Finally, there is the single-edge razor blade which is good only for straight cuts, as sharp turns require a much more pointed blade.

Saws to choose from

The main point to remember about saws for marquetry is that the thicker the blade, the cruder the cut and the wider the gap between pieces.

Thus the popular coping saw is definitely ruled out.

The author uses the double-bevel-cut method on a jig saw to cut a horizontal beam. Veneer for the beam is taped underneath and is being cut simultaneously.

Coping saw blades, which have pins at both ends, are too thick, but the coping saw frame cannot take the thinner but pin-less, jeweler's saw blades that do work. As a result, the most-used hand saw in marquetry is the fret saw. It has miniature clamp-like attachments for holding the pinless jeweler's blades.

The blades are five inches long and come in various sizes—No. 6/0 being the thinnest at 0.008 inches and No. 1/0 being the thickest at 0.011 inches (although there is a thicker "J" series). The No. 4/0 blade, with a thickness of 0.009 inches and a width of 0.018 inches, is a good compromise between being thin enough to produce a fine cut, but not so thin that it is always breaking. But sometimes the thinnest blade is required for extremely fine detail, and the thicker blades must be used for unusually hard woods. In any event, all the blades are quite small: they fit through the hole made by a sewing machine needle, so breakage is always a problem, and much practice is required to minimize it.

Jewelers partially overcome this by using a saw that can be adjusted to hold the shorter broken blades. These jeweler's saws can also be used for marquetry, but their limitation is in their throat size. The average fret saw has a throat of about 12 inches, meaning that a pattern 24 inches in diameter could be worked on. Jeweler's saws usually have a much smaller throat (2-1/2 inches is a popular size), but this may not be a limitation for those working on small pictures.

Whichever saw is used, a jig called a "bird's mouth" must be made or bought. It is a board with a narrow "V" (about eight inches long and three inches wide) cut in one end. When attached to the workbench, it serves as a sawing

Fret saw cuts veneer held on a "bird's mouth." Cutting is done near the apex where there is good support. Jig would be tilted for a bevel cut.

Jig saw modified for bevel marquetry cutting. Original work hold-downs are gone. Thin metal sheet with small hole for jeweler's blades to go through is glued to original top.

surface. The blade of the saw (with the teeth pointed down) is placed close to the vertex of the "V". The saw is moved up and down in a stationary position as the veneer is fed into the blade.

The main disadvantage with the hand-saw technique is that it takes much practice to hold the saw with one hand and move the veneer with the other so that an acccurate cut can be made on the pattern line.

This disadvantage is overcome (at considerable cost, however,) by the use of a power jig saw. For marquetarians, the main requirements in such a saw are special chucks for holding the jeweler's blades, a tilting table, and a foot switch that frees both hands. To my knowledge, only Rockwell makes a jig saw that can be adapted to take jeweler's blades. The popular Dremel saw does not adapt; neither does the Sears. Another desirable feature is tension adjustment, but if this is not available, a weaker spring can be substituted above the top clamp to help keep the blades from breaking too easily. Average throat size is usually between 16 and 24 inches.

The various cutting methods

The choice of the cutting method is partially determined by the tools available. If a power jig saw is available, then any of the four basic methods can be used; but if only a knife is available, the so-called double-cut methods are ruled out.

The single-piece method

The simplest of the methods (but the most difficult to get a perfect fit) is the single-piece method. Basically, one Xerox or carbon copy of the pattern must be made for each piece used in the pattern. The pattern (or portions of the pattern) are taped or glued to each of the selected veneers. (If glued, cut the picture from the back or in reverse; otherwise the glue will impregnate the veneer and show as blemishes in the final picture.) As each piece is cut, it is laid on a master pattern, and the pieces are held together temporarily with masking tape. The fret saw or power jig saw is recommended for this method, but a knife can also be used. The obvious

disadvantage of the method is the difficulty in cutting exactly on the lines to insure perfect fitting joints. Since each piece is cut independently of the others, a poor fit can easily occur.

The window method

A partial way around this disadvantage is through the so-called window method. Instead of cutting all the pieces independently of each other using many copies of one pattern, and then putting them together on a master pattern, the pieces are cut consecutively from a single pattern. The pattern is traced onto the background veneer using carbon paper. The background could be one or more pieces put together. (If the pattern is taped or hinged along the top of the background veneer, it will always be in register, should additional tracings be made onto the veneer.)

Larger pieces in the pattern are cut out of the background first. As each piece is cut and removed, a veneer selected for that part is placed under the opening and moved until the grain direction and figure are in their most pleasing and natural position. The piece is then taped temporarily on the back, turned over, and marked along the edge of the opening with a sharp pencil or knife. The veneer is then removed from the back and cut on the markings. It is then permanently placed in the opening and taped in place on the back side. Each part is done in this manner until the entire picture is completely cut.

The advantage of this popular method is that each veneer can be seen in position before it is cut, and both a knife or saw can be used. But the disadvantage, as with the previous method, is that accurate fitting is difficult because the pieces still are not cut simultaneously.

The pad method

A third method, the pad method, tries to get around this disadvantage by making a single cut; that is, by cutting all the pieces at once as in a jig saw puzzle.

Several pieces of soft waste veneer at least the size of the finished picture are stacked together into a "pad," and the good veneers are interleaved among them for the cutting. To

Veneer for house beam is taped in position to back of picture being cut by double-bevel method. Other tape is holding previously cut pieces that have been white glued.

Sewing needle s used to make hole along line of cut. Jeweler's saw blade will then be fed through and mounted on the jig saw for cutting out.

make up the pad, the good veneers are positioned on the waste veneer according to their place in the final picture and fastened with masking tape. Adjacent veneers are placed on different waste veneer layers so that there is no direct overlapping. In this way the pad is built up of alternate layers of waste and good veneers, and the assembled pad can be tightly compressed during the cutting. The top layer consists of a piece of waste veneer on which the cutting pattern is glued. The average picture may require a pad having six or so such layers.

During cutting, the pad is held together with the edges taped, stapled, or nailed. Power jig saws are recommended for this method and the blade used must be one of the thicker jeweler's blades, 1/0 or 2/0. Thinner blades would break too easily in cutting such a thick stack of veneers at one time.

This is the main disadvantage of this method: the thickness of the blade, slight as it is, prevents a tight fit. Another disadvantage is the wastage of veneers. But the main advantage is that once the pad is made up, the cutting goes quickly and the pieces all follow the same curve or contour because they are cut all at once. Ideally, if the saw blade had no thickness, the pad method would produce perfectly fitting joints.

After the cut is made, the beam is glued in place. Because the cut was made on a bevel, the pieces are not interchangeable. Notice difference in sizes of scrap pieces.

The double-bevel-cut method

This ideal can be reached by a fourth method, the double-bevel cut, but to do this, only two pieces of veneer can be cut at a time. By cutting the pieces at an angle, the gap caused by the blade thickness can be compensated for and eliminated in the final picture. The angle of the cut depends on both the blade thickness and veneer thickness, but usually an angle of 12 to 13 degrees does the job. If the angle is too great, the veneer tends to feather; if not great enough, the pieces won't fit tightly. The best way to find the proper angle is through experimentation.

Both the power jig saw or fret saw can be used with this method, assuming the jig saw table tilts. If a fret saw is used, the bird's mouth must be tilted and possibly modified to produce the same angle cut.

To start this method, proceed in the same manner as with

the window method. But before cutting out any piece of the background, tape the veneer that is to replace it to the back, in position. A sewing needle the same thickness as the blade and attached to a pin vise or handle is then pushed through both veneers on the cutting line. The jeweler's blade is passed through this hole (with teeth pointed downward) and then attached to the saw. The veneer is then consistently cut either in a clockwise or counter-clockwise manner, depending on which way the saw is tilted. The direction of the cut is very important because the cut pieces are not interchangeable. Again, it's best to experiment and then follow the results consistently. When the cut is completed, the new veneer will fit exactly in the place of the discarded veneer, even if the saw blade does not stay on the pattern line. The process is then repeated for the next piece in the picture.

After years of trying the various methods, I find the double-bevel cut by far the best method to use. It's also good with either hand or powered saws, so that expense is not a factor.

Most importantly, it consistently produces tight fitting joints requiring no wood filler. That frees my efforts for the more important aspect of marquetry: creating pictures that use the grain, figure and color of the woods to produce the most artistic and pleasing effect.

[Note: The fret saw and jeweler's blades can be obtained from Albert Constantine and Son, Inc., 2050 Eastchester Road, Bronx, N.Y. 10461. The scalpel can be obtained from the Brookstone Co., Peterborough, N.H., 03458.]

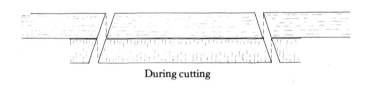

During cutting

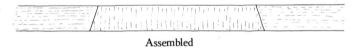

Assembled

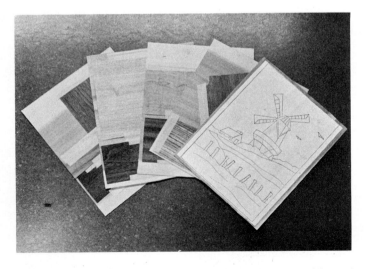

Photograph shows "pad" of veneers ready for assembly and cutting with pad method. Cross-sectional drawing shows how beveled saw kerf eliminates gap between pieces in double-bevel-cut method.

METHODS OF WORK

Raising arched panels

The shaper is the correct tool for making a raised panel door with an arched top. I don't have a shaper, so I do the job with the table saw and a chisel, the hard way.

Make the rails and stiles, with tenons and mortises, in the usual way and cut the panel to shape. Set up the table saw to cut the bevel, with the blade angled to the correct slope, the height set for the width of the bevel, and the fence placed to the edge thickness of the panel. The straight sides are no problem, just run them through. On the arched top, run the piece through resting on the top of the arch, then again

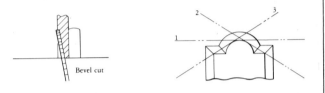

Bevel cut

resting on the top and one corner, and again resting on the top and the other corner.

Now set the table saw to cut the shallow shoulders on the bevels, thus removing the waste from the work. This com-

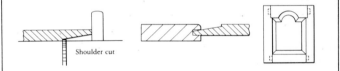

Shoulder cut

pletes the straight sides, except for cleanup with a rabbet plane, and removes most of the wood from the arched top.

Mark the shoulder line on the arched top and the 45° lines at the changes of direction. Use a wide, sharp chisel to carve the bevel down, making a neat, sharp juncture at the 45° line. Marking the correct thickness on the panel edge and carving back to the shoulder line is one way to do it.

The grooves that accept the panel in the straight sides are easily made with a dado blade in the table saw. To make the groove in the top rail, drill holes somewhat smaller than the desired thickness of the groove, then chisel out the groove to the line. Don't worry about the sloppy bottom of the groove, just make the sides nice and even.

Assemble the door dry, pin through the tenons with dowels, and fit it to its opening. Then take it apart and reassemble without the panel to round over the inside edge of the frame with a router. The panel should be finished before glue-up to prevent an unfinished edge from showing through as the door expands and contracts over the years. Make sure the panel is slightly loose on final assembly; that's the whole idea, allowing a little room for expansion and contraction.
—*Cary Hall, Hampton, Ga.*

Waxing saw tables

On all machine platens, such as saw tables and jointers, bottoms of planes and such: Use a good car wax such as Simonize, and you will be surprised how much better they perform. Wood will slide and not stick; rust will not form in wet weather. I use it on all of my chisels and any tool that comes in contact with the wood.
—*Ellis Thaxton, Arlington, Tex.*

SHAPING AND CARVING

Carving Fans

Reproductions gain richness, authenticity

by R. E. Bushnell

One characteristic of Queen Anne, Georgian and Chippendale furniture is the use of fans and shells as decoration. These are often found on the central drawers of highboys, lowboys and secretaries, on crests and knees of chairs, and on smaller pieces like mirrors and pipe boxes.

The addition of such carvings can make your reproductions more interesting and add richness and authenticity. Such forms are easy to carve and require only the minimum in tools and equipment.

Described here are the tools required and the procedures to be followed in making the simple convex fan and the more complicated concave-convex fan.

Convex fan

The first step is to lay out the form by drawing a base line on the item to be carved. This is generally 5/8 in. to 1 in. above the bottom of the board. Next, with proper proportion in mind, determine the overall size of the fan and mark the midpoint or center on the base line. From this point draw a half circle with the compass and erect a bisecting perpendicular center line.

Determine the approximate size of the rays desired, and with this as a starting point, use the dividers or compass to mark off the half circle into equal segments, by trial and error. Now, at the midpoint on the base line, draw a second and much smaller half circle. If you are making a drawer, the knob will be located at the center of this circle. Using a ruler, connect the equally divided marks on the outer circle with the midpoint on the base line and draw a line from each mark to

the inner circle line.

To start the actual carving, clamp the board to a working surface. Use a jackknife to outline the outer circle, making several passes until the cut is about 1/8 in. deep. Be sure to make these cuts exactly on the circle line. With the parting chisel, start precisely at the inner circle line and follow each ray line to the outer circle. Put considerable downward pressure on the chisel as the outer circle is reached to avoid making nicks or chisel marks beyond that point. Do the same when using the firmer chisel later on. About three passes with the parting chisel should do. If you wander slightly on the first pass, don't worry, as this can be corrected on the succeeding cuts.

If you do not have a parting chisel, you can use the jackknife to cut exactly on the ray lines before making the successive rounding cuts. Further, 1/4-in. and 1/2-in. cabinet chisels can be used in lieu of the 6-mm and 10-mm firmers.

With all the ray lines delineated, start rounding each of the rays with the 1/4-in. or 6-mm firmer chisel. You don't have to worry about grain direction with the two nearly perpendicular rays on each side of the center line because you are carving across the grain. As the rays progress downward, however, the grain direction must be carefully watched: one side of the ray will be carved from the inner to the outer circle; the other side of the same ray will be carved from the outer to the inner circle.

It is easiest to start each cut by inserting the corner of the chisel down to the proper depth with a shearing or slicing cut. Complete the rounding by making successive passes with the

Photo, cross-section drawing show sequential steps in carving of simple convex fan.

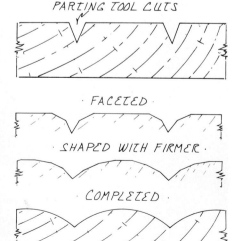

PARTING TOOL CUTS

· FACETED ·

· SHAPED WITH FIRMER ·

· COMPLETED ·

Author uses 6-mm #7 gouge to hollow concave portion of concave-convex fan. Simple convex fan enhances author's reproduction of Queen Anne lowboy, circa 1750.

chisel, each pass progressively less steep than the preceding cut until the form is as round as possible.

Each ray can now be smoothed by lightly scraping with the 1/2-in. or 10-mm chisel. If you own rifflers, these can also be used in the smoothing process.

To finish off the ends of the rays, draw a third circle about 1/8 in. inside the outer circle across the end of each ray. With the 1/2-in. or 10-mm chisel, make a sloping cut from the third to the outer circle. Sand the fan first with 100, then 150, and finally with 220 garnet paper before applying the finish.

Concave-convex fan

Slightly more complicated and time-consuming is the concave-convex fan. This is more than compensated for, however, by the added richness it conveys.

To make this fan we need three more chisels: a 2-mm firmer chisel, a 3-mm veiner and a 6-mm #7 gouge. Unlike carving the simple convex fan, it is not possible to substitute cabinet chisels.

The concave-convex fan is laid out in similar manner to the convex fan except that an odd number of rays is required to make the alternating concave-convex pattern. To accomplish this, determine the approximate size of the rays desired.

Then, by trial and error, use the dividers or compass to mark off the circle into equal segments. Start with the convex center ray, since it must be centered over the perpendicular line.

Carve this fan exactly as the convex fan but incise the outer circle only lightly with the jackknife to delineate the circumference. After the convex portion of the fan is carved, begin carving the concave portion by flattening every other ray. Use the 2-mm firmer chisel at the inner circle, followed by the 6-mm firmer as the rays widen toward the outer circle. Incise the outer circle quite heavily with the jackknife where each of the flattened rays ends.

When all alternate rays are flattened, start hollowing the flattened rays, beginning with the 3-mm veiner, followed by the 6-mm gouge. When cutting the concave portion, leave a shoulder approximately 1/32 in. wide on each side of the convex ray. You should do this by eye only, so work carefully. Be sure to work only with the grain, as the carving can easily be ruined at this point.

Judicious scraping and sanding will complete the carving.

Reg Bushnell is in charge of antique restoration at Old Sturbridge Village in Massachusetts.

Concave rays are outlined, flattened and hollowed after the convex portion has been carved.

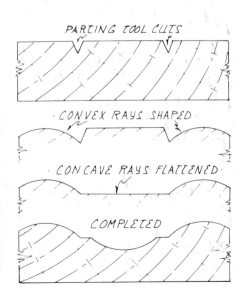

Gothic Tracery

Working with intriguing medieval designs

by Edward R. Hasbrouck

Sometime during the 12th century in Western Europe arose an architectural style which was later to be called Gothic. It developed through architects' and stonecarvers' efforts to raise their churches from squat Romanesque masses of stone to the towering, airy, light-filled cathedrals we admire today. The flowing, geometric lines and patterns which not only define but also decorate the structure were first called tracery by Sir Christopher Wren.

During the Gothic period (12th to 15th century), the Gothic style was common in most of Europe but was most fully developed in England, France and Germany. Various cultures and historical influences modified what was once an almost universal style. Ultimately the Renaissance swept over it. A brief revival in the 19th century seemed out of place and was short-lived.

The shapes used in tracery seem to derive from the sweeping structural lines of the arches and groined vaults invented by Gothic builders to open up stone walls and admit the mystical light. I get the impression that the spaces thus created were filled with lively and pleasing lines of stone or wood to support myriad tiny panes of colored glass. Craftsmen of the day were advised to study geometry, even to

Edward R. Hasbrouck is a biologist with the California Dept. of Agriculture. He took up carving eight years ago, and now carves Gothic-style furniture as a part-time business.

depict natural forms of plants and animals. Tracery on furniture mimics this architecture, and continued after the architectural style had passed.

The serious student of Gothic tracery can differentiate the cultural and historical influences with terms such as early English decorated, perpendicular, or French flamboyant. But these terms were applied long after the fact and for my purposes are merely academic. The Gothic style was more a feeling or intuitive concept than anything clearly delineated. I don't think the old carvers had very many verbalized rules.

English publications and illustrations of English work have been the best sources of designs for me. The use of wood in English churches was primarily decorative, although timber roofs, porches and doors are exceptions. The early work, even woodwork, was done by masons and smiths. Once carpenters and woodcarvers got into the act, screens, pews, galleries, choirs, thrones, font covers, pulpits, bosses, carved beams and spandrels grew, blossomed and ultimately filled the church interiors until the stonework became almost secondary. The very nature of wood allowed this decorative elaboration and proliferation.

Broad spaces were considered great opportunities to fill with decoration. Many of the design elements had symbolic meanings. The common ellipse probably refers to the Christian fish. Circles can be foliated three or four times: the Trinity or the cross. A circle with a quatrefoil can be twisted

A 14th-century monk's stool carved from California-grown English walnut is shown at left. The pierced top and uprights were drilled and sawed before carving. Above, one panel from a headboard carved in Eastern willow and stained. Drawing shows elements of gothic tracery.

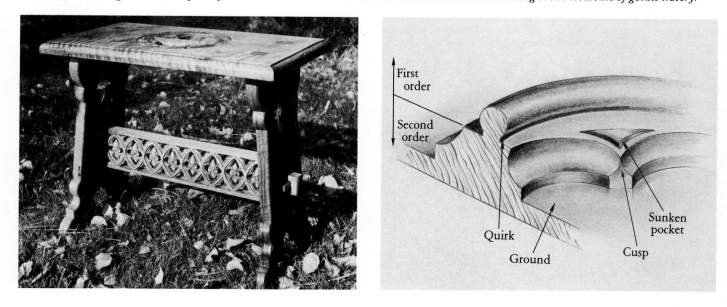

off-axis to make the "whirling cross," a reference to the martyrdom of St. Catherine. I think it was all to delight the eye, enthrall the hearts of generally illiterate and superstitious people, boost the prestige of the patrons who paid for the work, and give good employment to the craftsmen. Today we view the geometry, the moldings, the twining foliage, the saints and the gargoyles as symbols of a culture and life no longer our own.

Nevertheless, I enjoy tracery. I enjoy the process of carving it. In the current parlance, it is an esthetic and nostalgic "trip." I have used it on boxes, headboards, tables and stools, and will continue to use it wherever I have the chance.

Tracery can be carved in several ways, but each begins with a satisfactory pattern, usually involving several repeats. One can draw the design onto the wood, repeat by repeat, with ruler and compass (a technique I use on large pieces). In the example illustrated here, I made a template of one of the repeats and traced out the major foliations, then added small details and corrections freehand.

The design I used is taken from Brandon's *Analysis of Gothick Tracery* (1860). The square is divided into four foliated sections. This design has two orders. In this context the term "order" refers to the organization of design elements both spatially and in complexity.

The first order consists of the thick, sweeping lines close to the surface of the carving, the main elements in the design.

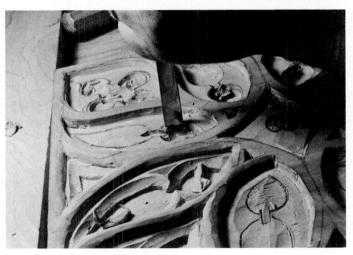

These lines trace out the four circles within the square, and divide each circle into three parts. The first-order lines are rounded and "quirked," or undercut, to form a bead.

The second order comprises the sharper lines and planes within the curves of the first order, from the ground of the carving up to the flat surface at the bottom of the bead. In pierced work the ground would be cut out. The second order is cusped where the curves intersect, and has sunken pockets setting off the cusps.

In executing the design, whittling is kept to a minimum. The shapes of the design result directly from the shape of the tools. The concave portions, or hollows, take their form from a given sweep of gouge; the convex elements are formed by back-bents.

The pattern can be set in either with stop cuts inside the lines or by outlining with a parting tool. I use both techniques, depending on the material. Well-placed stop cuts are a must where the grain is short, or the space too small or deep for the parting tool. Each order is bosted out in turn until the ground, or deepest part of the pattern, has been established. If the carving is to be pierced, I drill and saw out the pierced areas first. I use a saber saw with the narrowest, smoothest cutting blade I can get.

Starting from ground, the cove or hollow of the second order is run first. The amount of curvature in the hollow is a matter of choice. The longer I work, the deeper I want the hollows and the narrower I want the lines. The junction of two intersecting hollows cleans out nicely at obtuse angles, but at acute angles, must be worked with a 30-degree parting tool. The depth of the ground from the bottom edge of the hollow is controlled by eye, as is the width of the ledge outlining the top of the hollow. A pencil line makes that control a lot easier, however. Ideally the hollows can be run with clean, curving sweeps of the chisel, with maybe a little careful paring to tidy up the lines. (True joy is also a rare experience.) Where the grain is contrary, I whittle and then pare with the intent of leaving as few tool marks as I can. Straight-shank tools were sufficient for much of the design, but the equivalent long-bent tools would have been easier.

In tracery, the first order is frequently flat-surfaced. In this case I chose to mold and undercut the pattern until it approximated a bead. The bead can be run with straight-shank gouges, but I used a couple of back-bent tools, which simplified the job of rounding the top and sides of the bead. To cut the quirk I used a 1/4-inch 30-degree parting tool, with a small skew at the corners.

Once the overall design has been cleaned up and the acute angles tapered in, the sunken pockets at each of the cusps can be cut. These pockets lighten up the design by thinning the outline on each of the orders. They can be cut in with three strokes if the grain is right. Technical difficulties arise when the grain is very short between the pocket and the hollow. Some woods tend to crumble readily, such as pine and deodar cedar, which I chose for this carving. Oak was traditionally used in England, walnut in France, and basswood in both. Cherry and maple carve cleanly but are harder to work.

The success of this kind of carving depends on the regularity of the lines and shapes. Although machinelike perfection usually looks quite dead, irregular and uneven lines are even less desirable. I avoid using sandpaper because I don't like to sand. I also take an atavistic pride in good clean chisel work, an achievement I can sometimes claim.

METHODS OF WORK

Finishing clocks

I build hall and wall clocks. I use only walnut lumber. When I am finished with the case I don't fill the wood or stain it. I use only hot boiled linseed oil, nothing else. It makes a very beautiful finish. The grain seems to come to the surface in streaks of brown and some black. If there is a knot it turns black. For heating the oil I use an electric glue-pot of one quart size. I heat the oil to a point where it is too hot to put on with a rag, so I use a 1-in. nylon paintbrush. A brush also gets into the corners better than a rag. After the oil is applied, let it set until you see dry spots appear. This could take from 5 to 20 minutes, depending on room temperature and humidity. Then take a wool cloth or pad and rub the wood until the oil seems to disappear. What you are doing is forcing the oil into the wood. One or more coats can be applied. If one of my clocks is scratched or nicked, all it takes is a little sanding and a little hot oil and the scratch disappears.

—*George Eckhart, Kenosha, Wis.*

A router plane

You can build your own router plane that will work as well as a commercial one for the cost of a cheap offset screwdriver and a U-bolt. The cutting irons are ground from the screwdriver bits, a blade about ¼ in. wide at one end, and a

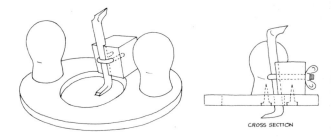

CROSS SECTION

narrow plow at the other. The blades sit almost flat to the work, like paring chisels. Relief under the heel of the blade is obtained by making the blade holder with a tilted face.

Dimensions and shape can be suited to the builder's fancy and to the materials at hand. The illustrated design is simple enough to be produced in a single evening at the workbench.

—*Van Caldwell, Cincinnati, Ohio*

Raising dents

To eliminate or reduce dents in wood use a soldering iron, a natural-fiber, smooth-finish cloth folded to a point, water and discretion.

Wet the dent, allowing the crushed fibers to soak up the water. Squeeze excess water out of the cloth. Bring the iron up to the boiling point, but not to full heat. Test the wet cloth until it steams. Press the wet cloth into the dent with the hot iron for as long as steam is still produced. Repeat, if necessary, until no further rising occurs. You cannot burn the wood as long as the cloth is wet, so press the iron for brief intervals and be sure the cloth is continually wet. This should be done only on raw wood; if there is finish on the piece, remove the finish first.

Raise the dent before final planing or scraping. Otherwise, the dent may rise above the planed surface. Make one or two passes with a plane at its finest setting after raising the dent.

This technique works as long as the dented fibers have been crushed and not torn.

—*Henry T. Kramer, Rye, N.Y.*

Tackling Carving

No need for a 'carving set'

by Robert L. Butler

Furniture makers have recently become aware of the role of sculpturing in fine woodworking. The sculptured furniture pioneered by Wharton Esherick and recently developed by Robert C. Whitley and others uses carving as a design essential to accent light and shadow, and to form such functional elements as handles and pulls. Some craftsmen have branched out into wood sculpture as art. They start with a background and feeling for wood that trained artists often lack. But for whatever reason, a craftsman who develops an interest in carving is faced with the problem of acquiring suitable tools.

Too frequently, the craftsman new to wood sculpture buys a set of carving tools that does not meet his needs. He should be guided by the principle he followed in equipping his shop: buy a rudimentary set and add to it as experience and knowledge increase. Since most suppliers of woodcarving tools carry at least 100 shapes and sizes, it is impossible to make specific recommendations without knowing the type, style and scale of carving he plans to do.

But without some guidance, the novice may not know where to begin. I feel that sculpture of moderate size provides a realistic starting point for beginners, especially for craftsmen who intend to sculpture furniture. I have arrived at this opinion through some early false starts and later during five years of teaching woodcarving and sculpture in local adult education courses. Small, intricate carvings do not provide the experience in line, movement and form that can be transferred to sculptured furniture.

For moderate-sized sculpture, I recommend five basic tools, plus a hard Arkansas slip stone to sharpen them. They are (1) a straight gouge with a cross-section curvature of #9, #10, or #11 and 25 to 30 mm. wide, (2) a smaller straight gouge, #5, #6, or #7 and 20 to 25 mm. wide, (3) a cylindrical Surform tool, (4) a fine-cutting wood rasp, and (5) a mallet. The first four will total about $30, and the mallet can be turned from any heavy hardwood such as maple or osage orange. A mallet could instead be cut from a branch and the handle roughed out on the band saw. The carver's mallet is preferable to the carpenter's mallet which is used to make mortises, because it carries more weight in the head and be-

Photos show what can be accomplished with four tools. Rough bosting out was done with a #11 30-mm straight gouge (top), followed by #5 25-mm straight gouge, which produced a smoother form (and smaller chips). Cylindrical Surform goes even further, while a fine, half-round wood rasp just about completes it (bottom). Area around the bird's beak will be finished with sandpaper of 80 garnet prior to the usual series of sandings and finishing as desired.

cause its cylindrical form gives the hand only a glancing blow when it misses the handle of the carving tool. There is much less damage to the knuckles.

The photos show what these tools can do. I began with a #11 gouge for bosting out the rough form of an abstract bird, after band-sawing a top and bottom view. This gouge makes deep cuts and removes excess wood rapidly. At this stage, the form has many valleys and humps. Next, I reduced the extremes of these humps and valleys with a gouge of flatter curvature, the #5. I then smoothed the piece with the Surform tool, which eliminated ridges and valleys left by the gouges and enabled me to make slight changes in the overall form. Before sandpapering, I used a fine rasp lightly so as not to pull any of the wood fibers. Sculptures may be left unsanded, with the texture and finish of the gouge, or rasped and sanded with garnet paper in the grit series 80, 120, 200 and polished with 400 or 500-weight wet-dry paper.

By now, it should be evident that sculpturing of moderate-sized pieces can be done well with this set of tools. I am sure that in my own carving, 95% of my time is spent with these five basic tools.

A craftsman who has mastered these tools may discover that he is more interested in smaller carvings. He can then buy tools of smaller sizes and different curvatures, and various types of hand-held knives and rifflers. With these, he can do small animal carvings, caricatures of cowboys and goldminers, or small religious items such as creches.

On the other hand, one may wish to carve much larger objects for the yard, foyer or a large room. Such carving is done with larger gouges and hand adzes. These tools, along with the basic five-piece set, can be used for carvings as large as totem poles or full-scale sculptures of human form. Some carvers are adept at using the chain saw for oversize and bold pieces.

As in all tool buying and usage, the limit is set only by the person and the work he contemplates. Other available tools include bent gouges, fluters, veiners, short-bent gouges, back-bent gouges and parting tools. The bent gouge is used extensively in free-form bowl carving. Fluters are semicircular in cross section. Veiners have u-shaped cross sections and make deep, continuous-cut lines. Spoons, front or short-bent gouges—they go by various names—are used for "spooning" wood, making deep, abrupt incisions. The back-bent gouge is the reverse of the short-bent, with the sharpened surface on the opposite edge. It is used to carve intricate flowers, leaves, etc. Parting tools make a v-shaped cut of various depths and angles.

Musical instrument makers use other specialized tools. The macaroni, fluteroni and backeroni gouges are designed for carving violin, viola and cello necks, backs and bellies. Like all carving tools, these may be short-bent, bent, etc. Some experienced woodcarvers even forge, grind and temper their own tools.

As in all craftsmanship, the ultimate is never achieved. A serious craftsman continues to improve his work and extend his horizons as he creates. Start with the simple set of tools and add to it as you find need and outgrow the limits of those you have already purchased.

Author's basic carving set (right) includes wooden mallet, hard Arkansas slip stone, #11 30-mm gouge, #5 25-mm gouge, fine rasp and cylindrical Surform. For smaller, more intricate work (below), add gouges, knives, chip carving tools and rifflers. For bigger work (far below), there are from bottom to top a #7 35-mm bent or long bent gouge, a #7 50-mm straight gouge, a #7 50-mm fishtail gouge, and an adze with two cutting faces—a gouge and a small ax. Carving tools other than straight gouges include (below right) a long bent gouge for deep carving, a front bent for deep incisive cutting, a back bent for carving leaves or petals, and a parting tool for deep angled and continuous cuts. Round lens cap shows relative size.

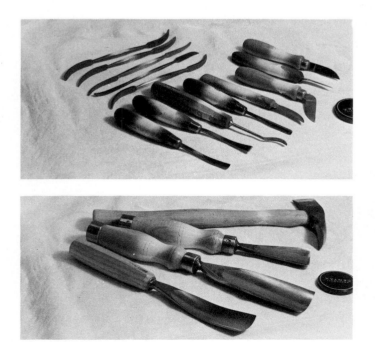

METHODS OF WORK

Making clamps

For many people who aren't professional cabinetmakers, wooden clamps are in the luxury-tool class. Good commercially-made handscrews cost at least $10 in the 8-in. size. Materials to make one cost less than $2.

Make the jaws from maple or another dense hardwood. The ½-in. holes must be carefully drilled square to the jaw surface and the same distance apart. The spindles are ⁵⁄₁₆-in. steel bar. Thread one end ⁵⁄₁₆-18 right-handed, and the opposite end ⁵⁄₁₆-18 left-handed. Make the 5-in. long thread right-

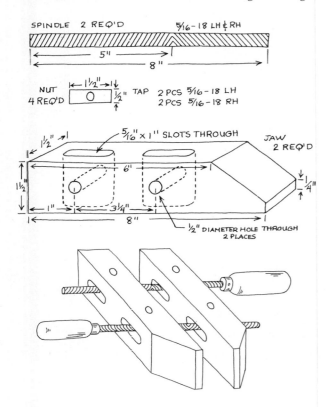

handed on one spindle, and left-handed on the other. The 3-in. thread is also reversed. Make the nuts from ½-in. round bar. Be sure the tapped holes are square to the axis of the bar. Small file handles will work well if you don't have a lathe. Drill through the ferrule and spindle and insert a small pin after assembly.

—*Richard E. Price, Seattle, Wash.*

EDITOR'S NOTE: The left-hand tap and die, necessary to make parallel-jaw clamps as shown, are not standard hardware items.

In Summer '77 you mention difficulty in locating a source of left-hand taps and dies. I have found them listed in the catalog of Manhattan Supply Co., Plainview, N.Y. 11803, as follows: ⁵⁄₁₆-in.—18 x 1 L.H. carbon-steel die, $3.25; ⁵⁄₁₆-in.—18 x 1 L.H. carbon-steel tap, $1.30.

They are also listed in the catalog of the Wholesale Tool Co., 12155 Stevens Drive, Warren, Mich. 48090, at $5.90 for the die and $2.20 for the tap.

—*Roger W. Curtis, Bethesda, Md.*

Bench-top clamps

My bench has two rows of holes along the front and back edges. These accommodate lengths of ¾-in. pipe, standing vertically, each fitted with extension clamps of the Sears variety. Two or more clamps may thus be mounted in conjunction with cross members for clamping frames, boxes, chests or chairs in gluing position. Four or more clamps form a light-duty veneer press against the bench top.

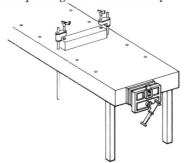

The advantage of this gluing method is that the work is always held true and square because the bench is a flat reference surface.

The holes for the pipe clamps are spaced about 8 in. apart. A crosspiece between two clamps may be used as a bench stop in conjunction with the stop on the tail vise, thereby holding long pieces of wood on the bench.

—*Harold F. Lathrop, Milan, Ill.*

More clamps

Here is a simple hand clamp that can be made without any threading or tapping—the only tools needed are a drill and a chisel. The idea is taken from old wooden handscrews that were given to me a few years back. There are no reverse threads and the jaws open and close parallel to each other. I hold the center handle in my left hand and spin the clamp around it clockwise to close the jaws; this keeps the jaws parallel until they are the desired distance apart. A turn or so on the rear handle then supplies enough pressure for any glue joint.

The threaded parts are ⅜-in. threaded rod sold at the hardware store. Get nuts to match and simply mortise them into

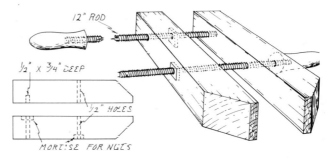

the hardwood jaws. If the mortises are loose, you can use epoxy glue to hold the nuts in place, just a dab, and keep it away from the threads. The holes are drilled ½ in. to allow easy passage of the rod. The turned handles are held firmly on the rod with epoxy glue pushed into a slightly oversize and overdeep hole.

—*Albert C. Landry, Richmond, Maine*

Lute Roses

Delicate patterns are cut or sawn

by Lyn Elder

Today there is a tremendous revival of interest in Renaissance and Baroque music. Naturally the demand for authentic copies of historical instruments has caused many craftsmen to specialize in their production. Much study has been devoted to these instruments and to discovering the design principles and working techniques of the old makers, so that high-quality reproductions can be built to satisfy exacting scholars and performers. As a builder of historical stringed instruments, mainly lutes, I have spent several years examining museum pieces and compiling data and design information to facilitate my work. A large part of my effort has been devoted to cataloging and studying lute roses.

During the Renaissance the lute occupied roughly the same position the piano does today. It was the instrument every serious musician was able to play; in addition to its immense solo repertoire it was used by composers and to accompany rehearsals and performances. In keeping with its role as a working instrument, it was usually quite plain in appearance, as the modern grand piano is usually stark black. The only decorative element found on all lutes was the rose, or carved soundhole. This feature is present in the earliest lutes we know of and changed very little between the Middle Ages and the Baroque period, when the popularity of the lute declined.

The word "lute" derives from *al-'ud,* an Arab musical instrument whose name means "the wood." The lute was probably introduced into Europe during the Middle Ages, either by returning Crusaders or by the Moorish conquerors of Spain. It was already a venerable instrument when the Europeans discovered it. Although European craftsmen continually modified the instrument over the next several hundred years, they never discarded the pierced rose or strayed far from its original style. Most 17th and 18th-century lute roses are identical with, or similar to, those seen in the earliest surviving lutes and in paintings of even earlier instruments. The Islamic character of these designs persists through many variations on the symmetrical geometric figures.

Although most historical lute builders probably carved their own roses, there is some evidence that at certain periods lute bellies could be bought with the roses already carved in. This may account for the prevalence of some patterns. In large shops the job was probably assigned to apprentices, as it is tedious and time-consuming.

There is considerable disagreement among lute builders and acousticians concerning the effect, if any, of the complex

Lyn Elder, 33, apprenticed with a master instrument maker and started his own workshop in 1968. He is craftsman-in-residence at Dominican College, San Rafael, Calif.

Lute made by author is decorated in style of early 17th century, with Venetian rose of fourfold symmetry.

rose on the sound of the instrument. The sound of a lute with a normal rose would certainly be different from that of the same instrument with a three-inch open hole, because the total open area of the former is smaller. But whether the sound would be changed with a smaller open hole equal to the total open area of the rose is questionable. Some think the sound must be strained through the sieve-like pattern, while others dismiss this idea as fantasy. Whatever effect there is, however, must be minimal, perhaps unnoticeable to the average listener.

The size and position of a historical lute rose bear a definite relationship to the geometry of the lute of which it is a part. Depending on the school to which the builder belonged, the rose is centered either five-eighths or five-ninths of the way from the bottom of the lute belly to the neck joint. Although some instruments do not conform exactly to these proportions, most old lutes seem to fall into one of the above categories. The diameter of the rose is usually between one-fourth and one-third the width of the belly at the rose center line. Occasionally the rose may seem larger than one-third, but this is usually because of a decorative border and not the open-work of the pattern itself.

Patterns

Dozens of historical rose patterns are known, but all may be categorized by their rotational symmetry, whether fourfold, sixfold or eightfold. Fourfold patterns are often seen in paintings of early lutes and were used by some Venetians and some Baroque builders. Sixfold patterns were by far the most common and varied during all historical periods. There are relatively few eightfold patterns, but one is the most famous of all lute roses: the Knot of Leonardo da Vinci, said to have been designed originally as an embroidery pattern but soon borrowed by lute makers.

Most common patterns contain both a straight-line geometrical design and some kind of curved line motif weaving through it. The main exceptions to this general rule are the roses of the Venetian builders mentioned above. Their roses are more flowery in appearance because of the almost total absence of straight lines. These delicate patterns are the most difficult to carve because of their many unsupported figures.

Most normal-size lutes seem to have plain, borderless roses. The relief-carved border was used to increase the apparent size of the rose for a larger instrument such as a bass lute or an archlute. Since the paper patterns had to be printed with hand-cut wood blocks, it was impractical to have the same rose in several different sizes.

Theorboes and chittarones, collectively known as archlutes, have somewhat larger bodies than normal lutes and extremely long necks with two separate pegboxes. These instruments often have a group of three roses carved all together in the normal position, probably originally for the reason mentioned above—to save making an entirely new pattern block. The style caught on and was used throughout the history of these instruments, along with larger single roses. Some of the

Rose of sixfold symmetry, below, is from a 16th-century bass lute. At right from top: triple rose from 17th-century chittarone; eightfold Knot of Leonardo, carved by author; 16th-century Italian rose by author. All are slightly smaller than actual size.

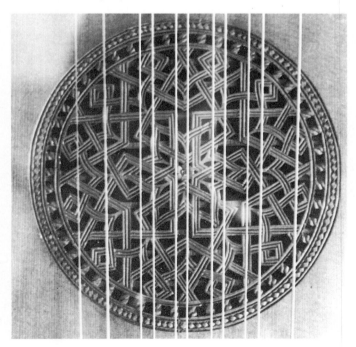

171

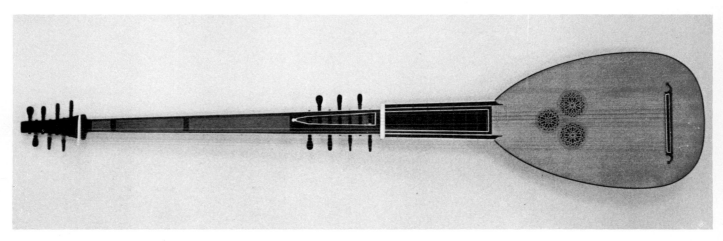

Chittarone by master luthier Donald Warnock of Boston University has two pegboxes, triple rose.

triple roses are combinations of familiar designs, but some are entirely new. Most have a carved decorative border.

A characteristic of all rose patterns is the weaving effect, achieved by cutting out minute chips crossing some elements of the pattern but not others. The visual impression is that the branches are, indeed, woven through each other. This effect often amazes the unsophisticated viewer.

Carving techniques

The belly of a good historical lute is made of very thin, very close-grained spruce, usually *Picea excelsa*. It is usually of two pieces, bookmatched and joined with the finer grain at the center. Many old lutes have small additional pieces or "wings" at the very edges, presumably because the main pieces were not quite wide enough or well-grained enough all the way across. The belly blank was planed and scraped to a final thickness of less than two millimeters. Often the area under and around the rose was further reduced to around one millimeter, for ease of carving.

From close examination of museum lutes and from workshop experimentation we can tell how the old makers must have executed their roses. All the work seems to have been done with a knife or a combination of knives. This method is still in use by many contemporary builders.

First a paper pattern of the rose is glued on the underside of the belly. Then work is begun with a very thin, sharp,

pointed knife, such as the small scalpel favored currently or a specially ground X-acto blade. The piercings are made from the underside with stabbing cuts through the pattern and the spruce into a soft backing of cork, hard felt or very soft wood. This is an extremely painstaking procedure, as a little too much pressure applied in the wrong direction will split the thin wood. After the initial piercing is complete the belly is turned over and the pattern is cleaned up from the front side.

Finally the weaving is done, with either the same knife or a slightly larger one. This process can be facilitated by the application of a little water to soften the spruce. If a border is to be carved it is left for last to ensure concentricity with the main pattern. The paper is usually left glued to the underside to provide some support for the delicate pattern.

It is possible, and often necessary, to repair minor mishaps in the carving. A small piece is merely glued into place and shaped to fit the missing element. Sometimes it is so small that it must be handled with needle-nosed tweezers. The very complexity of the pattern ensures that a small discrepancy of grain or color will never be detected by most observers.

Knife carving can produce a fine, clean-looking rose and is used by some of the finest modern builders. With some experience it is quick and neat: a rose can be finished in six to twelve hours, depending on its complexity, the carver's skill and the degree of precision desired.

Many modern makers prefer the method favored by the

Rose-carving tools: Chisel, X-acto knives and jeweler's fretsaw flank paper pattern pasted on spruce lute belly.

In German method, which author prefers, paper pattern is glued to front of belly and cut with a fretsaw.

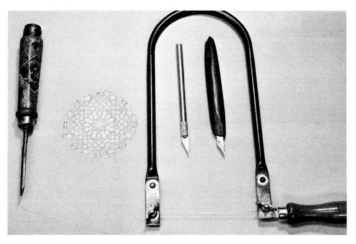

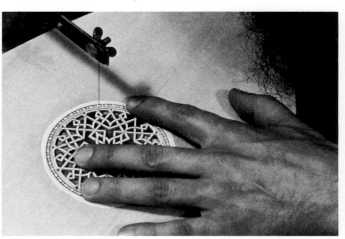

German school. It is much easier for a novice to use and can give extremely fine results. In experienced hands the German method is almost as fast as the knife method. The belly wood is prepared the same way.

First the paper pattern is glued onto the front side of the belly. (Many modern makers use zeroxed or offset-printed patterns.) Directly behind the rose, on the underside of the belly, a backing paper is glued, a little larger than the rose. If a border is required it is usually carved first. Then small holes are drilled through the belly to allow the introduction of the saw blade—most patterns require these holes to be 1/16 inch or smaller.

Piercing is done with a deep-throat fretsaw or jigsaw using jeweler's blades #0 or #00. With practice this can be done so precisely that little further work is necessary. After piercing, the pattern is cleaned up with small needle files, usually #4 or #6 cut. The most practical cross sections for rose files are triangular, square, half-round, flat and mousetail.

Weaving is done with a small chisel and a sharp knife, such as a pointed X-acto blade. The rose is finished off by sanding away the remains of the pattern paper with fine garnet paper and touching up wherever necessary. The paper backing is left for strength.

Before the belly is glued onto the lute shell it must be braced to resist the pull of the strings. One main brace runs directly under the rose; most old lutes also have two to nine smaller auxiliary braces under the rose. These auxiliary braces help to stiffen an otherwise weak area of the belly. All the braces are glued in place. Some makers dye them black with India ink so as not to confuse the pattern visually, while others leave them white.

Historically, lute bellies were not varnished, as were other parts of the instrument. They were either left bare or lightly sealed with thin sizing or egg white. They may have been waxed after sealing, but it is hard to tell from examining museum lutes. Most old lute bellies are quite dark and dirty after all these centuries.

Lute building is only one of the historical crafts that are being rediscovered today. We seem to be heading into a modern renaissance of hand work of all kinds. The techniques learned from studying historical crafts are useful not only in reconstructing authentic copies but also as inspiration for current designers and decorators.

Small gouge "weaves" a delicate rose of the 16th-century Bolognese style. Then remains of pattern will be sanded off.

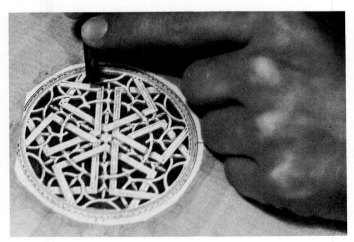

Shaped Tambours

Some design considerations

by Mark Sfirri

I wanted to design a cabinet with a tamboured front. Since I often feel that traditional tambours read visually as a bundle of sticks, my goal was to design something more imaginative than a simple rounding or beveling over the length of the tambour.

There are two limitations: The backs of the tambours must be flat and the width across their face must be uniform. These considerations insure a smooth, clean travel as the tamboured door "disappears" into the cabinet.

I designed a tambour which gracefully bellies out two-thirds of the way down the length. When determining the curve of the tambour, it is important to draw a plan view of the cabinet showing the track of the tambour, false sides, actual sides and the cap piece. This drawing is needed so that allowances can be made in the carcase for the curve of the tambour. The cap piece will have to be shaped on the inside to accommodate the curve. Because of the curve, more space is needed between the track and the actual side. It is also a good idea to make several tambours and mock them up in the curve of the tracks, paying particular attention to any tight radii. It may be necessary to ease off the radius so that the tambours will not splay open as much.

To reproduce the desired shape precisely on each tambour, I made a flush trimming jig for the shaper out of three pieces of plywood. The bottom piece (3/4 inch) has the exact shape of the tambour bandsawed out. The middle piece (1/4 inch) is notched out so that a tambour will fit in snugly. The top piece (3/4 inch) serves as a clamping surface for two eye bolts. The eye bolts also act as handles for the jig. The bottom part of the jig rides against a ball-bearing guide and the cutter shapes the tambour.

Each tambour was individually shaped in the jig. I then laid them out and realized that they still looked like flat sticks. The only place where the shaping could be seen was where the tambours disappeared behind the cap piece.

At this point I decided to bevel the tambours to bring out the three-dimensional quality of the shaping, for esthetic reasons and also out of necessity. The track that the tambours run in has a reverse curve. If the tambours were not beveled, they would bind at the points where they belly out. The beveling can be done on the table saw but a more effective method is to set up the router with a straight bit on a router table and tilt the router to the desired angle. Using the router leaves a smoother surface which requires less sanding. After beveling, the already shaped tambours are narrowest where they belly out the most and wider at the ends, where they are thinner.

Next I glued the tambours to #10 canvas with animal hide

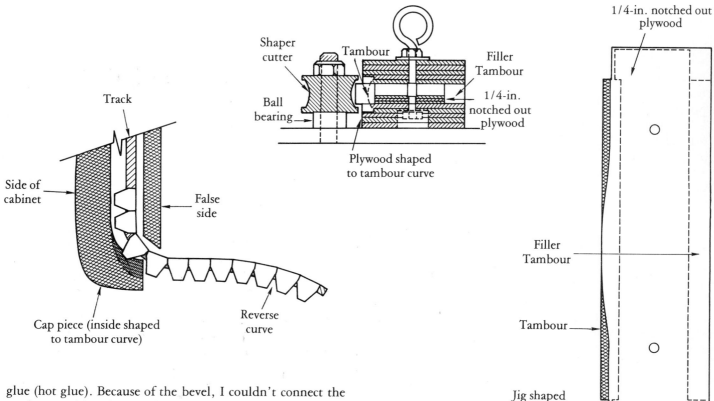

Track

Side of
cabinet

False
side

Cap piece (inside shaped
to tambour curve)

Reverse
curve

Shaper
cutter

Tambour

Ball
bearing

Filler
Tambour

1/4-in.
notched out
plywood

Plywood shaped
to tambour curve

1/4-in. notched out
plywood

Filler
Tambour

Tambour

Jig shaped
to tambour curve

glue (hot glue). Because of the bevel, I couldn't connect the tambours with wire, which would be visible when the tambours went around the curve of the track. After I got the tambours assembled and working in the cabinet, I realized that canvas was visible between the tambours where they turned a tight radius. I stained the canvas black to make it less noticeable behind the dark walnut. Fortunately the animal hide glue also took the stain. Had I used some other type of adhesive, this might not have happened. If you plan to stain the canvas, be sure that the glue you are using will take the stain.

When the shaped tambours are together, the subtle contrast of form and shadow creates an intriguing visual effect. This effect is illustrated in the liquor cabinet I have designed and constructed.

[*Author's note:* For readers interested in pursuing the subject of tambours, I recommend *The Encyclopedia of Furniture Making* by Ernest Joyce as the best source of general information.]

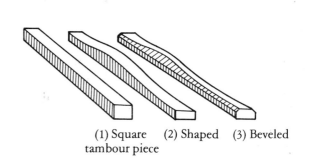

(1) Square   (2) Shaped   (3) Beveled
tambour piece

Walnut liquor cabinet by the author is 58 inches wide, 34 high. Plan drawing (upper left) is necessary to determine carcase clearances needed for shaped tambours (above). Flush trimming jig for shaping tambours is at top center and right.

Stacked Plywood

A fluid alternative to hardwood

by Ellen Swartz

Author with Surform

Making plywood furniture and understanding that process as a possible vehicle of social consciousness are primary concerns of mine. The material I use is secondary, although many people are struck by it first, foremost and finally. In 1970 I was searching for material to use in my simple shop and "found" plywood. It was easily available, inexpensive, strong when laminated, and could be worked with the basic tools I had. The more I used it, the more it appealed to me. I use it so there is very little waste (political appeal); it isn't rare or precious so my prices can reflect that (social appeal); I can scrounge plywood at construction sites for smaller works (economic appeal); and the simple and direct methods of construction allow me to concentrate more on concepts than technique (personal appeal; i.e., knowing your strong points and limitations). All said, we seem suited for each other.

The technique of making plywood by fastening thin strips of wood together and alternating the direction of the grain to give greater strength has been known since the time of the ancient Egyptians. At the Step Pyramid at Saqqara (2700 B.C.), plywood was found in which six 1/4-inch layers with alternating grain directions were fastened with wooden pegs. However, it was the demand for plywood for building ships and planes for the First and Second World Wars that brought about the product we know today. Until that time, the impermanency of casein, animal and vegetable starch glues retarded the development of plywood. The improved casein glues of the 1920s and 30s were used in airplane construction, but repeated cycles of wetting and drying caused eventual de-

terioration. The development of resin glues in 1935 made available an adhesive which is waterproof and immune to bacterial attack. It is unaffected by wet-dry cycles or intense heat and makes a permanent weld. In plywood glued with phenol resins, the glue lines are stronger than the wood. From an engineering standpoint, the advantages of plywood are impressive. It is extremely strong in comparison to its weight. It is durable, and it is permanently cured so there is no checking or splitting as with solid wood.

There are many ways of putting plywood together to make furniture. For the past 40 years, molded plywood has been well developed by industrial furniture designers. Veneer-covered plywood is widely used in panel and carcase construction and in cabinetmaking. But plywood can also be glued together in layers, building up to almost any form by laminating thin, cross-sectional slices. A stack of "side-view slices" can be face-glued together to block out the form of a chair that is then shaped and finished. Pieces of ply can be glued edge-to-face to make a right-angle joint, as long as the joining surface is large enough. If the area of contact is small I use screws or lag bolts for strength, as where the arms of a chair join the back. Sections can be hinged together. Laminated plywood lends itself especially to fluid, bending shapes because no joints are needed at the bends. As long as the material is thick enough for the stress it has to take, it will be extremely strong.

Plywood isn't suitable for traditional joinery, although pinned finger joints, as at the back of a chair rocker, work

High chair, coffee table, side chair: plywood's horizons open wide when the designer's mind escapes from the 4x8 sheet.

well. They need to be rather large because there are no complete long-grain to long-grain glue surfaces. I make each section three layers of plywood thick and stagger the layers to form the finger joint itself. It's very strong. To make a transition from horizontal to vertical, as in a table pedestal, I start by gluing the three vertical layers that form the column itself. Then I measure up four or five layers and glue a vertical lozenge-shaped piece to each side to form the transition, with its bottom edge square to the side of the column. I usually shape the column and the transition piece next, because there is still room to work, then I cut the base plate and screw it to the bottom of the column. Last, I cut the four or five layers that will fit between the transition piece and the base plate and glue them in place. If the measuring didn't work out and they're too thick, I plane off a layer of ply. If they're too thin, I add a piece of veneer. Then I carve away the stair steps and shape the whole base.

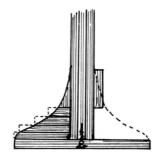

In terms of design, there are several ways I proceed. If an idea is quite clear, I make a small, three-dimensional and side-view sketch. Often I will ask the person I am working for whether he has any ideas to contribute, either verbally or through a drawing of his own. Other times I proceed with a rather vague idea and no sketch. This approach often evolves forms I'm sure I wouldn't ordinarily think up.

Once I determine the basic form I go directly to the plywood and draw up the first slice. This replaces the full-scale drawings many furniture makers use. The first and successive slices are cut out with a saber saw or band saw. The slices may be assembled from smaller pieces as long as the joints don't coincide from layer to layer. Usually I glue several slices at a time, sometimes as many as eight or ten. I use adjustable bar clamps and cee-clamps, placing one every 6 to 8 inches. I use Titebond yellow glue, which dries quickly, but 24 hours is still not too long to wait if much stress is going to be put on the joints.

For rough shaping I use a gouge and mallet, or a small electric chain saw. Then on larger pieces I use a high-speed sander—an auto body grinder, really—to take out the chain-

Chair begins with four side-view slices, clamped together without glue at the center.

When side has been shaped and four layers added to start the seat, gouge and Surform remove the stair-steps.

A wedge-shaped section will join the two halves, with dowels for reinforcement because the seat is supported only at the front.

Sinuous bend of three layers of plywood is made first; it is very strong and needs no reinforcement. Two small lozenges are glued and shaped for the transition atop the base, then the bottom plate is screwed on, and the half-layers of the base itself fit in between. Similarly the tabletop, except the surface piece hides the screws into the upright section.

saw marks. But I use the Surform and rasps to give all the shapes, curves and transitions their final form. Next I file to remove Surform marks. I fill checks, voids and splits in the plywood with oak-colored plastic wood and sand. I usually start with 30 grit, then finish with 50 or 60 grit. Sometimes I sand as fine as 80, but rarely. Because of the striations, plywood doesn't have to be sanded as finely as solid wood; because plywood doesn't expand and contract like solid, the plastic wood won't fall out as long as a sealing finish is used. I generally apply six coats of urethane varnish, sanding the second and fourth coats with worn 80-grit paper. The number of coats and the sanding builds a smooth finish on the rough-sanded ply.

The major difficulty in working with plywood is the chipping out caused by working your tools across layers going in different directions. Abrasive tools are better than sharp-edged ones for most operations because they cause less chip-out. And the abrasive nature of glue lines quickly dulls a sharp edge. Otherwise laminating plywood is a direct and easy method and a lot of technical background is not necessary before beginning.

Jewelry box is made of scrap. Cantilevered seat design of finished chair pushes material to its limits.

Rocking Chair with Message

Ellen Swartz made this rocking chair last year, when she was invited to show at a gallery of contemporary craft. Before applying the varnish, she wrote a message on the back:

In this society our responses to our work and to life in general are often conditioned by the cultural legacy of "rugged individualism," i.e. competitiveness. As a basic cultural tenet, competitiveness pits people against people and people against nature. A reordering of what we value which would place respect, equality and unity above divisiveness, could be a step toward re-establishing balance within society and within nature. I feel craftsmen/artists, as well as social thinkers, philosophers and doers, have a responsibility of evaluating their work and its relationship to the social, political and economic needs of society. If we remain on our ascribed pedestals and only feel we need to relate to the world of aesthetics, we remain part of the problem, not part of the solution.

Many viewers stopped cold, wondering why she had ruined the piece by writing all over it. But several inquired about the chair, and an art teacher eventually bought it—as much for the sentiment as for the chair itself. Swartz usually writes on the furniture she makes for invitational shows, aiming the messages at the audience such shows attract. "If I'm going to enter art shows," she says, "I want those people to listen to what I say, to react to it, even to say why did she ruin it."

Swartz, 31, is no raving revolutionary, but she believes American society needs some changes. She says that in traditional societies the artisan is an integral and necessary part of the culture, making the functional things everybody needs. In industrial society, mass production makes those things, often not very well, and only the rich can afford craftsmanship. As a result, she contends, the work becomes more sophisticated, elegant and technically elaborate—but also more hollow because its esthetic is "art for art's sake."

Thus she advocates using found materials and common construction plywood as a reaction against elegant, expensive rosewood or walnut. Her shop is simple; her only machine is a band saw, although she is a trained cabinetmaker.

The point of all this is to integrate her work as a craftsman with her life in the city. Her prices reflect the same ideas. When not bartering her work, she will build on commission for the same hourly rate that the buyer earns.

"I'd like to see craftsmen consider other ways of working," she says. "I'll try to use my work for good things, not all self-gain. Sure, I'm hooked into the system too, but it's a matter of degree. It's not to reject everything wholesale; it's small re-evaluations that may lead to bigger things." —J.K.

Stacking

The technique of building up wood forms for carving

by John Kelsey

The technique of stacking, by which layers of boards are glued together and carved to make furniture, was virtually unknown 15 years ago. Today it is part of the vocabulary of many professional furniture makers. Stacking makes possible the most arresting of contemporary designs. It is high-technology work, depending upon modern adhesives, clamps and power machinery.

Methods similar to stacking were used as early as medieval times, when sculptors occasionally glued baulks of wood together to build a block large enough to carve. Since the last century, carousel horses have been carved from laminated blocks of wood, with the legs and head attached by traditional joinery. Modern stacked furniture, however, relies on carefully preplanning the cross sections of the form at each elevation, and cutting the wood very near to the finished cross section before gluing it together. Wendell Castle of Scottsville, N.Y., believes he was the first to apply this technique to furniture, early in the 1960's. He has been doing it ever since, producing several dozen pieces a year, refining and developing his methods and forms.

Castle is trained as a sculptor and designer, but his interest in cross section goes back to his boyhood in Emporia, Kansas, during the 1930's. In the model airplane kits then popular, the fuselage was stacked balsa wood. The kit included a sheet of patterns and just enough 1/8-in. balsa to cut them all out. Then one would glue them together and sand smooth.

Most people, when first encountering Castles's work, conclude that he must glue together a rectangular block and slowly carve away the excess wood, like a sculptor with a block of stone. In fact, he tries to bandsaw each piece of wood to within 1/8 in. of the finished surface before gluing it. He works one layer at a time: cut, glue and clamp; cut, glue and clamp. The form is blocked out, more than half revealed, before it has been touched by a single carving tool.

Besides being esthetically satisfying, working this way is economical of time and material. Castle estimates his waste to be somewhat higher than that of a one-man cabinet shop, but lower than that of a furniture factory. In carving, he doesn't have to bash away pounds of material; he merely removes the stair steps of the stacked boards and refines the surface. This is the result of accurately visualizing cross sections from the start.

I followed the development of a stack dining-room table from a small clay model. Says Castle, ''This form started from a conch shell, although it has gone through about 50 variations over the past five years. Some of them looked much more like a conch shell than this. Bones are also nice sources of design. It's a mistake to try to interpret really literally, to make a big conch out of wood—you could have taken a photo. I use the conch as inspiration of form, to reinterpret and derive a new form. It ends up as a table base.''

As an aid to visualization, Castle often draws contour lines around his models. Throughout the work, the model is close at hand and he studies it frequently.

From the model, the first step is to draw a full-size plan of the bottom layer. He glues up a flat slab of wood, traces the

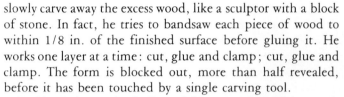

In photo sequence starting at left and going counter-clockwise—The clay model sits on the first two stacked layers. The shape for the next layer is traced. Castle applies glue and scrapes off the excess. He clamps across the work to prevent sliding. Clamps are placed about every three inches for even pressure and tight glue joints. The completed stack already resembles the model even before carving.

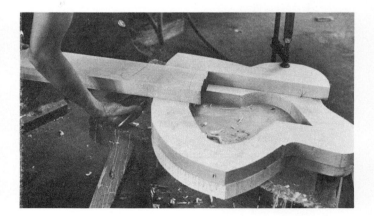

pattern onto it and bandsaws. With a new design such as this
one, he usually makes the bottom an inch larger than the
desired size. This gives an inch of material to play around
with while carving, and if he doesn't need the inch, the base
is just that much larger. No matter.

The wood for this table is 8/4 maple, planed to a uniform
1-5/8 in. thickness. While it might seem logical to work with
wide boards, Castle finds random widths ranging from 6 to 10
in. to be least wasteful. Kiln-dried lumber and careful
moisture control are essential to avoid unequal stresses and
consequent delamination.

The base and first stack are glued together, with the process
the same for every layer. First, Castle scrapes off the excess
glue and planes the top of the form to remove irregularities in
thickness and ensure a flat surface. The first board need only
have one true edge—the other edge will be sawed away. With
one eye on the model, Castle traces the outline of the stack on
the underside of the board and then modifies the pencil line
to account for the changes in the form at the new elevation.
The more accurate the shape now, the less time it will take to
carve the form later on. He goes to the bandsaw, cuts the
board and tacks it in place with a clamp.

Now he selects a board with square, parallel edges, holds it
in place, draws the inside cut on its top surface and traces
against the previous layer on its underside. Again, he adjusts
this line in tune with the evolution of the form, and
bandsaws. At this stage every piece looks alike and one bump
would scramble them irretrievably, if each weren't keyed to
its correct location with pencil lines on its face.

As he works, Castle varies randomly the cup of the end
grain both from layer to layer and from board to board and
makes sure the glue lines don't coincide. This tends to
equalize stresses throughout the mass as the wood expands
and contracts. And it avoids the regularity of a brick wall,
which would introduce visual confusion—the predictability
of the pattern would conflict with the perception of the form.

At this point, there are six pieces of wood in each layer. The
table base is hollow to save weight and allow the moisture
content to equalize. The bottom plate is solid now, but a hole
will be drilled in it later on. And the underside will be routed
out so the table rests on an edge, more stable than a slab.

A small ear left on the last board in the layer provides a

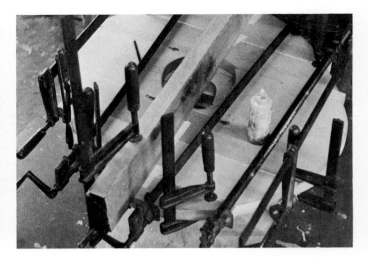

parallel surface for a clamp to bite in, drawing the edges of the boards together. Now is the time to check back with the model and make sure there is enough wood for the changes in the form; occasionally, Castle discards a piece of wood and saws another.

As the stack climbs, each layer twists with respect to the one below. In each, the grain remains at right angles to the long, curved edge. Castle explains that in this case the grain twists about 2 degrees per layer, to follow the twisting form and to allow carving downhill, with the grain, where there are grooves. The grain could twist as much as 5 degrees from layer to layer without danger of delamination—in a board, the fibers vary that much from parallel as the grain curves. Without such preplanning, one would be left trying to carve uphill, against the grain, from the bottom of a groove to the top. And that wouldn't be possible.

Castle uses both Titebond yellow glue and powdered plastic resin glue. The yellow glue comes ready-mixed and is convenient; powdered glue, while stronger, must be mixed anew for each job.

When the entire layer is cut, he carefully brushes the sawdust and chips from all the surfaces, lugs over a couple of dozen clamps from the rack in the middle of the shop, and begins to spread the glue. He uses a wooden shim for a spreader, starting on the stack and initially covering only the area of the first board. Then he coats the face and edge of that board and tacks it down with clamps, making sure it is in exactly the right place. Some of the clamps reach to the bottom of the form, and some go only to the next layer down; it doesn't matter. Then he quickly spreads glue across the rest of the stack and the other five boards in the layer, and plants them in place.

Quickly now, before the glue can set, two horizontal clamps pull the edges together. Without that little ear on the outside board, the clamp would have nowhere to bite. Another pair of horizontal clamps, reaching across at various angles, draws the joints tightly together and the glue oozes out. One glue line is recalcitrant, and a vertical clamp, set to bite at an angle, draws it snug. Castle calls this "applying a little East Indian."

Now more vertical clamps. A clamp every three inches all around the form, a clamp directly on every glue line, clamps alternately at the outer edge and near the center. Each clamp is twisted one-hand tight. When he is done, and it doesn't take long, there are 28 clamps. Any glue-squeeze wiped off

Chain saw, Surforms, pneumatic gouge and ball mill, gouges, rifflers and sanding disc are used for shaping. Then the top transition pieces are assembled and aligned.

The cavity of the first top layer is carved to remove weight, as it adds no useful glue surface. The top is clamped across to help keep the pieces level, and then laden with clamps until the glue sets.

now won't have to be scraped off later.

On a good day, Castle will stack a layer first thing in the morning, another at lunch time and a third at quitting time. The clamps stay on at least two hours with yellow glue, and overnight with powdered resin glue. Thus it will take about a week to build up the table base, although the total time each day isn't more than two hours.

A large piece of furniture, festooned with clamps holding 30 or more pieces of wood in a layer, may weigh 600 pounds. The weight of the clamps may cause it to tip. Get quickly out of the way; it's far too heavy to catch.

Some workers use a veneer press to stack. But while the press applies enormous pressure, it is uniform pressure and that's not what is needed. Hand clamps follow the irregularities in the wood, the tiny differences in thickness, the vagaries of warp, twist and cup, and still squeeze hard enough to produce a good joint. They also can be adjusted to apply pressure at an angle, and ganged to apply extra pressure when necessary—in general, they're a lot more flexible for this kind of work.

Wood coated with glue, especially yellow glue, is slippery. A combination of horizontal and vertical hand clamps controls slippage and keeps everything where it ought to be, but in a veneer press you'd have to use locating dowels. And then when you decided to change the form later on, to carve a little deeper, the dowel would surface.

When the entire base is stacked, it resembles a free-form staircase. If the pieces have been sawed accurately, what remains is to carve away the stair steps. Ideally, the desired surface lies just below the vee of each step. In practice, this is more true in some places than in others. A piece that has been made before can be stacked even more closely than a new one like this.

While it is possible to build a table from the top down, this one has to be done from the bottom up—otherwise, you'd need clamps with a three-foot throat. In general, Castle stacks as far as he can without impairing the carving, then carves as far as he can without making the rest of the clamping impossible. In this case, it is much easier to carve the base before adding the top. There is more room to work, more directions from which to work, and less mass to shift around.

The whole form could be carved by hand, with mallet and gouge, and smoothed with Surform, riffler and sandpaper. Castle, however, uses an array of power tools, most of them air driven, to save time. He begins with the chain saw, paring

away the stair steps, moves to the ball mill and pneumatic chisel to refine the main forms and block out details, and the body grinder to remove tool marks from large surfaces. The details are worked with mallet and gouge, and refined with Surform and riffler. He keeps Surform tools in sets, some to cut on the push stroke and some reversed in the handles to cut pulling.

Throughout the carving, he keeps the whole piece at the same stage; when one area is about right he moves to another. Thus the whole piece is brought at once from stepped layers to the general rough form, then each plane and hollow is defined, the sweeps of line adjusted and their starting and stopping points feathered imperceptibly to nothing. What makes a line is the intersection of two curved surfaces; what makes this form "read" is the lines. That means the surfaces have to be just right, so the lines will be just right. To change the curvature of a line, he has to change the surfaces that make it—he can't just whack a corner off. Finally, Surform and scraper remove the minute hollows and bumps and the piece is ready to sand.

The base of the table nears completion. It is remarkably like the model. Says Castle, "It's freeing for me to work in clay, and then figure out whether it's possible to make the form in wood. But in fact I find I make decisions early on, from my experience, and shy away from forms that would be too difficult to make, or too heavy to be practical. The forms I

*A ball mill helps shape the graceful transition from top to base.
After six coats of Watco the table is finished.*

draw and model fall into patterns that lend themselves to the things I know about doing; I don't do radical experiments that risk disaster. That experience, those patterns become my vocabulary and I work within it.''

The base was made without a definite top in mind, with the idea that it might fit a round top left over from an earlier project. ''I've never made a table this way before, with the top abruptly planted on the base. I've always said that was dumb. Tables should have an organic transition from base to top,'' Castle remarks. Then he plops the round top onto the base and it's clear he was right—it doesn't work. So he makes a cardboard pattern, a three-sided lozenge, and trims it to shape. Much better.

From the base as it was, it will take three layers to make the vertical-to-horizontal transition and complete the table top. And at that height, the table would be too high. So he chain-saws off a couple of laminations and glues on a slightly larger layer to create a clamping surface. Then he cuts and clamps the center three boards of the layer that is just under the top.

This layer has to be done in two stages because the boards at the perimeter are edge-glued to those at the center. The center three boards glue to the table base, but there isn't anything under the boards at the edge. In the end most of this layer will be carved away in the transition from vertical to

horizontal, but there must be enough wood to feather out so it is made nearly as large as the top itself. Since most of it will disappear, it is a good place to use up low-grade wood.

When the glue has set on the center three boards, Castle removes the clamps and begins to work out to the edge. He holds each board in position to lay out the cuts, marking them carefully for repositioning. As each is bandsawed, he tacks it in place with a couple of clamps atop the joint. An ear must be left on every board for the horizontal clamps that draw them together. A thick, straight plank, plus clamps directly on each glue line, keep the boards aligned. He puts paper under the plank to keep from gluing it to the table.

When the clamps come off, the surface is scraped to remove glue-squeeze and planed. The hole at the center is widened with gouge and chain saw to remove weight and because no useful clamping gluing surface is available there—no way to clamp. He vacuums the cavity to remove chips.

From the template, the wood for the top is cut and indexed. These boards are slightly thinner, about 1-1/4 in., to save a little weight and to achieve the correct table height. The long, tapered transition from base to top and the thin, rounded edge he plans make it impossible to detect the difference in thickness.

Castle next adjusts the placement of the top with reference to where the base provides support at the floor. The contour can still be changed later on, by chain saw and saber saw. He traces the previous layer on the underside to show where to spread glue and draws a line along the edge of a center board, keying it for precise relocation.

He changes to plastic resin glue to fix the top, at first brushing it only where the center board goes. This type of glue, mixed from powder each time, is more resistant to heat and moisture than yellow glue. Tabletop conditions won't cause yellow glue to fail, but may raise the glue lines or cause the boards to creep a little. And powdered glue gives a longer open time to work.

The dust is carefully brushed from all the surfaces, the center board positioned and clamped at each end. Then he spreads glue on one side of it and on those boards, positions them, and continues on the other side. The outer boards on each side aren't supported from underneath, so they wait on top until the horizontal clamps are applied. The first horizontal clamp goes from ear to ear across the whole top. A few vertical clamps go directly on the glue lines to tack the boards in place, with paper to prevent staining. They will be supplemented and tightened later. The deepest clamps in the shop reach in a foot from the edge. Castle and an assistant put clamps everywhere they will fit, in the end about 60 of them.

The clamps come off, the excess glue is scraped away, and the edge saber-sawed close to size. Castle carves the transition between base and top the same way he carved the base itself, with chain saw and ball mill, body grinder, Surform and gouge. The piece is ready for sanding.

The usual sanding sequence in Castle's shop begins with 32-grit rotary discs, then 80-grit discs, to remove digs and tears and bring the whole surface to the same degree of fineness. Then the whole form is carefully gone over with a sharp scraper to level the surfaces, remove bumps and hollows and minute irregularities. Then the wood is dampened to raise the grain, hand sanded at 150-grit, and finished off with 220-grit followed by six coats of Watco.

Bent Laminations

Slice and glue the wood to make it curve

by Jere Osgood

Samples of laminated wood have been found dating from the 15th century B.C. Lamination means a layering process. All the layers are aligned with the grain going in the same direction, and are held fast by a glue. Thin slices of wood can be laminated flat or to a curved form.

It is important to distinguish lamination from veneering. The grain of the laminate layers is always oriented in the same direction.

In contrast, in veneering or plywood the grain directions alternate and an odd number of layers must be used. In lamination the layers, when glued together, will act like solid wood, expanding and contracting across the long grain. In veneering, grain alteration stabilizes the unit and there is no movement across or with the grain. Another form of lamination, stacking, is really a separate subject. (See ''Stacking,'' *Fine Woodworking*, Winter '76.)

Furniture-related examples of lamination are flat or curved cabinet panels, tabletops, and curved leg blanks. The simplest lamination is the use of a fine figured wood as an outer layer on a tabletop or cabinet panel.

In many cases I find laminations more acceptable than solid construction. For example, one plank of an unusual figured wood could be resawn into many layers. These could perhaps

Jere Osgood teaches woodworking at Boston University. He lives in New Milford, Conn.

cover all the sides of a cabinet, if backed up by layers of wood of lesser quality or rarity. If used at full thickness, many planks of this unusual wood would be needed to achieve the same effect.

Lamination is an economical way of obtaining curved forms. Members can be thinner when laminated as opposed to sawn because of the inherent strength of parallel grain direction. Steam bending is of course an alternative for curves and is an important process. However, lamination offers the advantage in many cases of more accurate reproduction of the desired curve. Modern glues have eliminated the bugaboo of delamination—the glue lines are as strong as the wood itself. An excellent use of laminated wood is in chair or table legs

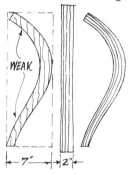

where short-grain weakness might inhibit design. It is important in some cases to make the layer stock thick enough so that any shaping or taper can be done in the outer two layers because going through the glue lines might be unsightly. In addition to counteracting short-grain weakness, laminating a curved leg also saves scarce wood, because a laminated leg can be cut from a much narrower plank than would be required for sawing the curved shape out of solid stock.

For flat panels such as a tabletop or a cabinet panel, a core of some stable wood (poplar or mahogany) is used. A face wood, which can be veneer or resawn stock, is glued on both sides with the grain directions the same. It is important to cover both sides to forestall warp and to use the same species

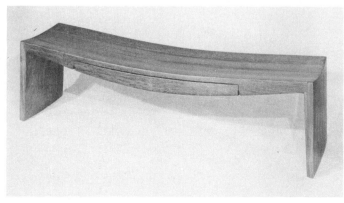

Dining table by James Schriber: Top is simple laminate faced with tamo veneer; apron and legs are laminated ash. Bench by Osgood: Curved ends, top and front are all bent laminates.

SEE PAGE 178

Chest of chair, laminated curly maple, by Jere Osgood.

on both sides. However, if the densities are kept the same, substitutions can be made. Typical veneer thicknesses are 1/30 in., 1/28 in., 1/16 in. and 1/8 in. Resawn stock is thicker—perhaps 1/8 in., 3/16 in., 1/4 in. or 3/8 in. The core thickness in a cabinet panel might be 1/2 in. and in a tabletop, 13/16 in. The core requirements disappear when laminating something like a drawer front, which might typically be two layers of 3/8-in. material or three layers of 1/4-in. stock.

When panels are curved the thickness of the layers is important. A thick core might not be possible. Whatever size layers are used, they must each be able to take the desired curve. For example, 1/16-in. layers might be needed to bend a 3-in. radius, but for a lesser bend of, say, 1-in. deflection over a 36-in. drawer front, 1/4 in. or 3/8 in. might be thin enough. The appearance of the visible edge of something like a drawer front is also a design factor to consider.

A general rule is to keep layers of the maximum thickness that will take the desired bend. This not only saves time and money (each time a lamination is cut, a slice the thickness of the saw blade turns into dust) but also aids in gluing evenly. A multitude of thin layers of, say, 1/28-in. veneers risks a surface unevenness from disparate clamp pressure marks resulting from a poorly bandsawn form or from unevenly spread glue. But you don't have any choice if you have 2000 square feet of very thin veneer that will fulfill the stock requirement for a specific piece of furniture.

First, determine the thickness needed by testing the bend with a sample. Narrow or simple cuts, say for chair legs, are usually possible with a single pass on a table saw, the limitation being the diameter of the saw blade. In many cases a carbide rip blade will give a good cut for gluing that will not need to be run through a thicknesser. Stock cut with a normal rip blade will need to be thickness-planed.

Wide laminations that can't be cut in one pass on the table saw can be cut on a band saw using a resaw jig. Another table-saw method involves dressing stock normally, cutting from opposite sides of the board with the blade height set to cut halfway, and thicknessing the cut-away pieces. Because there is one smooth face they can be surfaced as is, ignoring warp if they are thin. The center portion of the board is left rough and should be resurfaced before repeating the operation.

Resawn stock may warp or cup. If this is not desirable the stock must be left thick enough to plane warp out. There is a tendency to overestimate the number of resawn layers available from a board. Therefore take careful account of kerf loss and warp. Be sure to laminate resawn stock in the same order it was cut. A vee marked on the ends of the laminate boards makes it easy to keep them in this order when they are glued to the curve. For wide laminations, the resawn pieces can be folded apart, or bookmatched, to keep the grain in a pattern.

2-INCH STOCK SAWN INTO 5 LAYERS. VEE MARKED ON END BEFORE SAWING KEEPS LAMINATE IN ORDER.

Almost any glue works for flat laminations where the only stress is the seasonal movement of the wood. However, I prefer a slow-setting glue for a lot of layers or a large surface area. I do not recommend white glue for fine furniture because of the variation in quality from one brand to another. A yellow glue such as Franklin Titebond (an aliphatic naphtha-based glue) is good for shallow bends or curves without a lot of stress. Cold creep (slippage after drying) occurs to a lesser extent with yellow glue than with white glue. A chair leg laminated with yellow glue will slip minutely and show the layers after about nine months. The layers are trying to become straight again—you can see and feel the unevenness.

If a lamination is sharply bent and under stress, a urea formaldehyde glue such as Weldwood or Cascamite is called for. I have had good results with Urac 185, made by American Cyanamid Co., Industrial Chemicals and Plastics Division, Wayne, N.J. 07470. Unfortunately, it is available only in 55-gallon drums. I recommend a two-part resorcinol formaldehyde where wetness is a problem, but the dark glue line may be objectionable. These glues don't suffer cold creep.

Springback is normal as the layers try to straighten out against the formed curve. It is slightly greater with yellow glue than with urea glue. But the amount of springback is usually small and can be estimated with practice. In many cabinet or chair parts it can be ignored. Joint angles should be checked after laminated parts are made. Where a precise curve is needed one could use thinner (and therefore more) layers, which will tend to reduce or eliminate springback, or test-glue the part and adjust the form before laminating the actual piece.

In lamination, as in all gluing, there are four potential trouble areas: moisture content of the wood, temperature, oily woods, and dull thickness-planer blades. Opinions may vary, but below 6% moisture content is risky.

Temperature is another important factor. While yellow glue can set at a lower temperature, 70° F is about the lowest for the urea type, and at that temperature about 12 hours of clamping time are required. For urea-resin glue a temperature of 90° F reduces the pressure period to about five hours. One easy way to increase temperature in a workshop is to throw a drop cloth over the clamped work and put a 150-watt bulb underneath. Be careful, because most glues don't reach maximum strength for 48 hours.

Oily woods such as teak or rosewood can be laminated in several ways. Titebond is more likely to succeed than a urea glue. Another way to achieve a bond is to roughen the glue surfaces with a toothing plane or 40-grit garnet paper. Narrow pieces cut with a carbide table-saw blade which are not cleaned up or jointed may glue better. Another method is to clean the surface with lacquer thinner or carbon tetrachloride before gluing. Oily stock should be tested first, before committing an expensive lot of wood.

Another area of potential trouble that is often overlooked is a dull thickness-planer blade. Dull knives beat and mash down the wood fibers; sharp knives slice them off cleanly. Microscropic differences in the surface greatly affect gluing.

A simple flat lamination can be done with two cover boards and a few quick-action clamps. An alternative to this is a veneer press. In addition to flat pressing, the veneer press can be used for curved parts with a two-part form.

For simple parts a one-piece form can be used. The layers are held in place under pressure with quick-action clamps.

Free clamping without a heavy back-up form can be done for parts requiring a spiral or otherwise impossible compound curve. A lamination of several layers can be held in place with 1/4-in. Masonite strips as cover pieces on either side of the layers of wood. Masonite of this thickness twists easily.

On a wide piece, a good rule is to begin clamping from the center out to the sides or from one side to another so that air or glue pockets aren't trapped between the layers.

The cheapest material for making forms is particle board, chipboard or floor underlayment, all basically the same material. Fir plywood is the next most economical choice and should be used where strength is required. Particle board has an advantage over fir plywood in that the band saw won't track off the pencil line into some strong grain configuration.

I usually face my press or forms with Masonite to help obtain even gluing pressure and to compensate for slight irregularities in bandsawing. I use 1/8-in. or 1/4-in., depending on the severity of the curve. Masonite is cheap and its surface resists glue.

In determining the curve to be drawn on the form, the actual piece plus the thickness of the facing must be considered.

Forms five or six inches thick could be made from solid, but it is often more economical to make the form as a series of ribs with spacers in between each rib. The form can be made as a one-part, open-face jig or constructed as a two-part form. Usually the decision depends on the gluing process. Clamping pressure must be maintained approximately perpendicular to the work. While I prefer a two-part form that fits in a press for most work, there are many cases where the curve is too great or the piece is too large. For example, the semicircular apron for a round dining table can be made most easily with a one-piece form.

A two-part form with a shallow curve, such as for a drawer

Chair by Tom Hucker: Quick-action clamps hold thin layers of maple in two-part chipboard form, above. Outer part of form is segmented for easier assembly. Then eight identical staves are joined and shaped to make seat of chair. Legs are also laminated.

Hardwood board under screws of veneer press distributes pressure and keeps form from crumbling at center.

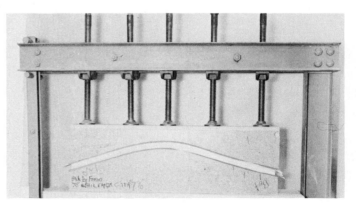

front with a one-inch deflection over a three-foot distance, requires bandsawing only along a single pencil line. The form will flex enough over that length to give even clamping pressure. For a drawer front of the same length but with a two-inch deflection, it would probably be necessary to calculate the various radii by the method described below.

The first step is to thickness-plane the laminates to the desired thickness and check the true combined thickness with calipers. For example, four 1/4-in. layers might actually measure 1-1/16 in. together, and a one-inch form would be off. The form needs to be that precise. The two band-saw lines are established by taking the curves of each side of the desired piece, adding the facing thickness to each side and transferring the total dimensioned curve to the form. For a compound shape, the bottom curve line is taken from a full-size shop drawing. Then a compass is set to the total laminate thickness plus the two layers of Masonite. The compass is lined up with the bottom line and small arcs are swung at the

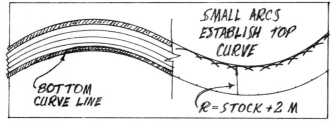

correct distance from points all along the bottom line. The crests of these small arcs are connected using a flexible curve, to establish the correct top line.

When laying out the curve onto the form, the normal inclination is to work from a vertical or horizontal reference on the drawing. This does not necessarily ensure perpendicular gluing pressure. Often the curve layout on the form must be tilted to center the curve.

Most of the directions so far have been for narrow furniture parts of up to five inches. Another method is suited to larger pieces such as door panels, cabinet ends and bench seats. The same method would be used to veneer the panels. After establishing the curve on the form, band-saw lines are drawn onto the end piece of a stack of ribs that have been carefully cut to the exact length and width and then dadoed. These ribs are not glued together, but held by four spacer strips press-fitted into the dadoes. The idea is to make a short, easy package to bandsaw. For example, a 20-in. form can be made of eleven 3/4-in. ribs which would make a stack 8-1/4 in. high to bandsaw. The stack can be kept uniform by inserting short, temporary spacer strips into the dadoes. After bandsawing, the short strips are replaced by strips of the total length. Masonite sheets are then used to line the form, and finally two sheets of particle board or plywood are cut for top and bottom plates.

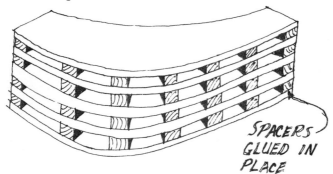

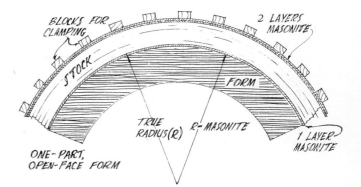

One-part, open-face form is used with quick-action clamps for parts that are too large for veneer press. Masonite regulates pressure, but must be accounted for in layout.

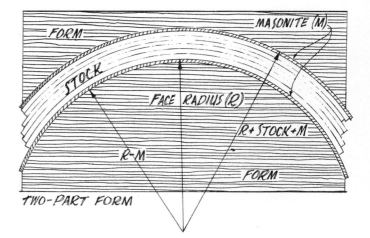

Two-part forms provide most even squeeze with either clamps or veneer press. Again, accurate layout is essential.

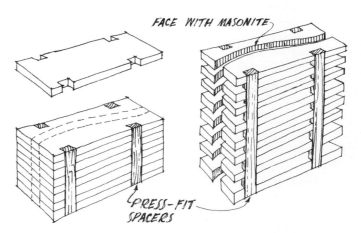

Rib-and-spacer forms bandsawn from a stack of boards are best for wide, curved panels. At left, an open-face ribbed form is made from chipboard with pine spacers.

INDEX

INDEX

Art Credits

14, 174 Loren McGurk
18, 32-34, 41-45, 54, 60-61, 64, 86, 89, 102-107, 108, 114-115, 126-128, 158, 169 Stan Tkaczuk, Image Area
27-28, 65-67, 92-95 William Zalkind
68-73 David Downs
74-80 Roger Barnes
81, 114, 122-125, 141, 154, 166, 169 Mathilde Anderson
109-113 B. D. Bittinger
145-148 John Kelsey
108, 114, 162-163, 169 Joseph Esposito

Photo Credits

8-12 Bruce Hoadley
35-38 Dave Elwell, Bob LaPree, Mark Lindquist
47-51 Timothy Ellsworth
58-59, 122-125 Rosanne Somerson
60-61 Charles Hall, Rodney Vowell
68-73 David Downs
74-80 Richard Starr, John Layton
109-113 B. D. Bittinger
116-119 Steve McDowell
141-144 Leeson's Photographic
145-148 John Kelsey
162-163 Donald F. Eaton
170-172 Lyn Elder, Donald Warnock
175-177 Joel Swartz
183-186 Jere Osgood